Light Desserts

Light Desserts

Beatrice Ojakangas

Oxmoor House®

Library of Congress Catalog Number: 88-64130
ISBN: 0-8487-0759-1

Manufactured in the United States of America
First Printing 1989

Published by Oxmoor House, Inc.
Book Division of Southern Progress Corporation
P.O. Box 2463, Birmingham, Alabama 35201

Executive Editor: Ann H. Harvey
Production Manager: Jerry Higdon
Associate Production Manager: Rick Litton
Art Director: Bob Nance

Light Desserts

Editor: Cathy A. Wesler, R.D.
Copy Editor: Melinda E. West
Editorial Assistant: Pam Beasley Bullock
Production Assistant: Theresa L. Beste
Test Kitchen Director: Julie Fisher
Test Kitchen Home Economists: Nancy C. Earhart, Vanessa Taylor Johnson, Christina A.
 Pieroni, Kathleen Royal, Gayle Hays Sadler, Paula N. Saunders, Jill Wills
Photographer: Jim Bathie
Photo Stylist: Kay E. Clarke
Designer: Design for Publishing

Cover: *Amaretto Cheesecake (page 57), Strawberry Champagne (page 17), and Chocolate Pots de Crème (page 238)*
Back Cover: *Old-Fashioned Marble Cake (page 30)*
Page 2: *Raspberry Cheesecake (page 57)*

To subscribe to *Cooking Light* magazine, write to *Cooking Light*, P.O. Box C-549, Birmingham, Alabama 35283.

Contents

Lightstyle Desserts

Light Desserts offers a lightened version of all-time favorites—cakes, pies, tarts, pastries and many other desserts—that contain under 200 calories per serving. There are ice milks, puddings, fruit desserts, sauces, and beverages as well as soufflés and mousses stylish enough to serve to company and healthy enough to be included in any menu.

Included arc tips on decreasing calories in traditional desserts as well as easy ideas for stunning presentations. Garnishing techniques and serving suggestions provide inspiration for creating that all-important final touch.

The step-by-step guidelines for special procedures used to achieve lighter desserts help guarantee successful results every time. These procedures have been standardized in each recipe so that even a novice baker can quickly become familiar with the techniques that are integral to preparing Light Desserts.

(Clockwise from right): Glazed Fruit Tart (page 159), Spicy Gingerbread Cut-Outs (page 233), and Chocolate Meringue Tarts (page 157) are just a sample of the variety of treats to be discovered in Light Desserts.

Healthy Eating

Perhaps more than any other course of a meal, desserts promise the pleasure of eating. For some, desserts have held the classic role of being a "reward," a sensuous luxury, the crowning glory of a meal or a between-meal treat. However, rich desserts, those masterpieces that traditionally are made of sugar, butter, whipped cream, eggs, and chocolate, run contrary to today's new interest in healthy eating.

However, with a few changes in ingredients and a few adjustments in cooking techniques, lighter desserts may be created that offer a sensible substitute for the richer, more traditional desserts.

Desserts for the health-conscious

Moderation is the key to healthy eating. Too much of any one food or any one nutrient can be unhealthy, especially too much fat, sugar, or cholesterol. While desserts can easily tip the scales toward the "excess" side of moderation, these light desserts do not. The nutritional analysis that accompanies each recipe can be used to balance the dessert with the other menu items. Tasty desserts that are lower in fat, calories, sodium, and sugar can then be enjoyed by the health-conscious, without guilt or frustration.

Desserts as a component of a meal

Natural, fresh ingredients, with less sugar, fat, cholesterol, and sodium, more dietary fiber and a higher nutrient value have been used in the development of these recipes. By using fresh fruits, decreasing the number of egg yolks, replacing whipped cream with whipped nonfat dry milk powder, and reducing the sugar content of the recipes, the flavors of the food are not hampered by extra fat and sugar and are more intense, clearer, and fresher.

As a result, lighter desserts can and should be incorporated as a component of a meal. The choices range from imaginative, new combinations to lightened old-fashioned favorites. Eliminating a dessert altogether can cause a psychological feeling of deprivation, but a beautiful ending to any meal is still possible with one of the lightened desserts. These are easy to prepare and a pleasure to eat yet provide nutritional advantages.

Light Desserts contains over 350 recipes designed to meet certain nutritional requirements for calcium, vitamins, and minerals by including ingredients such as low-fat milk and dairy products and fresh fruits. These lighter recipes can also help readjust taste buds so that one begins to prefer less sugar and less fat in all kinds of foods.

For general meal planning, it is most interesting to plan a simple, fresh dessert after a rather elaborate main course. Conversely, if the main course is a simple soup, a more elaborate dessert, such as a cake, pie, tart, or pastry can be an interesting addition to the meal.

In any menu, try to avoid the repetition of flavor and texture. If a main course has a fruit element, avoid repeating the same fruit in the dessert. If an entrée has a creamy sauce and smooth texture, plan a dessert with a fresh or crisp texture. And, if the entrée course is a pale color, select a colorful fruit dessert for an attractive contrast to the meal. Basically, there are few restrictions other than these simple, common-sense rules and, of course, following healthy dietary guidelines.

HOW THE RECIPES ARE ANALYZED

Calories per serving and a nutrient breakdown accompany every recipe. The nutrients listed include grams of carbohydrate, protein, and fat along with milligrams of cholesterol, calcium, iron, and sodium.

The recipes in *Light Desserts* were developed for people who are interested in lowering their intake of calories, sugar, fat, cholesterol, and sodium to maintain healthy eating patterns. The levels of these restricted nutrients in some recipes may be higher than those prescribed by a physician for specific health problems. The calorie and nutrient breakdown of each recipe is derived from computer analysis, based primarily on information from the U.S. Department of Agriculture. The values are as accurate as possible and reflect certain assumptions:

• All nutrient breakdowns are listed per serving.
• When a range is given for an ingredient (e.g. 3 to 3½ cups flour), the lesser amount is calculated.
• Alcohol calories evaporate when heated, and this reduction is reflected in the calculations.
• When a marinade is used, only the amount of marinade used (not discarded) is calculated.
• Fruits and vegetables listed in the ingredients are not peeled unless otherwise specified.

Finishing Touches

Edible flowers add a crowning touch to a dessert, whether simple or elaborate. Check with your florist on the availability of edible flowers in your area.

Clockwise from right: Spearmint, mint, orange mint, Best mint, and lemon balm can be colorful garnishes for beverages or desserts.

To make an apricot rose, flatten dried apricots; roll one into a cone. Press additional apricots to form petals. Secure with a wooden pick.

For chocolate garnishes, make a design on wax paper. Using pastry bag, pipe melted chocolate over design. Place in refrigerator until firm.

For a quick garnish for cakes or bar cookies, place a doily on top of cake; sift powdered sugar over doily to create a lacy design.

Fresh berries and citrus rind offer color and appeal as a garnish. Select ripe, unblemished fruit to use as an accent on desserts.

Light Techniques

Whipped instant nonfat dry milk powder

Whipped milk powder is a healthy alternative to whipped cream. The procedure is easy, but it requires that the equipment and ingredients be very cold. Select a small, narrow bowl, making sure that the beaters of the electric mixer will fit comfortably down to the bottom of the bowl.

Unflavored gelatin

Unflavored gelatin provides structure for chiffons, Bavarians, soufflés, and other desserts containing beaten egg whites or whipped instant nonfat dry milk powder. Be sure that the gelatin granules have time to soften or swell. This allows the gelatin to dissolve when heated.

Measure water or other liquid into a small, narrow glass bowl.

In a small saucepan, sprinkle unflavored gelatin over cold water.

Place bowl with water in freezer 25 minutes or until a ⅛-inch layer of ice forms on the surface.

Let stand 1 minute to "soften" gelatin.

Add milk powder and beat at high speed of an electric mixer 5 minutes or until stiff peaks form.

Add additional liquid according to the recipe and heat, stirring to dissolve gelatin.

Pastry dough

Cake flour is used in most of the pastry recipes as it contains less gluten and requires less fat to produce a tender crust. When margarine is used, it should be chilled; if it becomes too soft, the pastry may be less flaky.

The use of heavy-duty plastic wrap eliminates the need for additional flour to roll the pastry. Chilling the dough is essential in many of the recipes to make the dough easier to handle and to prevent shrinkage during baking.

Preparing a soufflé dish

A soufflé is a light and delicate dessert made with beaten egg whites; because of it lightness, it requires the use of a collar to support it, whether it is baked or chilled.

A soufflé makes an impressive dessert, especially when presented in the appropriate size dish. Use the size specified in each recipe, preparing it first with an aluminum foil collar extending up from the rim. This technique can be used with either chilled or baked soufflés.

Using a pastry blender, cut the chilled margarine into the flour until the mixture resembles coarse meal.

Sprinkle cold water, 1 tablespoon at a time, over surface. Stir with a fork until dry ingredients are moistened. (Do not form into a ball.)

Cut a piece of aluminum foil long enough to fit around the soufflé dish, allowing a 1-inch overlap. Fold foil into thirds.

Lightly spray one side of folded foil with vegetable cooking spray.

Gently press dough between 2 sheets of heavy-duty plastic wrap into a 4-inch circle. Chill 15 minutes.

Roll dough, still covered, as specified in each recipe. Freeze 5 minutes or until bottom layer of plastic wrap can be removed easily.

Wrap foil, coated side against dish, so that foil extends 3 inches above rim of dish.

Secure foil with a string.

Beverages

In frosted glasses or steaming cups, beverages can add cooling refreshment or a welcome warmth to a meal or snack. The beverages in this chapter are made with fruits, yogurts, fruit juices, and skim milk and are ideal nutrition boosters for both children and adults. Several of them are also appropriate for brunches and parties.

Some can be prepared ahead of time; others can be partially prepared, saving precious minutes just before serving.

Recipes calling for the use of alcohol or liqueurs can be easily modified by consulting the Alcohol Substitution Chart on page 249.

(Clockwise from left): Flaming Café Royal (page 21), Spiced Tea (page 19), Fresh Mint Tea (page 20), Viennese Coffee (page 21), and Cranberry Tea (page 19) make special after-dinner drinks.

Banana Sunset

2 medium-size ripe bananas,
   peeled and sliced
⅓ cup instant nonfat dry milk
   powder
2 tablespoons frozen orange juice
   concentrate, thawed and
   undiluted
1 cup water
8 ice cubes
2 tablespoons grenadine syrup
Orange rind strips (optional)

Combine first 4 ingredients in container of an electric blender; top with cover, and process until smooth. Add ice cubes, and process until smooth. Add grenadine syrup, and process just until blended. Pour into serving glasses, and garnish with orange rind strips, if desired. Serve immediately. Yield: 4 cups (118 calories per ½-cup serving).

PROTEIN 4.4 / FAT 0.4 / CARBOHYDRATE 25.8 / CHOLESTEROL 2 / IRON 0.3 / SODIUM 54 / CALCIUM 133

Banana Smoothie

2 medium-size ripe bananas,
   peeled and sliced
2 cups unsweetened orange juice
2 cups vanilla low-fat yogurt
2 cups crushed ice

Combine first 3 ingredients in container of an electric blender; top with cover, and process until smooth. Add crushed ice, and process until smooth. Pour into glasses, and serve immediately. Yield: 6 cups (132 calories per 1-cup serving).

PROTEIN 4.6 / FAT 1.1 / CARBOHYDRATE 27.1 / CHOLESTEROL 4 / IRON 0.2 / SODIUM 51 / CALCIUM 139

Cranberry Cream

⅔ cup fresh or frozen cranberries,
   thawed
1 cup vanilla low-fat yogurt
4 ice cubes

Combine all ingredients in container of an electric blender or food processor; top with cover, and process until smooth. Pour into 4 stemmed glasses, and serve immediately. Yield: 2 cups (112 calories per ½-cup serving).

PROTEIN 5.7 / FAT 1.5 / CARBOHYDRATE 19.7 / CHOLESTEROL 6 / IRON 0.1 / SODIUM 75 / CALCIUM 196

These refreshing fruit beverages are attractively served: (left to right) Orange Julia (page 17), Grapefruit Cooler (page 16), Banana Sunset, Cranberry Cream, and Kiwifruit Daiquiri (page 16).

Grapefruit Cooler

(pictured on page 15)

3 cups unsweetened apple cider,
  chilled
2 cups unsweetened grapefruit
  juice, chilled
1 (23-ounce) bottle lime-flavored
  sparkling mineral water, chilled
Lime slices (optional)
Fresh mint sprigs (optional)

Combine first 3 ingredients in a large pitcher; stir well. Pour over ice in serving glasses. If desired, garnish with lime slices and fresh mint sprigs. Serve immediately. Yield: 2 quarts (67 calories per 1-cup serving).

PROTEIN 0.4 / FAT 0.2 / CARBOHYDRATE 16.4 / CHOLESTEROL 0 / IRON 1.6 / SODIUM 21 / CALCIUM 11

Kiwifruit Daiquiri

(pictured on page 15)

1 cup unsweetened kiwifruit juice
1 tablespoon plus 1 teaspoon lime
  juice
½ teaspoon rum extract
16 ice cubes, crushed
Kiwifruit slices (optional)

Combine first 4 ingredients in container of an electric blender; top with cover, and process until smooth. Garnish with kiwifruit slices, if desired. Serve immediately. Yield: 2½ cups (64 calories per 1¼-cups serving).

PROTEIN 0.0 / FAT 0.0 / CARBOHYDRATE 14.5 / CHOLESTEROL 0 / IRON 0.0 / SODIUM 6 / CALCIUM 1

Peaches and Cream

2 medium-size ripe peaches,
  peeled and sliced
¼ cup instant nonfat dry milk
  powder
¼ cup plus 1 tablespoon peach
  nectar
4 ice cubes
½ teaspoon vanilla extract
2 whole strawberries

Combine peaches, milk powder, peach nectar, ice cubes, and vanilla in container of an electric blender; top with cover, and process until smooth. Pour into 2 stemmed glasses. Top each serving with a strawberry. Yield: 2 cups (126 calories per 1-cup serving).

PROTEIN 6.3 / FAT 0.3 / CARBOHYDRATE 25.7 / CHOLESTEROL 3 / IRON 0.3 / SODIUM 83 / CALCIUM 198

Orange Julia

(pictured on page 15)

2 cups water
1 (6-ounce) can frozen orange
   juice concentrate, thawed and
   undiluted
1/3 cup instant nonfat dry milk
   powder
1 teaspoon vanilla extract
2 cups crushed ice
10 orange slices (optional)

Combine first 4 ingredients in container of an electric blender; top with cover, and process until smooth. Add crushed ice, and process until smooth. Pour into glasses, and garnish with orange slices, if desired. Serve immediately. Yield: 5 cups (86 calories per ½-cup serving).

PROTEIN 3.7 / FAT 0.1 / CARBOHYDRATE 17.4 / CHOLESTEROL 2 / IRON 0.1 / SODIUM 44 / CALCIUM 111

Strawberry-Banana Smoothie

5 cups whole fresh strawberries,
   washed and hulled
2 medium-size ripe bananas,
   peeled and sliced
1/2 cup instant nonfat dry milk
   powder
1/2 cup vanilla low-fat yogurt
1 cup ice cubes
2 teaspoons vanilla extract
6 whole strawberries
Fresh mint sprigs (optional)

Combine first 6 ingredients in container of an electric blender; top with cover, and process until smooth. Pour into 6 stemmed glasses. Top each serving with a strawberry, and garnish with mint sprigs, if desired. Yield: 6 cups (127 calories per 1-cup serving).

PROTEIN 5.6 / FAT 0.9 / CARBOHYDRATE 25.3 / CHOLESTEROL 3 / IRON 0.6 / SODIUM 67 / CALCIUM 176

Strawberry Champagne

(pictured on cover)

1 quart fresh strawberries,
   washed and hulled
1 (6-ounce) can frozen pink
   lemonade concentrate, thawed
   and undiluted
1/3 cup instant nonfat dry milk
   powder
2 cups crushed ice
1 (25.4-ounce) bottle pink
   champagne, chilled

Combine strawberries and lemonade in container of an electric blender; top with cover, and process until smooth. Add milk powder and ice; blend mixture until smooth and thickened.

To serve, combine strawberry mixture and champagne in a large pitcher or punch bowl; stir well. Serve immediately. Yield: 7½ cups (121 calories per ¾-cup serving).

PROTEIN 2.1 / FAT 0.3 / CARBOHYDRATE 15.8 / CHOLESTEROL 1 / IRON 0.8 / SODIUM 26 / CALCIUM 63

Hot Apple Cider Nog

3 cups skim milk
1 cup unsweetened apple cider
¼ cup sugar
2 eggs, lightly beaten
¼ teaspoon ground cinnamon
¼ teaspoon ground nutmeg, divided
6 (6-inch) sticks cinnamon (optional)

*P*lace milk in a medium saucepan; cook over low heat until warm.

Combine cider, sugar, eggs, cinnamon, and ⅛ teaspoon nutmeg in a large saucepan. Cook over medium heat, stirring constantly, 5 minutes or until thoroughly heated (do not boil). Slowly add warm milk, stirring with a wire whisk until frothy. Pour into individual mugs, and sprinkle with remaining nutmeg. Garnish with cinnamon sticks, if desired. Serve immediately. Yield: 4½ cups (121 calories per ¾-cup serving).

PROTEIN 6.2 / FAT 2.1 / CARBOHYDRATE 19.4 / CHOLESTEROL 94 / IRON 0.6 / SODIUM 88 / CALCIUM 164

Cranberry Tea
(pictured on pages 12 and 13)

2 quarts water
2 quarts reduced-calorie cranberry juice cocktail
4 regular-size tea bags
4 (3-inch) sticks cinnamon
¼ cup sugar
¾ teaspoon cardamom seeds
¾ teaspoon whole cloves

*P*our water and cranberry juice cocktail into a 30-cup electric percolator. Place tea bags, cinnamon sticks, sugar, cardamom, and cloves in percolator basket. Perk through complete cycle of electric percolator. Serve warm. Yield: 4 quarts (36 calories per 1-cup serving).

PROTEIN 0.0 / FAT 0.0 / CARBOHYDRATE 9.0 / CHOLESTEROL 0 / IRON 2.8 / SODIUM 4 / CALCIUM 7

Spiced Tea
(pictured on pages 12 and 13)

4 orange pekoe tea bags
2 tablespoons sugar
1 (3-inch) stick cinnamon
½ teaspoon whole cloves
¼ cup unsweetened orange juice
1 tablespoon lemon juice
4 cups boiling water

*C*ombine first 6 ingredients in a 1-quart glass measure; gradually add boiling water to mixture. Steep 8 to 10 minutes. Strain liquid; discard tea bags and spices. Serve tea warm or over ice. Yield: 4 cups (34 calories per 1-cup serving).

PROTEIN 0.1 / FAT 0.0 / CARBOHYDRATE 9.1 / CHOLESTEROL 0 / IRON 0.0 / SODIUM 0 / CALCIUM 2

Take the chill off winter days with Hot Apple Cider Nog, a cross between hot apple cider and eggnog.

Fresh Mint Tea

(pictured on pages 12 and 13)

½ cup Fresh Mint Tea Extract
3 cups sparkling mineral water,
　chilled
Fresh mint sprigs (optional)

Fresh Mint Tea Extract

2 cups packed fresh mint leaves,
　finely chopped
Dash of salt
2 cups sugar
2 cups water

*P*lace 2 tablespoons Fresh Mint Tea Extract over crushed ice in each of 4 serving glasses. Add ¾ cup mineral water to each glass, stirring well. Garnish with fresh mint sprigs, if desired. Yield: 3½ cups (72 calories per serving).

*P*lace mint leaves in a medium-size glass bowl. Sprinkle with salt; cover and set aside.

Combine sugar and water in a medium saucepan; bring mixture to a boil, and cook until sugar dissolves. Pour boiling syrup over mint leaves. Cover and let stand 1 hour.

Line a colander or sieve with a double layer of cheese-cloth that has been rinsed out and squeezed dry, allowing cheese-cloth to extend over outside edges of colander. Pour mint mixture through sieve into a 2-quart glass measure. Discard mint leaves. Cover and store in refrigerator. Yield: 2¾ cups.

PROTEIN 0.2 / FAT 0.0 / CARBOHYDRATE 36.9 / CHOLESTEROL 0 / IRON 0.7 / SODIUM 54 / CALCIUM 14

Slimmer Irish Coffee

⅓ cup water
⅓ cup instant nonfat dry milk
　powder
2 tablespoons plus 2 teaspoons
　sugar
3 cups strong, hot brewed coffee
½ cup Irish whiskey

*P*lace water in a small, narrow glass or stainless steel bowl; freeze 25 minutes or until a ⅛-inch-thick layer of ice forms on surface.

Add milk powder to partially frozen water; beat at high speed of an electric mixer 5 minutes or until stiff peaks form. Add sugar; beat well.

Divide coffee among 4 coffee cups. Spoon 2 tablespoons whiskey over coffee. Top with whipped milk mixture. Yield: 3 cups (124 calories per serving.)

PROTEIN 3.9 / FAT 0.1 / CARBOHYDRATE 17.1 / CHOLESTEROL 2 / IRON 0.8 / SODIUM 57 / CALCIUM 130

Flaming Café Royal

(pictured on pages 12 and 13)

2 cups strong, hot brewed coffee
6 sugar cubes
6 (2-inch) strips lemon rind
¼ cup plus 2 tablespoons brandy

*P*our hot coffee into 6 demitasse cups. Add 1 sugar cube and 1 strip lemon rind to each cup.

Place brandy in a small, long-handled saucepan; heat until warm (do not boil). Remove from heat. Gently spoon 1 tablespoon warm brandy over coffee in each cup (do not stir). Ignite with a long match; serve immediately. Yield: 2 cups (10 calories per ⅓-cup serving).

PROTEIN 0.1 / FAT 0.0 / CARBOHYDRATE 2.4 / CHOLESTEROL 0 / IRON 0.3 / SODIUM 2 / CALCIUM 2

Cappuccino

1½ cups skim milk
¼ cup instant nonfat dry milk powder
1 tablespoon plus 1 teaspoon espresso powder
2 teaspoons sugar
⅛ teaspoon ground cinnamon
¼ teaspoon grated semisweet chocolate

*C*ombine skim milk and milk powder in a medium saucepan. Bring to a boil, stirring constantly with a wire whisk. Remove from heat.

Divide espresso powder among 4 coffee cups. Divide milk mixture evenly among coffee cups. Add ½ teaspoon sugar to each serving. Sprinkle evenly with cinnamon and grated chocolate. Serve immediately. Yield: 4 cups (71 calories per 1-cup serving).

PROTEIN 6.0 / FAT 0.3 / CARBOHYDRATE 10.6 / CHOLESTEROL 3 / IRON 0.1 / SODIUM 88 / CALCIUM 210

Viennese Coffee

(pictured on pages 12 and 13)

⅓ cup water
⅓ cup instant nonfat dry milk powder
1 tablespoon sugar
3 cups strong, hot brewed coffee
⅛ teaspoon ground nutmeg

*P*lace water in a small, narrow glass or stainless steel bowl; freeze 25 minutes or until a ⅛-inch-thick layer of ice forms on surface.

Add milk powder to partially frozen water; beat at high speed of an electric mixer 5 minutes or until stiff peaks form. Add sugar; beat well.

Divide coffee among 4 coffee cups. Top with whipped milk mixture. Sprinkle with nutmeg. Serve immediately. Yield: 3 cups (52 calories per serving).

PROTEIN 3.8 / FAT 0.1 / CARBOHYDRATE 9.1 / CHOLESTEROL 2 / IRON 0.8 / SODIUM 57 / CALCIUM 129

Cakes

Cakes, a traditional symbol of celebration, are a welcome accompaniment for birthdays, anniversaries, and holidays. And for healthy eating, cakes need not be eliminated from these occasions.

Although the ingredients may vary slightly from those customarily used in baking, the texture, flavor, and appearance of these "light" cakes will be pleasingly familiar. Lighter cakes are possible with careful balancing of ingredients. For a fine, tender texture, cake flour is used in many of the recipes; this reduces the sugar and fat, thereby reducing the total calories of the cake.

This chapter introduces new combinations of ingredients as well as a number of old favorites: angel food, sponge and chiffon cakes, rolled cakes, cheesecakes, pound cakes, layer cakes, and quick-to-mix cakes—all "lightened," attractive, and flavorful!

When it's time for dessert, no one will be able to resist these light offerings: (clockwise from upper left) a serving of "Mile High" Peach Meringue Torte (page 54), Poppy Seed Cake With Lemon Filling (page 50), and Orange Custard Cake (page 51).

Old-Fashioned Sponge Cake

4 eggs, separated
²/₃ cup cold water
1 cup sugar
1½ cups sifted cake flour
¼ teaspoon salt
2 teaspoons grated lemon rind
1 teaspoon lemon extract
1 teaspoon cream of tartar
1 tablespoon powdered sugar

Combine egg yolks and cold water in a large bowl; beat at high speed of an electric mixer 5 minutes. Gradually add 1 cup sugar, 2 tablespoons at a time, and beat an additional 5 minutes or until thick and lemon colored.

Sift flour and salt together. Sift again over egg yolk mixture, and blend at low speed. Stir in lemon rind and lemon extract.

Beat egg whites (at room temperature) at high speed of an electric mixer until foamy. Add cream of tartar, and beat until stiff peaks form. Gently fold egg whites into egg yolk mixture.

Pour batter into an ungreased 10-inch tube pan. Bake at 325° for 55 to 60 minutes or until cake springs back when lightly touched. Invert pan; cool 2 hours or until cake is cooled completely. Loosen cake from sides of pan using a narrow metal spatula; remove from pan. Sift powdered sugar over cake. Yield: 12 servings (140 calories per serving).

PROTEIN 3.0 / FAT 2.0 / CARBOHYDRATE 27.0 / CHOLESTEROL 91 / IRON 0.4 / SODIUM 89 / CALCIUM 12

Old-Fashioned Angel Food Cake

¾ cup all-purpose flour
1¼ cups sugar, divided
12 egg whites
1½ teaspoons cream of tartar
¼ teaspoon salt
1½ teaspoons vanilla extract

Combine flour and ¾ cup sugar in a small bowl; set mixture aside.

Beat egg whites (at room temperature) in an extra-large bowl at high speed of an electric mixer until foamy. Add cream of tartar and salt; beat until soft peaks form. Gradually add remaining ½ cup sugar, 2 tablespoons at a time, beating until stiff peaks form. Sift flour mixture over egg white mixture, ¼ cup at a time, folding in carefully after each addition. Gently fold in vanilla.

Pour batter into an ungreased 10-inch tube pan; spread evenly with a spatula. Bake at 375° for 30 to 35 minutes or until cake springs back when lightly touched. Remove cake from oven. Invert pan; cool 1 hour. Loosen cake from sides of pan using a narrow metal spatula; remove from pan. Yield: 12 servings (130 calories per serving).

PROTEIN 4.2 / FAT 0.1 / CARBOHYDRATE 27.9 / CHOLESTEROL 0 / IRON 0.3 / SODIUM 125 / CALCIUM 5

Piña Colada Angel Food Cake

1¼ cups sugar, divided
¾ cup all-purpose flour
11 egg whites
1½ teaspoons cream of tartar
¼ teaspoon salt
1 teaspoon coconut extract
Piña Colada Filling
¼ cup unsweetened coconut

Combine ¾ cup sugar and flour; set aside. Beat egg whites (at room temperature) in an extra-large mixing bowl at high speed of an electric mixer until foamy. Add cream of tartar and salt; beat until soft peaks form. Add remaining sugar, one tablespoon at a time, beating until stiff peaks form. Sift flour mixture over egg whites; fold in carefully. Fold in coconut extract.

Pour batter into an ungreased 10-inch tube pan. Cut through batter with a knife to remove air bubbles. Bake at 375° for 30 to 35 minutes or until golden brown. Invert pan; cool completely. Loosen cake from sides of pan using a narrow metal spatula; remove from pan.

Split cake into 3 layers. Place first layer in tube pan. Spread half of Piña Colada Filling on layer; top with second layer and remaining filling. Top with remaining cake layer. Cover and chill 8 hours or overnight. Invert cake onto serving platter. Spread reserved 2 tablespoons pineapple yogurt over top; sprinkle with coconut. Slice cake with an electric knife. Yield: 12 servings (173 calories per serving).

Piña Colada Filling

1 package unflavored gelatin
¼ cup cold water
1 (8-ounce) can unsweetened
    crushed pineapple, undrained
1 (8-ounce) carton pineapple
    low-fat yogurt
2 egg whites

Soften gelatin in cold water. Drain pineapple, reserving fruit and juice. Place pineapple juice in a small saucepan over medium heat; add gelatin, stirring to dissolve. Add reserved pineapple; chill until mixture mounds from a spoon. Reserve 2 tablespoons yogurt for topping; stir remaining yogurt into pineapple mixture. Beat egg whites (at room temperature) at high speed of an electric mixer until stiff peaks form. Fold into pineapple mixture. Yield: 3⅓ cups.

PROTEIN 6.0 / FAT 1.4 / CARBOHYDRATE 34.6 / CHOLESTEROL 1 / IRON 0.4 / SODIUM 141 / CALCIUM 35

Angel food cake contains no egg yolk or shortening, making it low in fat and calories. For the highest volume of angel food cake, beat egg whites (at room temperature) at high speed of an electric mixer until stiff but not dry.

Chocolate Angel Food Cake

¾ cup sifted cake flour
¼ teaspoon baking soda
¼ cup unsweetened cocoa
1 cup sugar, divided
11 egg whites
1½ teaspoons cream of tartar
¼ teaspoon salt
1½ teaspoons vanilla extract
1 tablespoon powdered sugar

Sift flour, soda, cocoa, and ⅓ cup sugar together 3 times; set aside.

Beat egg whites (at room temperature) in an extra-large bowl at high speed of an electric mixer until foamy. Add cream of tartar, salt, and vanilla; beat until soft peaks form. Gradually add ⅔ cup sugar, beating until stiff peaks form. Sprinkle flour mixture over egg white mixture, ¼ cup at a time; fold in carefully.

Pour batter into an ungreased 10-inch tube pan, spreading evenly. Bake at 350° for 35 to 40 minutes or until cake springs back when lightly touched. Invert pan; cool 40 minutes or until completely cooled. Loosen cake from sides of pan using a narrow metal spatula; remove from pan. Sift powdered sugar over cooled cake. Yield: 12 servings (113 calories per serving).

PROTEIN 4.0 / FAT 0.3 / CARBOHYDRATE 23.5 / CHOLESTEROL 0 / IRON 0.4 / SODIUM 138 / CALCIUM 11

Orange Chiffon Cake

1 cup sifted cake flour
⅔ cup sugar
1½ teaspoons baking powder
¼ teaspoon salt
2 egg yolks
⅓ cup water
3 tablespoons vegetable oil
1 teaspoon grated orange rind
1 teaspoon vanilla extract
6 egg whites
¼ teaspoon cream of tartar
1 tablespoon powdered sugar
Edible flowers (optional)

Combine flour, sugar, baking powder, and salt in a large mixing bowl. Combine egg yolks, water, oil, orange rind, and vanilla in a small bowl; stir well with a wire whisk. Make a well in center of dry ingredients; add egg yolk mixture, stirring until smooth.

Beat egg whites (at room temperature) and cream of tartar in a large mixing bowl at high speed of an electric mixer until stiff peaks form. Gently fold egg whites into batter. Pour batter into an ungreased 10-inch tube pan, spreading evenly with a spatula. Bake at 325° for 50 to 60 minutes or until cake springs back when lightly touched. Remove from oven; invert pan, and cool completely. Loosen cake from sides of pan using a narrow metal spatula; remove from pan. Sift powdered sugar over cooled cake. Garnish with edible flowers, if desired. Yield: 12 servings (125 calories per serving).

PROTEIN 2.7 / FAT 4.4 / CARBOHYDRATE 18.5 / CHOLESTEROL 45 / IRON 0.2 / SODIUM 117 / CALCIUM 32

*Dress Orange Chiffon Cake for company with powdered sugar and edible flowers;
it tastes as light and delicious as it looks.*

Quarter Pound Cake

2 cups all-purpose flour
1 cup sugar
2 teaspoons baking powder
⅛ teaspoon salt
¾ cup skim milk
½ cup margarine, softened
1 egg
2 egg whites
1 teaspoon lemon extract
1 teaspoon vanilla extract
Vegetable cooking spray

Combine first 10 ingredients in a large bowl; beat 3 minutes at medium speed of an electric mixer.

Pour batter into an 8-cup tube pan that has been coated with cooking spray. Bake at 350° for 55 to 60 minutes or until a wooden pick inserted in center comes out clean. Cool in pan 15 minutes; remove from pan, and let cool completely on a wire rack. Yield: 16 servings (176 calories per serving).

PROTEIN 3.0 / FAT 6.3 / CARBOHYDRATE 26.3 / CHOLESTEROL 17 / IRON 0.6 / SODIUM 140 / CALCIUM 45

Brown Sugar Applesauce Cake

1¾ cups sifted cake flour
⅓ cup firmly packed brown sugar
1 teaspoon baking powder
1 teaspoon pumpkin pie spice
½ teaspoon baking soda
½ teaspoon ground cinnamon
1 cup unsweetened applesauce
¼ cup plus 1 tablespoon
   vegetable oil
1 egg
1 tablespoon vanilla extract
⅓ cup currants
Vegetable cooking spray

Combine cake flour, brown sugar, baking powder, pumpkin pie spice, soda, and cinnamon in a large bowl; stir until well blended. Make a well in center of mixture. Add applesauce and next 3 ingredients, stirring until smooth. Stir in currants.

Spoon batter into a 6-cup Bundt pan that has been coated with cooking spray. Bake at 350° for 35 minutes or until a wooden pick inserted in center comes out clean. Cool in pan 5 minutes; invert cake onto a wire rack, and cool completely. Yield: 12 servings (155 calories per serving).

PROTEIN 1.7 / FAT 6.4 / CARBOHYDRATE 22.6 / CHOLESTEROL 23 / IRON 0.6 / SODIUM 69 / CALCIUM 39

Unfrosted cakes containing pureed fruit or fruit juice generally freeze well. Slice and freeze any leftovers to use as individual servings; the slices will be as fresh as they were when first prepared.

Chocolate-Zucchini Cake

Vegetable cooking spray
¼ cup sugar, divided
¾ cup firmly packed brown sugar
¼ cup margarine, softened
¼ cup plus 1 tablespoon
  vegetable oil
3 eggs
½ cup nonfat buttermilk
1½ teaspoons vanilla extract
2½ cups sifted cake flour
¼ cup unsweetened cocoa
1 teaspoon baking powder
1 teaspoon baking soda
2 teaspoons ground cinnamon
¼ teaspoon salt
¼ teaspoon ground nutmeg
1 medium zucchini, shredded
  (about ½ pound)
2 teaspoons powdered sugar

Coat a 10-inch Bundt pan with cooking spray. Dust with 2 teaspoons sugar. Set aside.

Combine remaining sugar, brown sugar, margarine, and oil in a large bowl. Beat at medium speed of an electric mixer until well blended. Add eggs, one at a time, beating well after each addition. Stir in buttermilk and vanilla.

Combine flour and next 6 ingredients, stirring well. Add to batter, mixing well. Press zucchini between paper towels to remove excess moisture. Stir into batter. Pour batter into prepared pan.

Bake at 325° for 45 to 55 minutes or until a wooden pick inserted in center comes out clean. Let cool in pan 10 minutes. Remove from pan; invert onto a wire rack, and cool completely. Sift powdered sugar over cooled cake. Yield: 16 servings (198 calories per serving).

PROTEIN 3.1 / FAT 8.6 / CARBOHYDRATE 27.3 / CHOLESTEROL 51 / IRON 1.0 / SODIUM 165 / CALCIUM 48

Gingerbread Cake

2 cups sifted cake flour
1 teaspoon baking powder
1 teaspoon ground ginger
½ teaspoon baking soda
½ teaspoon ground cinnamon
½ teaspoon ground nutmeg
¾ cup water
⅓ cup firmly packed brown sugar
¼ cup light molasses
2 tablespoons vegetable oil
Vegetable cooking spray
¼ cup sugar
⅓ cup water
2 tablespoons lemon juice
½ teaspoon grated lemon rind

Combine first 6 ingredients in a large bowl; stir well.

Combine water, brown sugar, molasses, and oil in a small bowl; stir well with a wire whisk. Add molasses mixture to flour mixture, stirring just until blended.

Pour batter into a 6½-cup ring mold that has been coated with cooking spray. Bake at 350° for 35 to 40 minutes or until a wooden pick inserted in center comes out clean.

Combine sugar, water, lemon juice, and lemon rind in a small saucepan; bring to a boil over medium heat, stirring often. Pour over hot cake. Let stand 5 minutes or until sauce is absorbed. Unmold onto a serving plate; serve warm. Yield: 12 servings (137 calories per serving).

PROTEIN 1.2 / FAT 2.5 / CARBOHYDRATE 27.7 / CHOLESTEROL 0 / IRON 0.6 / SODIUM 63 / CALCIUM 44

Old-Fashioned Marble Cake

(pictured on back cover)

2½ cups all-purpose flour
1 cup sugar
2½ teaspoons baking powder
¼ teaspoon salt
1 cup skim milk
⅓ cup vegetable oil
¼ cup water
1 teaspoon vanilla extract
¼ cup unsweetened cocoa
1 teaspoon ground cinnamon
⅛ teaspoon baking soda
8 egg whites
Vegetable cooking spray
2 teaspoons powdered sugar
Fresh raspberries (optional)

Combine first 4 ingredients in a large bowl. Add skim milk, oil, water, and vanilla. Beat at low speed of an electric mixer until blended. Remove half of batter, and add cocoa, cinnamon, and soda; stir until well blended.

Beat egg whites (at room temperature) at high speed of an electric mixer until stiff peaks form. Fold half of egg whites into chocolate mixture. Fold remaining half into plain batter.

Spoon half of plain batter into a 10-inch fancy tube pan that has been coated with cooking spray. Top with half of chocolate batter. Repeat layers, ending with chocolate batter. Gently swirl batter with a knife to create marble effect.

Bake at 375° for 35 to 40 minutes or until a wooden pick inserted in center comes out clean. Cool in pan 5 minutes; remove from pan, and let cool completely on a wire rack. Sift powdered sugar over cooled cake. Garnish with fresh raspberries, if desired. Yield: 16 servings (189 calories per serving).

PROTEIN 4.8 / FAT 5.0 / CARBOHYDRATE 30.9 / CHOLESTEROL 0 / IRON 0.9 / SODIUM 124 / CALCIUM 59

Golden Raisin Orange Cake

½ cup margarine, softened
½ cup sugar
¼ cup firmly packed brown sugar
2 eggs
1¾ cups plus 2 tablespoons
    all-purpose flour
2¼ teaspoons baking powder
¾ teaspoon pumpkin pie spice
½ cup water
¼ cup plus 2 tablespoons golden
    raisins
1 tablespoon plus 1½ teaspoons
    grated orange rind
1½ teaspoons vanilla extract
Vegetable cooking spray
3 tablespoons Triple Sec or other
    orange-flavored liqueur

Cream margarine in a large bowl; gradually add sugars, beating well at medium speed of an electric mixer. Add eggs, beating well.

Combine flour, baking powder, and pumpkin pie spice; add to creamed mixture, blending well. Add water, raisins, orange rind, and vanilla; beat at low speed for 1 minute.

Spoon batter into a 6-cup fancy tube pan that has been coated with cooking spray. Bake at 350° for 35 to 40 minutes or until a wooden pick inserted in center comes out clean. Sprinkle liqueur over cake; cool in pan 5 minutes. Remove from pan. Yield: 16 servings (179 calories per serving).

PROTEIN 2.7 / FAT 6.6 / CARBOHYDRATE 26.2 / CHOLESTEROL 34 / IRON 0.8 / SODIUM 120 / CALCIUM 41

Honey-Orange Cake

Vegetable cooking spray
1 tablespoon all-purpose flour
2 eggs
¾ cup sugar
⅛ teaspoon salt
1 tablespoon grated orange rind
1 teaspoon orange extract
1 tablespoon margarine
2 tablespoons honey
⅓ cup water
1 cup sifted cake flour
1 teaspoon baking powder
⅓ cup unsweetened orange juice
1 tablespoon honey
1 navel orange, peeled and sliced
  (optional)

Coat a 9-inch tube pan with cooking spray; dust lightly with 1 tablespoon flour. Set aside.

Combine eggs and next 4 ingredients in a large mixing bowl. Beat at medium speed of an electric mixer until well blended.

Combine margarine, honey, and water in a small saucepan; bring to a boil, stirring constantly. Slowly add to egg mixture, beating at low speed. Stir in cake flour and baking powder.

Pour batter into prepared pan. Bake at 375° for 30 minutes or until a wooden pick inserted in center comes out clean. Remove from oven; cool in pan 5 minutes on a wire rack. Remove from pan, and invert onto serving plate.

Combine orange juice and honey in a small saucepan; bring to a boil. Slowly spoon orange mixture over top of cake, allowing it to be absorbed.

Cut orange slices in half; garnish top of cake with halved orange slices, if desired. Serve warm or cool. Yield: 8 servings (185 calories per serving).

PROTEIN 2.7 / FAT 3.0 / CARBOHYDRATE 37.4 / CHOLESTEROL 69 / IRON 0.4 / SODIUM 109 / CALCIUM 38

When possible, freeze cakes unfrosted as they will keep 4 to 6 months in freezer if wrapped properly. Remove from pan, or remove from pan to cool, and replace in pan for freezing. Wrap airtight in aluminum foil or heavy-duty plastic wrap. For frosted cakes (or leftovers), freeze unwrapped until frosting is firm. Then wrap and freeze. Frosted cakes can be kept 2 to 3 months in freezer if properly wrapped. Cream fillings and fluffy frostings are not recommended for freezing because they break down and become soggy when thawed.

Spiced Cake With Orange Topping

3 eggs
1 tablespoon plus 1½ teaspoons
    unsalted margarine
½ cup firmly packed brown sugar
4 egg whites
⅛ teaspoon salt
¾ cup sifted cake flour
1 teaspoon pumpkin pie spice
Vegetable cooking spray
1 tablespoon all-purpose flour
Orange Topping

Combine eggs, margarine, and brown sugar in top of a double boiler; bring water to a boil. Reduce heat to low; beat mixture at high speed of an electric mixer until sugar dissolves and mixture is warm. Remove from heat, and continue beating at high speed 5 to 10 minutes or until mixture is very thick.

Beat egg whites (at room temperature) and salt in a large bowl at high speed of electric mixer until stiff but not dry. Fold beaten egg whites into yolk mixture.

Sift ¾ cup cake flour and pumpkin pie spice together. Sift one-third of flour mixture over egg mixture; gently fold in. Repeat procedure with remaining flour mixture, adding one-third of the mixture at a time. Spoon batter into a 10-inch Bundt pan that has been coated with cooking spray and dusted with 1 tablespoon all-purpose flour. Bake at 350° for 30 minutes or until a wooden pick inserted in center comes out clean. Remove from pan; invert onto a wire rack. Cut cake into 12 servings. Dollop each serving with 2 tablespoons Orange Topping; serve warm. Yield: 12 servings (111 calories per serving).

Orange Topping

¼ cup unsweetened orange juice
¼ cup instant nonfat dry milk
    powder
2 teaspoons Cointreau or other
    orange-flavored liqueur

Place orange juice in a narrow, glass or stainless steel bowl; freeze 25 minutes or until a ⅛-inch-thick layer of ice forms on surface.

Add milk powder to partially frozen orange juice; beat at high speed of an electric mixer 5 minutes or until stiff peaks form. Stir in liqueur. Yield: 1½ cups.

PROTEIN 4.1 / FAT 2.9 / CARBOHYDRATE 16.6 / CHOLESTEROL 69 / IRON 0.7 / SODIUM 75 / CALCIUM 51

Using the correct size cake pan will help assure a successful product. Too large a pan causes cake to bake too fast, resulting in a dark bottom, pale top, and a tough, coarse texture. Too small a pan may cause the cake batter to run over the edge as it bakes, resulting in a sunken center and coarse texture with a sticky center layer.

Rum Baba

1 package dry yeast
1½ cups all-purpose flour
¼ cup sugar
¼ teaspoon salt
½ cup water
3 tablespoons margarine
2 eggs
Vegetable cooking spray
¼ cup sugar
⅓ cup water
3 tablespoons dark rum

Combine yeast, flour, ¼ cup sugar, and salt; set aside. Combine water and margarine in a small saucepan; heat until margarine melts. Cool to 120°. Add to yeast mixture, and beat at medium speed of an electric mixer 2 minutes.

Add eggs, one at a time, beating well after each addition. Spoon batter into an 8-cup mold that has been coated with cooking spray. Cover and let rise in a warm place (85°), free from drafts, 1 hour or until doubled in bulk. Bake at 350° for 30 to 40 minutes or until a wooden pick inserted in center comes out clean.

Combine ¼ cup sugar and ⅓ cup water in a saucepan. Bring mixture to a boil over medium heat; reduce heat, and simmer 10 minutes. Remove from heat, and cool slightly; stir in rum. Spoon sauce over warm cake. Yield: 10 servings (175 calories per serving).

PROTEIN 4.0 / FAT 4.8 / CARBOHYDRATE 26.4 / CHOLESTEROL 55 / IRON 1.1 / SODIUM 114 / CALCIUM 11

Streusel-Topped Cupcakes

1 cup all-purpose flour
2 tablespoons instant nonfat dry milk powder
1 teaspoon baking powder
¼ teaspoon baking soda
Dash of salt
¼ cup plus 1 tablespoon margarine
3 ounces Neufchâtel cheese, softened
½ cup sugar
1 egg
⅓ cup water
½ teaspoon vanilla extract
¼ cup firmly packed brown sugar
3 tablespoons all-purpose flour
½ teaspoon ground cinnamon
1 tablespoon margarine, softened

Combine first 5 ingredients in a small bowl, stirring well; set mixture aside.

Cream ¼ cup plus 1 tablespoon margarine and Neufchâtel in a large bowl. Gradually add sugar, beating well at medium speed of an electric mixer. Add egg and water, beating well. Add reserved dry ingredients; beat until smooth. Stir in vanilla.

Spoon batter evenly into 12 paper-lined muffin cups. Combine brown sugar, 3 tablespoons flour, and cinnamon; cut in 1 tablespoon margarine with a pastry blender until crumbly. Sprinkle brown sugar mixture evenly over batter. Bake at 350° for 25 minutes. Remove from pans, and cool completely on wire racks. Yield: 1 dozen cupcakes (180 calories each).

PROTEIN 3.2 / FAT 8.0 / CARBOHYDRATE 24.2 / CHOLESTEROL 28 / IRON 0.7 / SODIUM 164 / CALCIUM 52

Spiced Crumb Cake

1¼ cups all-purpose flour
½ cup plus 2 tablespoons firmly
  packed dark brown sugar
1 teaspoon ground cinnamon
¼ teaspoon ground cloves
3 tablespoons vegetable oil
2 tablespoons instant nonfat dry
  buttermilk powder
1 teaspoon baking powder
1 teaspoon baking soda
½ teaspoon salt
½ cup water
1 egg, beaten
1 teaspoon vanilla extract
½ teaspoon lemon extract
Vegetable cooking spray

Combine flour, brown sugar, cinnamon, cloves, and vegetable oil in a large bowl. Stir just until dry ingredients are moistened. Remove 1 cup flour mixture, and set aside. Add buttermilk powder and next 7 ingredients to remaining flour mixture. Beat at medium speed of an electric mixer until smooth. Spoon batter into an 8-inch square baking pan that has been coated with cooking spray. Sprinkle evenly with reserved 1 cup flour mixture. Bake at 350° for 30 minutes or until a wooden pick inserted in center comes out clean. Yield: 9 servings (187 calories per serving).

PROTEIN 3.3 / FAT 5.5 / CARBOHYDRATE 30.7 / CHOLESTEROL 31 / IRON 1.3 / SODIUM 277 / CALCIUM 85

Blueberry Cake With Lemon Glaze

3 cups sifted cake flour
2 teaspoons baking powder
¼ teaspoon salt
1½ cups fresh blueberries
1 cup sugar
2 eggs
1 cup skim milk
3 tablespoons vegetable oil
1 teaspoon vanilla extract
1 teaspoon lemon extract
Vegetable cooking spray
1 tablespoon sifted cake flour
1 cup sifted powdered sugar
1 tablespoon plus 1 teaspoon
  lemon juice
1 teaspoon grated lemon rind
Lemon curls (optional)

Combine 3 cups cake flour, baking powder, and salt in a medium bowl. Sprinkle 1 tablespoon flour mixture over blueberries, and toss gently to coat; set aside.

Beat sugar and eggs in a large bowl at medium speed of an electric mixer 5 minutes or until light and fluffy. Combine milk and oil. Add flour mixture to sugar mixture alternately with milk mixture, beating at low speed of an electric mixer until blended. Stir in flavorings. Fold in blueberries.

Pour batter into a 10-cup fancy tube pan that has been coated with cooking spray and dusted with 1 tablespoon cake flour. Bake at 350° for 50 to 55 minutes or until a wooden pick inserted in center comes out clean. Cool cake in pan 10 minutes; remove from pan, and cool completely on a wire rack.

Combine powdered sugar and lemon juice; stir well. Stir in lemon rind. Drizzle glaze over cooled cake. Garnish with lemon curls, if desired. Yield: 16 servings (194 calories per serving).

PROTEIN 2.8 / FAT 3.5 / CARBOHYDRATE 37.6 / CHOLESTEROL 35 / IRON 0.3 / SODIUM 92 / CALCIUM 51

Cake flour gives Blueberry Cake With Lemon Glaze a light texture and the glaze provides a sweet topping.

Apple Mix-in-the-Pan Cake

2 cups chopped apple
⅔ cup sugar
1 cup all-purpose flour
1 teaspoon ground cinnamon
½ teaspoon baking powder
½ teaspoon baking soda
¼ teaspoon salt
¼ cup brewed coffee
3 tablespoons vegetable oil
1 egg
1 teaspoon vanilla extract
¼ cup chopped walnuts or pecans

*P*lace chopped apple in an ungreased 8-inch square baking pan. Sprinkle with sugar. Let stand 10 minutes.

Combine flour, cinnamon, baking powder, soda, and salt. Add to apples; toss gently. Combine coffee, oil, egg, and vanilla; stir well. Add to apple mixture in pan. Stir gently until well blended. Stir in nuts.

Bake at 350° for 45 minutes or until a wooden pick inserted in center comes out clean. Let cool on a wire rack. Cut into squares to serve. Yield: 9 servings (200 calories per serving).

PROTEIN 3.1 / FAT 7.2 / CARBOHYDRATE 31.5 / CHOLESTEROL 30 / IRON 0.8 / SODIUM 136 / CALCIUM 33

Banana Crunch Cake

1 tablespoon margarine
1 tablespoon brown sugar
1 tablespoon honey
⅔ cup unsweetened banana chips
Vegetable cooking spray
½ cup margarine, softened
¾ cup sugar
2 eggs
1 tablespoon lemon juice
1 teaspoon vanilla extract
¼ cup skim milk
¼ cup crème de banana liqueur
1½ cups all-purpose flour
2 tablespoons instant nonfat dry
    buttermilk powder
¾ teaspoon ground nutmeg
¼ teaspoon baking powder
¼ teaspoon baking soda
¼ teaspoon salt

*M*elt 1 tablespoon margarine in a medium skillet; stir in brown sugar, honey, and banana chips. Sauté over low heat, stirring constantly, 2 to 5 minutes or until mixture is golden and chips are coated. Remove from heat, and spread in a 13- x 9- x 2-inch baking pan that has been coated with cooking spray. Chill until firm; break into pieces. Position knife blade in food processor bowl; add banana chip mixture. Top with cover, and process 30 seconds or until coarsely chopped. Set aside.

Cream ½ cup margarine; gradually add sugar, beating well at medium speed of an electric mixer. Add eggs, one at a time, beating well after each addition. Add lemon juice and vanilla; mix well.

Combine milk and liqueur; set aside. Combine flour and remaining ingredients; add to creamed mixture alternately with milk mixture, beginning and ending with flour mixture. Mix well after each addition.

Spread batter in a 13- x 9- x 2-inch baking pan that has been coated with cooking spray. Sprinkle prepared banana crunch topping over batter. Bake at 350° for 30 to 35 minutes or until a wooden pick inserted in center comes out clean. Yield: 16 servings (169 calories per serving).

PROTEIN 2.4 / FAT 7.4 / CARBOHYDRATE 21.7 / CHOLESTEROL 35 / IRON 0.5 / SODIUM 146 / CALCIUM 30

Oat-Apple Coffee Cake

1½ cups regular oats, uncooked
⅔ cup sugar
⅓ cup margarine, softened
1 cup nonfat buttermilk
1 egg
¾ cup all-purpose flour
½ cup whole wheat pastry flour
1 teaspoon baking powder
½ teaspoon baking soda
1 teaspoon ground cinnamon
½ teaspoon ground nutmeg
Vegetable cooking spray
1 large apple, peeled, cored, and thinly sliced (about ½ pound)
Orange Glaze

Combine first 5 ingredients in a large bowl; stir well. Combine all-purpose flour and next 5 ingredients; add to oat mixture, stirring just until blended. Spoon batter into a 13- x 9- x 2-inch baking pan that has been coated with cooking spray. Press apple slices into batter to make evenly spaced rows.

Bake at 375° for 35 to 40 minutes or until a wooden pick inserted in center comes out clean. Cool cake 15 minutes. Drizzle Orange Glaze over cake. Yield: 16 servings (179 calories per serving).

Orange Glaze

1 cup sifted powdered sugar
1 tablespoon plus 2 teaspoons unsweetened orange juice

Combine powdered sugar and orange juice in a small bowl; stir until mixture is smooth. Yield: ⅓ cup.

PROTEIN 3.1 / FAT 4.9 / CARBOHYDRATE 31.4 / CHOLESTEROL 17 / IRON 0.7 / SODIUM 110 / CALCIUM 28

Toasted Walnut Cake

1 cup sifted cake flour
½ cup sugar
1½ teaspoons baking powder
⅛ teaspoon salt
¼ cup skim milk
3 tablespoons vegetable oil
1 egg
1 teaspoon vanilla extract
Vegetable cooking spray
¼ cup chopped walnuts, toasted
Sliced fresh strawberries (optional)

Combine first 4 ingredients in a large bowl. Combine milk, oil, and egg. Add to dry ingredients. Stir in vanilla. Beat at low speed of an electric mixer until blended. Continue beating at high speed 2 minutes.

Pour batter into a 9-inch square pan that has been coated with cooking spray. Cut through batter with a knife to remove air bubbles. Sprinkle walnuts over batter. Bake at 350° for 25 minutes or until a wooden pick inserted in center comes out clean. Cut into squares to serve. Garnish with strawberries, if desired. Yield: 9 servings (155 calories per serving).

PROTEIN 2.5 / FAT 7.1 / CARBOHYDRATE 20.6 / CHOLESTEROL 31 / IRON 0.3 / SODIUM 94 / CALCIUM 47

Caribbean Banana Loaf Cake

Vegetable cooking spray
2 teaspoons all-purpose flour
2 large ripe bananas, peeled and
  sliced
¾ cup sugar
¼ cup plus 1 tablespoon
  margarine, softened
1 egg
2 cups all-purpose flour
2 teaspoons baking powder
¼ teaspoon baking soda
⅛ teaspoon salt
2 tablespoons dark rum
1 teaspoon powdered sugar

Coat a 9- x 5- x 3-inch loafpan with cooking spray. Dust with 2 teaspoons flour; set aside.

Combine banana, sugar, margarine, and egg in container of an electric blender or food processor. Top with cover, and process until smooth.

Combine 2 cups flour, baking powder, soda, and salt in a large bowl. Add banana mixture, and stir just until dry ingredients are moistened.

Pour batter into prepared pan. Bake at 350° for 40 to 50 minutes or until a wooden pick inserted in center comes out clean. Cool in pan 5 minutes. Spoon rum over cake. Let cool an additional 5 minutes. Turn cake out onto a wire rack to cool completely. Sift powdered sugar over cooled cake. Yield: 16 servings (159 calories per serving).

PROTEIN 2.4 / FAT 4.2 / CARBOHYDRATE 27.3 / CHOLESTEROL 17 / IRON 0.6 / SODIUM 115 / CALCIUM 34

Tropical Fruit Cake

½ cup chopped pistachios
½ cup golden raisins
½ cup chopped candied papaya
½ cup chopped candied pineapple
⅓ cup light rum
2 cups all-purpose flour
¾ cup sugar
½ teaspoon baking powder
¼ teaspoon salt
3 tablespoons vegetable oil
1 teaspoon vanilla extract
6 egg whites
Vegetable cooking spray
3 tablespoons light rum

Combine first 5 ingredients, stirring well. Let stand overnight.

Combine flour and next 3 ingredients in a large bowl. Add fruit mixture; stir to coat evenly. Stir in oil and vanilla.

Beat egg whites (at room temperature) at high speed of an electric mixer until stiff peaks form. Fold into batter.

Spoon batter into an 8½- x 4½- x 3-inch loafpan that has been coated with cooking spray and lined with parchment paper. Bake at 350° for 55 minutes to 1 hour or until a wooden pick inserted in center comes out clean. Cool in pan 10 minutes; remove from pan. Remove parchment. Let cake cool completely on a wire rack.

Moisten several layers of cheesecloth with 3 tablespoons rum; wrap cake in cheesecloth. Wrap with aluminum foil. Refrigerate at least 3 days before cutting. Yield: 24 servings (154 calories per serving).

PROTEIN 2.9 / FAT 3.6 / CARBOHYDRATE 21.6 / CHOLESTEROL 0 / IRON 0.7 / SODIUM 44 / CALCIUM 16

Colonial Spice Cake

¾ cup sugar
1 cup water
1 teaspoon ground cinnamon
½ teaspoon salt
¼ teaspoon ground cloves
¼ teaspoon ground allspice
¼ cup vegetable oil
¼ cup raisins
2 tablespoons chopped pecans
2 cups all-purpose flour
2 teaspoons baking powder
Vegetable cooking spray
2 tablespoons margarine, melted
2 tablespoons brown sugar
¼ cup grated fresh coconut
2 tablespoons chopped pecans

*C*ombine first 9 ingredients in a medium saucepan. Cook over medium heat until mixture comes to a boil; cook 1 minute. Remove from heat; cool 15 minutes. Add flour and baking powder, stirring well with a wooden spoon. Spoon batter into an 8½- x 4½- x 3-inch loafpan that has been coated with cooking spray. Bake at 350° for 35 to 40 minutes or until a wooden pick inserted in center comes out clean.

Combine margarine, brown sugar, coconut, and 2 tablespoons pecans; stir well. Spread over top of hot cake. Broil 6 inches from heat 2 to 3 minutes or until topping bubbles. Cool in pan 10 minutes. Remove from pan; cool completely on a wire rack. Yield: 16 servings (174 calories per serving).

PROTEIN 2.1 / FAT 7.1 / CARBOHYDRATE 26.1 / CHOLESTEROL 0 / IRON 0.7 / SODIUM 129 / CALCIUM 33

Blueberry Cake

1⅓ cups all-purpose flour
½ cup plus 2 tablespoons sugar, divided
2 teaspoons baking powder
¼ teaspoon salt
¼ cup margarine, softened
½ cup skim milk
1 egg, beaten
½ teaspoon vanilla extract
Vegetable cooking spray
1 cup fresh blueberries

*C*ombine flour, ½ cup sugar, baking powder, salt, and margarine in a large bowl. Beat at low speed of an electric mixer until well blended. Add milk, egg, and vanilla, beating until smooth. Pour into a 9-inch square baking pan that has been coated with cooking spray. Sprinkle blueberries over top. Sprinkle with remaining 2 tablespoons sugar. Bake at 375° for 25 to 30 minutes or until a wooden pick inserted in center comes out clean. Serve warm. Yield: 9 servings (197 calories per serving).

PROTEIN 3.4 / FAT 6.0 / CARBOHYDRATE 32.5 / CHOLESTEROL 31 / IRON 0.8 / SODIUM 208 / CALCIUM 69

Store single-layer cakes in baking pan, tightly sealed with the pan's cover, aluminum foil, or heavy-duty plastic wrap. Store layer cakes in a deep plastic or metal pan or under a glass dome. Cakes with dairy products in the filling or frosting should be stored in the refrigerator to prevent spoilage.

Cranberry Cake With Brown Sugar Sauce

1 cup all-purpose flour
1/2 cup sugar
1 teaspoon baking powder
1/2 teaspoon salt
1/2 cup skim milk
2 tablespoons margarine, melted
1 1/2 cups fresh cranberries
Vegetable cooking spray
1/4 cup water
2 tablespoons sugar
1 tablespoon plus 1 1/2 teaspoons
  margarine
1 tablespoon brown sugar

Combine flour, sugar, baking powder, and salt in a large bowl; stir well. Add skim milk and margarine. Beat at low speed of an electric mixer until well blended. Gently stir in cranberries. Pour batter into a 9-inch square pan that has been coated with cooking spray. Bake at 375° for 30 minutes or until a wooden pick inserted in center comes out clean.

Combine water and remaining ingredients in a small saucepan. Bring to a boil, stirring constantly. Pour boiling sauce mixture over warm cake. Let stand 5 to 10 minutes before serving. Yield: 9 servings (167 calories per serving).

PROTEIN 2.2 / FAT 4.7 / CARBOHYDRATE 29.6 / CHOLESTEROL 0 / IRON 0.5 / SODIUM 224 / CALCIUM 45

Cocoa Crazy Cake

1 1/2 cups all-purpose flour
1/2 cup plus 2 tablespoons sugar
1/4 cup unsweetened cocoa
1 teaspoon baking soda
1/4 teaspoon salt
1 cup water
3 tablespoons plus 1 teaspoon
  vegetable oil
1 teaspoon lemon juice
1 teaspoon vanilla extract
2 teaspoons powdered sugar

Combine first 5 ingredients in an ungreased 8-inch square baking pan, stirring well. Combine water, oil, lemon juice, and vanilla. Add to dry ingredients, stirring with a fork until batter is smooth.

Bake at 350° for 30 minutes. Let cool in pan on a wire rack. Sift powdered sugar over cooled cake. Yield: 9 servings (196 calories per serving).

PROTEIN 3.1 / FAT 5.6 / CARBOHYDRATE 33.2 / CHOLESTEROL 0 / IRON 1.1 / SODIUM 157 / CALCIUM 27

Check a cake for doneness as directed in each recipe. Begin checking for doneness 5 minutes ahead of the specified baking time to allow for differences in ovens.

One-Bowl Cocoa Cake

2 cups sifted cake flour
1 cup sugar
½ cup unsweetened cocoa
1 teaspoon baking powder
1 teaspoon baking soda
½ teaspoon salt
¾ cup strong brewed coffee
½ cup vegetable oil
½ cup nonfat buttermilk
Vegetable cooking spray
1 tablespoon powdered sugar

Combine first 6 ingredients in a large bowl; stir well. Add coffee, oil, and buttermilk, stirring until well blended. Pour batter into a 13- x 9- x 2-inch baking pan that has been coated with cooking spray. Bake at 350° for 35 minutes or until a wooden pick inserted in center comes out clean. Let cake cool completely. Sift powdered sugar over cooled cake. Yield: 16 servings (167 calories per serving).

PROTEIN 1.7 / FAT 7.3 / CARBOHYDRATE 23.9 / CHOLESTEROL 0 / IRON 0.6 / SODIUM 144 / CALCIUM 30

Spicy Gingerbread With Lemon Sauce

1 cup all-purpose flour
¼ cup sugar
1½ teaspoons pumpkin pie spice
⅛ teaspoon salt
1 egg, beaten
2 tablespoons light molasses
½ cup hot water
1 teaspoon baking soda
Vegetable cooking spray
Lemon Sauce

Combine flour, sugar, pumpkin pie spice, and salt in a mixing bowl. Combine egg and molasses; set aside. Combine water and soda. Add molasses mixture and water mixture to flour mixture, stirring until dry ingredients are moistened. Pour batter into an 8-inch square baking pan that has been coated with cooking spray. Bake at 350° for 20 minutes or until a wooden pick inserted in center comes out clean. Cool slightly. Cut into 9 squares; spoon 1 tablespoon Lemon Sauce over each serving. Yield: 9 servings (121 calories per serving).

Lemon Sauce

3 tablespoons sugar
2 teaspoons cornstarch
½ teaspoon grated lemon rind
½ cup water
1 tablespoon plus 1½ teaspoons
    lemon juice
1 teaspoon margarine

Combine all ingredients in a small saucepan. Cook over medium heat, stirring constantly, until thickened. Yield: ½ cup plus 1 tablespoon.

PROTEIN 2.3 / FAT 1.3 / CARBOHYDRATE 25.3 / CHOLESTEROL 30 / IRON 0.8 / SODIUM 138 / CALCIUM 35

Chocolate Cupcakes

(pictured on pages 44 and 45)

⅓ cup margarine, softened
¾ cup firmly packed brown sugar
2 eggs
1 cup all-purpose flour
¼ cup unsweetened cocoa
1 teaspoon baking soda
¼ teaspoon salt
½ cup skim milk
1 teaspoon vanilla extract
Chocolate Frosting

Cream margarine; gradually add brown sugar, beating well at medium speed of an electric mixer. Add eggs, one at a time, beating well after each addition.

Combine flour, cocoa, soda, and salt; add to creamed mixture alternately with skim milk, beginning and ending with flour mixture. Mix after each addition. Stir in vanilla.

Spoon batter into paper-lined muffin pans, filling each cup two-thirds full. Bake at 375° for 20 minutes. Remove from pans, and cool completely on wire racks. Frost with Chocolate Frosting. Yield: 14 cupcakes (168 calories each).

Chocolate Frosting

¾ cup sifted powdered sugar
1 tablespoon unsweetened cocoa
1 teaspoon vanilla extract
Dash of salt
1 tablespoon hot water

Combine all ingredients in a small bowl. Stir well until frosting is of spreading consistency. Yield: ¼ cup.

PROTEIN 2.8 / FAT 5.5 / CARBOHYDRATE 26.9 / CHOLESTEROL 39 / IRON 1.2 / SODIUM 180 / CALCIUM 44

Lady Baltimore Cake

(pictured on pages 44 and 45)

Vegetable cooking spray
¼ cup margarine, softened
⅔ cup sugar
2 cups sifted cake flour
2 teaspoons baking powder
⅛ teaspoon salt
¾ cup skim milk
1 teaspoon vanilla extract
2 egg whites
¼ cup raisins
2 tablespoons chopped walnuts
1 dried fig, chopped
1 teaspoon Frangelica or other
  hazelnut-flavored liqueur
Frosting (recipe follows)

Coat two 8-inch round cakepans with cooking spray; line with wax paper. Set aside.

Cream margarine; gradually add sugar, beating well at medium speed of an electric mixer. Combine flour, baking powder, and salt; add to creamed mixture alternately with milk, beginning and ending with flour mixture. Mix just until blended after each addition. Stir in vanilla.

Beat egg whites (at room temperature) at high speed of an electric mixer until stiff peaks form; fold into batter. Spoon batter evenly into prepared pans. Bake at 375° for 20 to 25 minutes or until a wooden pick inserted in center comes out clean. Cool in pans 10 minutes; remove from pans, and cool completely on wire racks.

Position knife blade in food processor bowl. Add raisins, walnuts, and fig; top with cover, and process 30 seconds or until finely chopped. Remove cover and stir in liqueur and ⅓ cup

Lady Baltimore Cake
(CONTINUED)

Frosting

1 teaspoon unflavored gelatin
1 tablespoon cold water
⅓ cup light corn syrup
1 teaspoon vanilla extract
1 teaspoon Frangelica or other hazelnut-flavored liqueur
1 egg white
¼ teaspoon cream of tartar

frosting. Spread fruit-nut filling between layers; spread remaining frosting on top and sides of cake. Yield: 12 servings (196 calories per serving).

*S*prinkle gelatin over cold water in a small saucepan; let stand 1 minute. Add corn syrup, and cook, stirring constantly, over medium heat just until mixture boils and gelatin dissolves. Remove from heat, and stir in vanilla and liqueur.

Beat egg white (at room temperature) and cream of tartar in a small mixing bowl at high speed of an electric mixer until foamy. Slowly add syrup mixture, and continue beating until stiff peaks form and frosting is of spreading consistency. Yield: 2 cups.

PROTEIN 3.2 / FAT 4.8 / CARBOHYDRATE 34.7 / CHOLESTEROL 0 / IRON 0.2 / SODIUM 156 / CALCIUM 59

Ring of Gold Cake
(pictured on pages 44 and 45)

¼ cup margarine, softened
½ cup sugar
1 egg
2 tablespoons instant nonfat dry milk powder
1 tablespoon grated orange rind
¼ cup water
1½ teaspoons lemon juice
1⅓ cups all-purpose flour
1 teaspoon baking powder
½ teaspoon baking soda
¼ cup chopped pecans
2 egg whites
Vegetable cooking spray
3 tablespoons sugar
2 tablespoons unsweetened orange juice
1 tablespoon Grand Marnier or other orange-flavored liqueur
1 pint fresh strawberries
1 pint blueberries
2 tablespoons sugar

*C*ream margarine; gradually add ½ cup sugar, beating well at medium speed of an electric mixer. Add egg, milk powder, and orange rind. Beat well. Combine water and lemon juice. Combine flour, baking powder, and soda. Add dry ingredients to creamed mixture alternately with water mixture, beginning and ending with flour mixture. Stir in pecans.

Beat egg whites (at room temperature) at high speed of an electric mixer until stiff peaks form. Gently fold beaten egg whites into batter.

Pour batter into a 6½-cup ring mold that has been coated with cooking spray. Bake at 350° for 25 minutes or until a wooden pick inserted in center comes out clean.

Combine 3 tablespoons sugar, orange juice, and liqueur in a small saucepan. Bring to a boil. Remove from heat. Drizzle syrup mixture over hot cake. Let cake cool in pan. Invert onto a serving platter. Fill center of ring with strawberries and blueberries. Sprinkle with 2 tablespoons sugar. Yield: 12 servings (197 calories per serving).

PROTEIN 3.7 / FAT 6.4 / CARBOHYDRATE 32.4 / CHOLESTEROL 23 / IRON 0.7 / SODIUM 127 / CALCIUM 52

Overleaf: *(left to right) Ring of Gold Cake, Lady Baltimore Cake, and Chocolate Cupcakes add up to an irresistible choice of cakes.*

Caramel-Glazed Hot Milk Cake

¾ *cup skim milk*
1 *tablespoon plus 1½ teaspoons*
  margarine
1 *cup sugar*
3 *eggs*
1 *teaspoon vanilla extract*
1½ *cups sifted cake flour*
1½ *teaspoons baking soda*
½ *teaspoon salt*
Vegetable cooking spray
Caramel Glaze

Combine milk and margarine in a small saucepan; cook over medium heat until margarine melts, stirring occasionally. Cool to 120°.

Combine sugar and eggs in a large bowl; beat at high speed of an electric mixer until light and fluffy. Add vanilla, beating well. Combine flour, soda, and salt. Sift flour mixture over egg mixture, beating at low speed. Gradually add milk mixture to egg mixture, beating at high speed. Spoon batter into a 13- x 9- x 2-inch baking dish that has been coated with cooking spray. Bake at 350° for 25 to 30 minutes or until cake is golden brown. Immediately spread Caramel Glaze over warm cake. Yield: 16 servings (141 calories per serving).

Caramel Glaze

¼ *cup plus 1 tablespoon firmly*
  packed brown sugar
2 *tablespoons margarine*
2 *tablespoons skim milk*
1 *teaspoon vanilla extract*

Combine brown sugar, margarine, and milk in a saucepan. Cook over medium heat, stirring constantly, until mixture boils; cook 30 seconds. Remove from heat, and stir in vanilla. Yield: ½ cup.

PROTEIN 2.3 / FAT 3.7 / CARBOHYDRATE 24.8 / CHOLESTEROL 52 / IRON 0.4 / SODIUM 201 / CALCIUM 45

Fresh Plum-Filled Cake

Vegetable cooking spray
½ *cup skim milk*
2 *tablespoons margarine*
1 *cup sugar*
2 *eggs*
1 *teaspoon vanilla extract*
1 *cup all-purpose flour*
1 *teaspoon baking powder*
¼ *teaspoon salt*
Plum Filling
Glaze (recipe follows)

Coat two 9-inch round cakepans with cooking spray, and line with wax paper. Coat wax paper with cooking spray; set pans aside.

Combine milk and margarine in a small saucepan; heat until margarine melts, stirring occasionally. Cool mixture to 120° to 130°. Combine sugar, eggs, and vanilla; beat at high speed of an electric mixer until light and fluffy. Combine flour, baking powder, and salt; add to creamed mixture alternately with milk mixture, beginning and ending with flour mixture. Mix after each addition.

Spoon batter evenly into prepared pans. Bake at 350° for 20 to 25 minutes or until a wooden pick inserted in center comes

Fresh Plum-Filled Cake
(CONTINUED)

out clean. Remove layers from pans; peel off wax paper, and cool completely on wire racks. Spread Plum Filling between cake layers. Drizzle glaze over cake. Yield: 12 servings (200 calories per serving).

Plum Filling

¾ pound fresh plums, quartered and pitted
½ cup Burgundy or other dry red wine
3 tablespoons sugar

Combine plums and wine in a medium saucepan. Cook over medium heat, stirring constantly, until mixture is reduced to 1 cup. Add sugar; continue cooking over medium heat until mixture measures ⅔ cup. Cool slightly. Yield: ⅔ cup.

Glaze

⅔ cup sifted powdered sugar
1 tablespoon kirsch or other cherry-flavored liqueur
1 tablespoon hot water

Combine powdered sugar, liqueur, and hot water, blending until smooth. Yield: ⅓ cup.

PROTEIN 2.8 / FAT 3.2 / CARBOHYDRATE 39.9 / CHOLESTEROL 46 / IRON 0.6 / SODIUM 114 / CALCIUM 38

Lazy Daisy Cake

½ cup skim milk
2 tablespoons margarine
2 eggs
1 cup sugar
1 cup all-purpose flour
1 teaspoon baking powder
¼ teaspoon salt
1 teaspoon vanilla extract
Vegetable cooking spray
½ cup fresh grated coconut
¼ cup plus 1 tablespoon firmly packed brown sugar
3 tablespoons margarine, melted
2 tablespoons skim milk

Combine ½ cup skim milk and 2 tablespoons margarine in a small saucepan; cook over medium heat, stirring constantly, until margarine melts.

Beat eggs at high speed of an electric mixer until foamy. Gradually add 1 cup sugar, beating until mixture is thick and lemon colored (about 5 to 6 minutes). Combine flour, baking powder, and salt in a small bowl, stirring well. Add dry ingredients to egg mixture alternately with hot milk mixture, beginning and ending with dry ingredients. Mix well after each addition. Stir in vanilla.

Spoon batter into a 13- x 9- x 2-inch baking pan that has been coated with cooking spray. Bake at 350° for 30 minutes or until a wooden pick inserted in center comes out clean.

Combine coconut and remaining ingredients in a small bowl; stir well. Top hot cake with coconut mixture. Broil 1 to 2 minutes or until lightly browned. Cool in pan; cut into squares to serve. Yield: 16 servings (158 calories per serving).

PROTEIN 2.2 / FAT 6.0 / CARBOHYDRATE 24.4 / CHOLESTEROL 34 / IRON 0.6 / SODIUM 113 / CALCIUM 34

Heavenly Pineapple Roll

Vegetable cooking spray
¾ cup sugar
4 eggs, separated
¾ cup sifted cake flour
1 teaspoon baking powder
¼ cup skim milk
2 tablespoons unsalted margarine
1 tablespoon powdered sugar
Pineapple Filling
1 teaspoon powdered sugar

Coat a 17- x 11- x 1-inch jellyroll pan with cooking spray, and line with wax paper. Coat wax paper with cooking spray; set pan aside.

Combine sugar and egg yolks in top of a double boiler. Place over boiling water, and cook, stirring constantly with a wire whisk, until thickened. Remove from heat. Beat at high speed of an electric mixer 5 minutes.

Combine flour and baking powder; set aside. Combine milk and margarine in a small saucepan. Cook over medium heat until margarine melts. Cool to 120°. Add flour mixture to yolk mixture alternately with milk mixture, beginning and ending with flour mixture. Set aside.

Beat egg whites (at room temperature) at high speed of an electric mixer until stiff peaks form. Gently fold into yolk mixture. Pour into prepared pan. Bake at 400° for 10 minutes or until golden brown. Invert onto a linen towel that has been dusted with 1 tablespoon powdered sugar; cool. Remove paper from cake. Spread cake with Pineapple Filling; starting at wide end, roll cake jellyroll fashion. Freeze until ready to serve. Let stand at room temperature 5 minutes before serving. Sift 1 teaspoon powdered sugar over cake. Slice with an electric knife. Yield: 16 servings (115 calories per serving).

Pineapple Filling

1 (8-ounce) can unsweetened
  crushed pineapple
1½ teaspoons unflavored gelatin
1 tablespoon cold water
½ cup instant nonfat dry milk
  powder
1 tablespoon rum

Drain pineapple, reserving pineapple; add water to juice if necessary, to yield ½ cup liquid. Place in a small, narrow glass or stainless steel bowl; freeze 25 minutes or until a ⅛-inch-thick layer of ice forms on surface. Sprinkle gelatin over cold water in a small saucepan; let stand 1 minute. Place over medium heat, stirring to dissolve. Add to reserved pineapple, and chill.

Add milk powder to partially frozen juice; beat at high speed of an electric mixer 5 minutes or until stiff peaks form. Beat in rum. Fold into pineapple mixture. Yield: 2 cups.

PROTEIN 3.7 / FAT 3.0 / CARBOHYDRATE 18.1 / CHOLESTEROL 69 / IRON 0.3 / SODIUM 59 / CALCIUM 74

Heavenly Pineapple Roll is a delicate sponge-type cake filled with a light, creamy pineapple filling.

Poppy Seed Cake With Lemon Filling

(pictured on pages 22 and 23)

Vegetable cooking spray
2 teaspoons all-purpose flour
6 egg whites
1 teaspoon cream of tartar
1¾ cups sifted cake flour
¾ cup sifted powdered sugar
2 teaspoons baking powder
2 teaspoons poppy seeds
1 teaspoon grated lemon rind
½ cup vegetable oil
½ cup water
1 teaspoon vanilla extract
Lemon Filling
Light Lemon Frosting

Coat two 9-inch round cakepans with cooking spray. Dust with 2 teaspoons flour. Set aside.

Beat egg whites (at room temperature) in a large bowl until foamy. Add cream of tartar, and beat at high speed of an electric mixer until stiff peaks form.

Combine cake flour and next 4 ingredients in a large bowl. Combine oil and water. Add to dry ingredients. Mix at low speed until well blended. Stir in vanilla. Gently fold in beaten egg whites. Pour batter into prepared pans.

Bake at 350° for 20 to 25 minutes or until cake springs back when lightly touched. Cool in pans 10 minutes. Remove layers from pans, and cool completely on wire racks.

Spread Lemon Filling between cake layers. Frost top and sides of cake with Light Lemon Frosting. Yield: 16 servings (179 calories per serving).

Lemon Filling

¼ cup sugar
2 tablespoons cornstarch
⅛ teaspoon salt
1 cup skim milk
1 egg yolk, lightly beaten
¾ teaspoon grated lemon rind
2 tablespoons lemon juice

Combine sugar, cornstarch, and salt in a medium saucepan. Gradually add milk. Cook over medium heat until mixture thickens, stirring constantly. Remove from heat. Gradually stir about one-fourth of hot mixture into egg yolk. Add to remaining hot mixture. Cook over medium-low heat 2 minutes. Remove from heat. Let cool slightly. Stir in lemon rind and lemon juice. Cover and chill thoroughly. (Mixture will become very thick.) Yield: 1 cup.

Light Lemon Frosting

1 egg white
⅓ cup light corn syrup
1 tablespoon lemon juice
½ teaspoon lemon extract

Beat egg white (at room temperature) at high speed of an electric mixer until soft peaks form. Bring corn syrup and lemon juice to a boil in a small saucepan. Continue beating egg white, and slowly pour boiling syrup mixture over egg white in a slow, steady stream. Beat at high speed 6 to 8 minutes or until light and fluffy. Beat in lemon flavoring. Yield: 2 cups.

PROTEIN 3.1 / FAT 7.5 / CARBOHYDRATE 24.7 / CHOLESTEROL 17 / IRON 0.2 / SODIUM 108 / CALCIUM 54

Orange Custard Cake

(pictured on pages 22 and 23)

1 cup all-purpose flour
1 teaspoon baking powder
¼ teaspoon salt
2 eggs
¾ cup sugar
½ cup skim milk
2 tablespoons margarine
Vegetable cooking spray
1½ teaspoons all-purpose flour
2 tablespoons Triple Sec or other
   orange-flavored liqueur
Custard Topping
Orange curls (optional)
Orange slices (optional)
Kiwifruit slices (optional)

Combine first 3 ingredients in a small bowl; stir well and set aside. Beat eggs in a large mixing bowl at high speed of an electric mixer 4 minutes or until thick and lemon colored. Gradually add sugar, beating at medium speed 5 minutes. Fold dry ingredients into egg mixture. Combine milk and margarine in a saucepan; cook over low heat until margarine melts, stirring occasionally. Cool to 120°. Add to batter, and mix well.

Pour batter into a 10-inch tiara pan that has been coated with cooking spray and dusted with 1½ teaspoons flour. Bake at 350° for 20 to 25 minutes or until a wooden pick inserted in center comes out clean. Cool in pan 10 minutes; remove from pan, and let cool completely on a wire rack.

Pour liqueur evenly over cooled cake. Spread chilled Custard Topping over cake. If desired, garnish with orange curls, orange slices, and kiwifruit slices. Yield: 12 servings (158 calories per serving).

Custard Topping

1 tablespoon plus 1½ teaspoons
   all-purpose flour
2 tablespoons sugar
⅛ teaspoon salt
¾ cup skim milk
1 egg, lightly beaten

Combine flour, sugar, and salt in a medium saucepan. Add milk, stirring well with a wire whisk. Cook over medium heat, stirring constantly, 5 minutes or until thickened and bubbly. Gradually stir about one-fourth of hot mixture into beaten egg; add to remaining hot mixture, stirring well. Cook over low heat, stirring constantly, 2 minutes. Remove from heat; cover and chill thoroughly. Yield: 1⅔ cups.

PROTEIN 3.8 / FAT 3.6 / CARBOHYDRATE 26.6 / CHOLESTEROL 69 / IRON 0.7 / SODIUM 152 / CALCIUM 57

For ease in removing cake layers from the baking pan, allow layers to cool slightly (about 10 minutes) and run a thin knife or spatula around the edge of the pan to loosen layers. If removed too soon, the cake may break. If allowed to cool too long before removing, the cake may stick to the pan.

Orange Cake With Apricots

Vegetable cooking spray
1½ teaspoons all-purpose flour
1¾ cups sifted cake flour
⅓ cup sugar
1½ teaspoons baking powder
⅛ teaspoon salt
½ cup water
⅓ cup vegetable oil
1 teaspoon grated orange rind
2 teaspoons vanilla extract
6 egg whites
1 teaspoon cream of tartar
1 (16-ounce) can apricot halves
  in light syrup, drained
Apricot Frosting
Dried apricot roses (optional)
Edible flowers (optional)

Coat two 8-inch round or heart-shaped cakepans with cooking spray; dust with flour.

Combine cake flour and next 3 ingredients in a large mixing bowl, stirring well. Make a well in center of dry ingredients. Add water, vegetable oil, orange rind, and vanilla extract, stirring well.

Beat egg whites (at room temperature) and cream of tartar in a large mixing bowl at high speed of an electric mixer until stiff but not dry. Fold one-third of egg whites into flour mixture. Gently fold flour mixture into remaining egg whites. Spread batter evenly into prepared pans. Bake at 350° for 25 minutes or until cake springs back when touched. Cool in pans 10 minutes. Carefully remove cakes from pans to wire racks. Cool completely.

Place apricot halves on top of one cake layer. Spread ½ cup Apricot Frosting over apricot halves. Top with remaining cake layer. Spread remaining frosting on top and sides of cake. If desired, garnish with dried apricot roses and edible flowers. Yield: 12 servings (149 calories per serving).

Apricot Frosting

1 teaspoon unflavored gelatin
1 tablespoon cold water
⅓ cup apricot syrup
1 egg white
¼ teaspoon cream of tartar
Dash of salt

Sprinkle gelatin over cold water in a small saucepan; let stand 1 minute. Add apricot syrup. Cook over low heat, stirring constantly, until gelatin dissolves. Bring mixture to a boil. Remove from heat.

Beat egg white (at room temperature), cream of tartar, and salt in a medium bowl at high speed of an electric mixer until soft peaks form. Continue beating egg white, and slowly pour hot syrup mixture over egg white in a slow, steady stream. Beat at high speed about 7 minutes or until stiff peaks form and frosting is thick enough to spread. Yield: 1½ cups.

PROTEIN 3.5 / FAT 6.2 / CARBOHYDRATE 19.7 / CHOLESTEROL 0 / IRON 0.2 / SODIUM 130 / CALCIUM 32

Apricot Frosting spreads into pretty swirls on Orange Cake With Apricots. Roses made from dried apricots add a finishing touch of elegance.

"Mile High" Peach Meringue Torte

(pictured on pages 22 and 23)

¼ cup margarine, softened
¼ cup firmly packed brown sugar
1 egg
2 egg yolks
1 cup all-purpose flour
1 teaspoon baking powder
¼ teaspoon salt
3 tablespoons skim milk
2 teaspoons almond extract
Vegetable cooking spray
2½ cups sliced fresh peaches
2 tablespoons sugar
6 egg whites
1 teaspoon lemon juice
¾ cup plus 2 tablespoons sugar
Fresh peach slices (optional)

Cream margarine in a medium bowl; add brown sugar, beating well at medium speed of an electric mixer. Add egg and egg yolks, beating well. Add flour, baking powder, salt, milk, and almond extract; mix well.

Spoon batter into a 13- x 9- x 2-inch baking pan that has been coated with cooking spray. (Batter will be thin in pan.) Press peach slices into batter; sprinkle with 2 tablespoons sugar. Bake at 375° for 30 minutes or until a wooden pick inserted in center comes out clean.

Beat egg whites (at room temperature) in a large bowl at high speed of an electric mixer until foamy. Add lemon juice; continue beating until soft peaks form. Gradually add sugar, 1 tablespoon at a time, beating until stiff peaks form. Spread over hot cake; bake an additional 15 to 20 minutes or until meringue is golden brown. Garnish with fresh peach slices, if desired. Yield: 16 servings (151 calories per serving).

PROTEIN 3.2 / FAT 4.1 / CARBOHYDRATE 25.6 / CHOLESTEROL 51 / IRON 0.6 / SODIUM 116 / CALCIUM 29

Fresh Strawberry Cream Torte

1 cup sifted cake flour
½ cup sugar
3 tablespoons instant nonfat dry
  milk powder
1 teaspoon baking powder
⅛ teaspoon salt
3 tablespoons vegetable oil
½ cup water
1 teaspoon vanilla extract
2 egg whites
Vegetable cooking spray
4 cups fresh strawberries, washed
  and hulled
Topping (recipe follows)
Fresh mint sprigs (optional)

Combine first 5 ingredients; stir well. Combine oil, water, and vanilla, beating with a wire whisk; add to flour mixture, stirring until dry ingredients are moistened.

Beat egg whites (at room temperature) at high speed of an electric mixer until stiff but not dry; fold into cake batter.

Spoon batter into a 9-inch springform pan that has been coated with cooking spray. Bake at 350° for 25 to 30 minutes or until a wooden pick inserted in center comes out clean. Remove from pan, and cool completely on a wire rack.

Return cooled cake to reassembled springform pan.

Set aside 6 strawberries for garnish. Cut in half enough strawberries to make a ring around cake; arrange cut side against pan. Stand remaining berries on top of cake. Pour topping over berries; cover with heavy-duty plastic wrap and chill 3 to 4 hours.

Remove cake from pan; place on serving plate. Cut

Fresh Strawberry Cream Torte
(CONTINUED)

Topping

⅓ *cup unsweetened orange juice*
1 *envelope unflavored gelatin*
½ *cup cold water*
¼ *cup plus 1 tablespoon sugar*
¼ *cup lemon juice*
⅓ *cup instant nonfat dry milk*
  powder
1 *egg white*

reserved strawberries in half. Arrange strawberry halves on top of cake. Garnish plate with fresh mint sprigs, if desired. Yield: 12 servings (157 calories per serving).

Place orange juice in a small, narrow glass or stainless steel bowl; freeze 25 minutes or until a ⅛-inch-thick layer of ice forms on surface.

Sprinkle gelatin over cold water in a small saucepan; let stand 1 minute. Cook over low heat, stirring constantly, until gelatin dissolves. Add sugar and lemon juice; stir until sugar dissolves. Chill until the consistency of unbeaten egg white.

Add milk powder to partially frozen orange juice; beat at high speed of an electric mixer 5 minutes or until stiff peaks form.

Beat egg white (at room temperature) in a small bowl at high speed of an electric mixer until soft peaks form. Fold egg white and whipped milk mixture into gelatin mixture. Yield: about 2 cups.

PROTEIN 4.2 / FAT 3.7 / CARBOHYDRATE 27.3 / CHOLESTEROL 1 / IRON 0.3 / SODIUM 91 / CALCIUM 91

For an attractive dessert, garnish Fresh Strawberry Cream Torte with strawberries and fresh mint sprigs.

Fruit and Custard-Filled Torte

4 eggs
¾ cup sugar
1 cup sifted cake flour
1½ teaspoons baking powder
1 teaspoon vanilla extract
Vegetable cooking spray
Custard Filling
1 cup fresh strawberries, hulled
  and sliced
1 small banana, thinly sliced
1 tablespoon sifted powdered
  sugar
3 fresh whole strawberries,
  (optional)

*B*eat eggs in a large bowl 5 minutes at high speed of an electric mixer. Gradually add sugar, 1 tablespoon at a time, beating an additional 5 minutes or until mixture is thick and lemon colored.

Sift together flour and baking powder. Sprinkle one-fourth of flour mixture over egg mixture. Fold in gently. Repeat procedure with remaining flour mixture, adding one-fourth mixture at a time. Stir in vanilla.

Spoon batter into two 9-inch cakepans that have been coated with cooking spray and lined with parchment paper. Bake at 400° for 15 minutes or until a wooden pick inserted in center comes out clean. Cool in pan 10 minutes. Remove to a wire rack; peel off parchment paper. Cool completely.

Spread half of Custard Filling over one layer of cake. Arrange sliced strawberries and banana over filling. Spread remaining filling over fruit. Cover with remaining cake layer. Sift powdered sugar over top; garnish with whole strawberries, if desired. Yield: 12 servings (159 calories per serving).

Custard Filling

3 tablespoons sugar
2 tablespoons cornstarch
⅛ teaspoon salt
1½ cups skim milk
1 egg
2 teaspoons vanilla extract

*C*ombine sugar, cornstarch, and salt in a medium saucepan. Gradually add milk, stirring until blended. Cook over medium heat, stirring constantly, until mixture thickens and comes to a boil. Boil 1 minute, stirring constantly. Remove from heat.

Beat egg at high speed of an electric mixer until thick and lemon colored. Gradually stir one-fourth hot mixture into beaten egg; add to remaining hot mixture, stirring constantly. Cook over medium heat, stirring constantly, 2 to 3 minutes. Remove mixture from heat; stir in vanilla. Cover and chill 3 hours or until set. Yield: 1⅔ cups.

PROTEIN 4.4 / FAT 2.6 / CARBOHYDRATE 29.5 / CHOLESTEROL 115 / IRON 0.6 / SODIUM 107 / CALCIUM 77

Thaw frozen unfrosted cakes, unwrapped, at room temperature, 1 hour or in 350° oven 10 to 15 minutes. Thaw frosted cakes unwrapped, under a cover or dome.

Amaretto Cheesecake

(pictured on cover)

¼ cup crushed amaretti cookies
Vegetable cooking spray
2 (15-ounce) cartons part-skim
   ricotta cheese, drained
⅓ cup sugar
1 teaspoon vanilla extract
1 tablespoon amaretto
⅛ teaspoon salt
2 eggs
1½ cups fresh strawberries,
   halved
2 kiwifruit, sliced
1 tablespoon reduced-calorie apple
   spread, melted

*P*osition knife blade in food processor bowl; add cookies. Top with cover, and process until crumbs measure ¼ cup. Spread crumbs in a 9-inch springform pan that has been coated with cooking spray.

Place ricotta cheese and next 4 ingredients in food processor bowl; top with cover, and process 5 minutes or until mixture is smooth. Add eggs; process until blended. Slowly pour mixture over crumbs in pan. Bake at 350° for 50 minutes (center may be soft but will firm when chilled). Turn oven off; crack oven door and allow cheesecake to cool to room temperature. Chill at least 2 hours. Remove sides of pan. Arrange fruit on top; brush fruit with apple spread to glaze. Yield: 12 servings (165 calories per serving).

PROTEIN 9.6 / FAT 7.2 / CARBOHYDRATE 14.6 / CHOLESTEROL 68 / IRON 0.6 / SODIUM 140 / CALCIUM 205

Raspberry Cheesecake

(pictured on page 2)

¼ cup graham cracker crumbs
1 tablespoon reduced-calorie
   margarine
Vegetable cooking spray
2 (15-ounce) cartons part-skim
   ricotta cheese, drained
⅓ cup sugar
1 teaspoon vanilla extract
1 tablespoon raspberry schnapps
⅛ teaspoon salt
2 eggs
1 ounce semisweet chocolate,
   melted
¾ cup fresh raspberries
Edible flowers (optional)

*C*ombine cracker crumbs and margarine in a small bowl; stir well. Spread mixture in a 9-inch springform pan that has been coated with cooking spray.

Place ricotta cheese and next 4 ingredients in food processor bowl; top with cover, and process 5 minutes or until mixture is smooth. Add eggs; process until blended. Slowly pour mixture over crumbs in pan. Bake at 350° for 50 minutes (center may be soft but will firm when chilled). Turn oven off; crack oven door and allow cheesecake to cool to room temperature. Chill at least 2 hours. Remove sides of pan.

Place melted chocolate in a small pastry bag that has been fitted with round tip No. 2. Pipe chocolate on top of cheesecake. Top with raspberries. Garnish with edible flowers, if desired. Yield: 12 servings (164 calories per serving).

PROTEIN 9.4 / FAT 8.2 / CARBOHYDRATE 13.4 / CHOLESTEROL 68 / IRON 0.7 / SODIUM 147 / CALCIUM 201

Creamy Cranberry Cheesecake

Vegetable cooking spray
10 vanilla wafers, crushed
1 (10½-ounce) package soft tofu, drained
1 cup low-fat cottage cheese
1 (8-ounce) package light process cream cheese product
¾ cup sugar
1 cup skim milk
1 tablespoon cornstarch
2 teaspoons vanilla extract
½ teaspoon almond extract
1 egg
Cranberry Sauce
Fresh cranberries (optional)
Fresh mint sprig (optional)

Cranberry Sauce

2 cups fresh cranberries
½ cup sugar
¾ cup water
1½ teaspoons cornstarch
¼ cup water

Coat a 9-inch springform pan with cooking spray. Dust bottom and sides of pan with crushed vanilla wafers.

Combine soft tofu and cottage cheese in a large mixing bowl. Beat at medium speed of an electric mixer until smooth. Add cream cheese and next 5 ingredients. Beat just until blended. Add egg; beat until blended. Pour batter into prepared pan. Bake at 325° for 50 minutes or until set but center is still creamy (do not overbake). Remove from oven, and cool to room temperature; cover and refrigerate until thoroughly chilled.

Remove from springform pan. Top with Cranberry Sauce. If desired, garnish with fresh cranberries and a mint sprig. Yield: 16 servings (146 calories per serving).

Wash cranberries and drain well. Combine cranberries, sugar, and water in a medium saucepan; bring mixture to a boil, and cook 7 to 10 minutes or until cranberry skins pop. Remove from heat; press cranberry mixture through a sieve. Discard skins. Return puree to saucepan. Combine cornstarch and water; add to puree. Cook over medium heat, stirring constantly, until mixture thickens; cover and refrigerate until thoroughly chilled. Yield: 1 cup.

PROTEIN 5.3 / FAT 4.3 / CARBOHYDRATE 22.4 / CHOLESTEROL 18 / IRON 0.4 / SODIUM 161 / CALCIUM 83

Cheesecake lovers will savor these desserts: (from top) Marble Cheesecake (page 60), Creamy Cranberry Cheesecake, and Ginger-Orange Cheesecake (page 61).

Lemon Cheesecake

Vegetable cooking spray
2 tablespoons graham cracker
  crumbs
1 (10½-ounce) package soft tofu,
  drained
1 (8-ounce) package light process
  cream cheese product
1 cup 1% low-fat cottage cheese
½ cup sugar
¼ cup honey
1 teaspoon grated lemon rind
2 tablespoons lemon juice
1 teaspoon lemon extract
1 teaspoon vanilla extract
2 eggs
1 cup sliced fresh strawberries
2 small lemons, thinly sliced

Coat a 9-inch springform pan with cooking spray. Dust with graham cracker crumbs.

Combine tofu and next 8 ingredients in container of an electric blender or food processor. Top with cover, and process until smooth. Add eggs, one at a time; process just until blended. Pour into prepared pan.

Bake at 300° for 1 hour. Turn off oven. Cool cheesecake in oven for 1 hour. Cover and chill. Remove sides of pan. Top cheesecake with sliced strawberries and lemon. Yield: 12 servings (153 calories per serving).

PROTEIN 7.0 / FAT 5.6 / CARBOHYDRATE 20.0 / CHOLESTEROL 46 / IRON 0.7 / SODIUM 204 / CALCIUM 91

Marble Cheesecake

(pictured on page 58)

Vegetable cooking spray
4 chocolate wafer cookies, crushed
1 (16-ounce) carton low-fat sour
  cream
1 (8-ounce) package light process
  cream cheese product
⅔ cup sugar
2 teaspoons vanilla extract
4 eggs
¼ cup unsweetened cocoa

Coat a 9-inch springform pan with cooking spray. Dust bottom of pan with cookie crumbs. Set aside.

Combine sour cream, cream cheese, sugar, and vanilla in a large mixing bowl. Beat at medium speed of an electric mixer until smooth. Add eggs, one at a time, beating at low speed just until blended.

Transfer 1½ cups batter to a medium bowl. Add cocoa. Beat at low speed of an electric mixer until well blended.

Pour remaining cheesecake mixture into prepared pan. Pour chocolate mixture over top of cheesecake mixture; gently swirl with a knife.

Bake at 325° for 45 minutes or until set; remove from oven. Let cool; chill thoroughly. Remove sides of pan and cut into wedges to serve. Yield: 12 servings (194 calories per serving).

PROTEIN 6.0 / FAT 11.1 / CARBOHYDRATE 18.4 / CHOLESTEROL 110 / IRON 0.8 / SODIUM 165 / CALCIUM 84

Ginger-Orange Cheesecake

(pictured on page 58)

Vegetable cooking spray
5 gingersnaps, crushed (about ¼
   cup)
1 pound soft tofu
2 (8-ounce) packages Neufchâtel
   cheese, softened
1 envelope unflavored gelatin
½ cup unsweetened orange juice
2 eggs
⅔ cup sugar
1 tablespoon grated orange rind
1 tablespoon vanilla extract
½ cup plain low-fat yogurt
2 tablespoons powdered sugar
1 teaspoon vanilla extract
Mandarin oranges (optional)
Fresh mint sprig (optional)

Coat a 9-inch springform pan with cooking spray, and dust with gingersnap crumbs; set aside.

Drain tofu and pat dry. Combine tofu and Neufchâtel in container of an electric blender or food processor; top with cover, and process until smooth. Transfer to a bowl.

Sprinkle gelatin over orange juice in a small bowl; let stand 5 minutes. Combine gelatin mixture, eggs, sugar, orange rind, and 1 tablespoon vanilla in electric blender; top with cover, and process until smooth. Add cheese mixture, and process until combined. Pour into prepared pan. Bake at 325° for 55 minutes or until nearly set.

Combine yogurt, powdered sugar, and 1 teaspoon vanilla. Spread on hot cheesecake. Let cool to room temperature on a wire rack; chill thoroughly. Remove sides of pan before serving. If desired, garnish with mandarin oranges and a mint sprig. Yield: 16 servings (160 calories per serving).

PROTEIN 6.1 / FAT 8.9 / CARBOHYDRATE 14.1 / CHOLESTEROL 57 / IRON 0.7 / SODIUM 131 / CALCIUM 92

Tofu, a soft curd made from soybeans, is usually found in the produce departments of supermarkets. Free of fat and high in protein, tofu has no distinct flavor of its own. It readily takes on the flavors of accompanying ingredients while it adds a smooth creaminess to cheesecakes.

Cookies

Homemade cookies have long been a symbol of caring, a hand-held treat not to be underestimated. So, it's good to know that cookies that are easy to make and fun to eat can also be nutritious. A blend of whole grains, dried fruits, and natural ingredients provides a variety of cookies that are sure to please.

And all of these cookies keep well when refrigerated or frozen; just pack them in sturdy plastic containers in layers separated by wax paper. They can then be removed a few at a time or by the layer for a snack or dessert, thereby leaving the remainder frozen and unbroken.

A tiered server displays (from top) Meringue Kisses (page 72), Pecan Icebox Cookies (page 73), and Sugar Cookies (page 75), while Italian Cookie Rusks (page 73) accompany fresh brewed coffee.

Black Walnut-Apple Bars

½ cup all-purpose flour
½ cup sugar
1 teaspoon baking powder
1 teaspoon ground cinnamon
¼ teaspoon salt
1 egg
1 teaspoon vanilla extract
1 cup chopped apple
¼ cup chopped black walnuts
Vegetable cooking spray
¼ cup sifted powdered sugar
2 teaspoons hot water
⅛ teaspoon black walnut-flavored
    extract

Combine first 5 ingredients in a large bowl, stirring well. Add egg and vanilla; stir until blended. Stir in chopped apple and black walnuts. Spoon batter into an 8-inch square pan that has been coated with cooking spray. Bake at 400° for 15 to 20 minutes or until a wooden pick inserted in center comes out clean. Let cool on a wire rack.

Combine powdered sugar, water, and black walnut extract; stir until smooth. Drizzle glaze over top, and cut into 2- x 1-inch bars. Yield: 32 bars (35 calories each).

PROTEIN 0.7 / FAT 0.8 / CARBOHYDRATE 6.5 / CHOLESTEROL 9 / IRON 0.2 / SODIUM 30 / CALCIUM 9

Apricot Bars

½ cup dried apricots
1 cup water
½ cup sugar
1½ cups all-purpose flour
½ cup firmly packed brown sugar
1¼ cups quick-cooking oats,
    uncooked
⅓ cup plus 1 tablespoon
    margarine
Vegetable cooking spray

Combine apricots and water in a small saucepan; bring to a boil. Cover; reduce heat and simmer 15 minutes or until tender. Remove from heat. Let cool, covered. Pour apricot mixture into container of an electric blender. Add sugar; top with cover, and blend until pureed.

Combine flour, brown sugar, and oats in a large bowl, stirring well. Cut in margarine with a pastry blender until mixture resembles coarse meal.

Pat two-thirds of oat mixture into a 13- x 9- x 2-inch baking pan that has been coated with cooking spray. Bake at 350° for 10 minutes.

Spread apricot mixture evenly over crust, spreading to within ¼ inch from edge of pan. Sprinkle with remaining oat mixture. Bake at 350° for 30 to 35 minutes or until lightly browned. Let cool in pan; chill. Cut into approximately 1¼- x 2-inch bars. Store in refrigerator. Yield: 36 bars (77 calories each).

PROTEIN 1.1 / FAT 2.3 / CARBOHYDRATE 13.3 / CHOLESTEROL 0 / IRON 0.5 / SODIUM 25 / CALCIUM 7

Ladyfinger Bars

4 eggs, separated
¼ cup sugar
3 tablespoons water
1 teaspoon vanilla extract
¾ cup sifted cake flour
½ teaspoon baking powder
Vegetable cooking spray

*B*eat egg yolks in a large bowl at high speed of an electric mixer 5 minutes or until thick and lemon colored. Add sugar, water, and vanilla, mixing just until blended. Combine flour and baking powder. Sift flour mixture over yolk mixture; gently fold in flour mixture.

Beat egg whites (at room temperature) at high speed of an electric mixer until stiff peaks form. Gently fold egg whites into yolk mixture. Spread batter evenly in a 15- x 10- x 1-inch jellyroll pan that has been coated with cooking spray and lined with parchment paper. Bake at 325° for 15 minutes or until cake springs back when lightly touched.

Remove from oven, and cool completely in pan. Gently cut into 1- x 2½-inch bars, using a sharp knife. Yield: 60 ladyfingers (13 calories each).

PROTEIN 0.5 / FAT 0.4 / CARBOHYDRATE 1.9 / CHOLESTEROL 18 / IRON 0.1 / SODIUM 7 / CALCIUM 4

Fresh Apple Cookies

½ cup margarine, softened
½ cup firmly packed brown sugar
2 egg whites
1¾ cups sifted cake flour
¾ teaspoon baking soda
1½ teaspoons pumpkin pie spice
1 cup finely chopped apple
¼ cup currants

*C*ream margarine in a medium bowl; gradually add brown sugar, beating at medium speed of an electric mixer until light and fluffy. Stir in egg whites. Combine flour, soda, and pumpkin pie spice; add to sugar mixture, stirring well. Stir in chopped apple and currants.

Drop dough by rounded teaspoonfuls 2 inches apart onto cookie sheets lined with parchment paper. Bake at 400° for 6 to 8 minutes or until edges are lightly browned. Remove from cookie sheets, and cool completely on wire racks. Yield: 68 cookies (30 calories each).

PROTEIN 0.3 / FAT 1.4 / CARBOHYDRATE 4.2 / CHOLESTEROL 0 / IRON 0.1 / SODIUM 27 / CALCIUM 5

When baking cookies, use parchment paper to cover baking sheets, thereby eliminating the need to add additional fat to baked goods. Parchment paper will also keep the baking sheets clean.

Banana-Oat Bran Cookies

2 cups all-purpose flour
²/₃ cup unsweetened grated
    coconut
½ cup regular oats, uncooked
½ cup oat bran
½ teaspoon baking soda
½ teaspoon ground cinnamon
⅛ teaspoon salt
½ cup margarine
½ cup firmly packed brown sugar
3 tablespoons vegetable oil
1 egg white
1 cup mashed ripe banana
1 teaspoon vanilla extract
Vegetable cooking spray

Combine first 7 ingredients; stir well and set aside.

Combine margarine, sugar, and oil in a medium bowl; beat at medium speed of an electric mixer until smooth. Add egg white, banana, and vanilla, mixing well. Gradually add dry ingredients to creamed mixture; mix well.

Drop dough by rounded teaspoonfuls 2 inches apart onto cookie sheets that have been coated with cooking spray. Bake at 375° for 10 to 12 minutes. Remove from cookie sheets, and cool completely on wire racks. Yield: 62 cookies (57 calories each).

PROTEIN 0.9 / FAT 2.9 / CARBOHYDRATE 7.2 / CHOLESTEROL 0 / IRON 0.3 / SODIUM 30 / CALCIUM 6

Carrot-Oat Bran Cookies

1¼ cups all-purpose flour
⅓ cup oat bran
½ cup firmly packed brown sugar
½ teaspoon baking soda
½ teaspoon ground cinnamon
⅛ teaspoon salt
1 cup grated carrot
½ cup vegetable oil
1 egg white
½ cup golden raisins
Vegetable cooking spray
Glaze (recipe follows)

Glaze

½ cup sifted powdered sugar
½ teaspoon coconut extract
1 tablespoon water

Combine first 6 ingredients in a large mixing bowl; stir well. Add carrot, oil, and egg white, stirring with a wooden spoon until dough is stiff. Add raisins; stir well.

Drop dough by rounded teaspoonfuls 2 inches apart onto cookie sheets that have been coated with cooking spray. Bake at 375° for 8 to 10 minutes. Remove from cookie sheets; drizzle with glaze. Yield: 4 dozen cookies (56 calories each).

Combine sugar, extract, and water in a small bowl. Stir until smooth. Yield: 3 tablespoons.

PROTEIN 0.6 / FAT 2.4 / CARBOHYDRATE 8.2 / CHOLESTEROL 0 / IRON 0.3 / SODIUM 18 / CALCIUM 7

(Clockwise from top): Oatmeal-Oat Bran Cookies (page 70), Pineapple-Walnut Cookies (page 72), Lemon Cornmeal Cookies (page 69), and Banana-Oat Bran Cookies.

Chinese Fortune Cookies

¼ cup plus 2 tablespoons
    margarine, softened
¼ cup plus 2 tablespoons sugar
Dash of salt
2 egg whites
½ teaspoon almond extract
⅔ cup all-purpose flour
Vegetable cooking spray

Cut colored paper into 3- x ¾-inch strips; write the fortunes, and fold strips in half lengthwise. Set aside.

Cream margarine in a medium bowl; gradually add sugar, beating well at medium speed of an electric mixer. Add salt, egg whites, and almond extract, beating at high speed of an electric mixer until light and fluffy. Stir in flour.

Drop dough by rounded teaspoonfuls 4 inches apart onto cookie sheets that have been coated with cooking spray. Spread each cookie into a 3-inch circle. Bake at 400° for 5 minutes or until edges are lightly browned. Remove from oven. Working quickly, loosen cookies with a spatula; leave cookies on warm cookie sheets.

Working one at a time, place fortune in center of cookie. Gently fold cookie in half. Bend folded edge of cookie downward. Place in muffin pan to harden. Repeat with remaining cookies. If cookies cool and become too brittle to fold, return to warm oven briefly to soften. Yield: 3 dozen cookies (36 calories each).

PROTEIN 0.5 / FAT 2.0 / CARBOHYDRATE 4.0 / CHOLESTEROL 0 / IRON 0.1 / SODIUM 29 / CALCIUM 1

Chocolate-Sour Cream Drops

½ cup margarine, softened
⅔ cup sugar
½ cup plus 2 tablespoons low-fat
    sour cream
1 teaspoon vanilla extract
1 egg white
1 tablespoon water
1¾ cups all-purpose flour
3 tablespoons unsweetened cocoa
½ teaspoon baking powder
1 teaspoon baking soda
½ teaspoon ground cinnamon
Vegetable cooking spray
1 teaspoon powdered sugar

Cream margarine; gradually add sugar, beating at medium speed of an electric mixer until light and fluffy. Add sour cream, vanilla, egg white, and water; beat well.

Combine flour, cocoa, baking powder, soda, and cinnamon; stir well. Add to creamed mixture, mixing well.

Drop dough by rounded teaspoonfuls 2 inches apart onto cookie sheets that have been coated with cooking spray. Bake at 350° for 10 to 12 minutes. Cool on wire racks. Sift powdered sugar over cooled cookies. Yield: 5½ dozen cookies (38 calories each).

PROTEIN 0.6 / FAT 1.7 / CARBOHYDRATE 5.1 / CHOLESTEROL 1 / IRON 0.2 / SODIUM 33 / CALCIUM 8

Lemon Cornmeal Cookies

(pictured on page 66)

1/4 cup margarine, softened
2 tablespoons vegetable oil
3/4 cup sifted powdered sugar
3 egg whites
1 tablespoon plus 1 1/2 teaspoons
   grated lemon rind
1 teaspoon vanilla extract
1 1/4 cups all-purpose flour
3/4 cup yellow cornmeal
1/2 teaspoon baking powder
1/4 teaspoon salt
Vegetable cooking spray

Cream margarine and oil in a medium bowl; gradually add sugar, beating well at medium speed of an electric mixer. Add egg whites, lemon rind, and vanilla, mixing well. Combine flour, cornmeal, baking powder, and salt; gradually add to creamed mixture, mixing well.

Drop dough by rounded teaspoonfuls 2 inches apart onto cookie sheets that have been coated with cooking spray; flatten to 1/4-inch thickness. Bake at 375° for 10 to 12 minutes. Remove from cookie sheets, and cool completely on wire racks. Yield: 40 cookies (51 calories each).

PROTEIN 0.9 / FAT 1.9 / CARBOHYDRATE 7.4 / CHOLESTEROL 0 / IRON 0.2 / SODIUM 36 / CALCIUM 4

Maple-Fruit Whole Grain Crisps

1/2 cup margarine, softened
1/4 cup sugar
1/4 cup firmly packed brown sugar
1 egg white
1 tablespoon dark molasses
1 teaspoon maple flavoring
1/3 cup unsweetened applesauce
1 cup all-purpose flour
1 cup quick-cooking oats,
   uncooked
1/3 cup oat bran
1/4 cup wheat germ
2 tablespoons currants
1/2 teaspoon baking soda
1/2 teaspoon cream of tartar
Vegetable cooking spray

Cream margarine; gradually add sugars, beating at medium speed of an electric mixer until light and fluffy. Add egg white, molasses, and maple flavoring; beat mixture well. Stir in applesauce.

Combine flour and next 6 ingredients; add to creamed mixture, and mix well.

Drop dough by rounded teaspoonfuls 2 inches apart onto cookie sheets that have been coated with cooking spray. Bake at 350° for 10 minutes or until cookies are lightly browned. Cool on wire racks. Yield: 4 1/2 dozen cookies (54 calories each).

PROTEIN 1.1 / FAT 2.2 / CARBOHYDRATE 7.6 / CHOLESTEROL 0 / IRON 0.4 / SODIUM 32 / CALCIUM 8

Oatmeal-Oat Bran Cookies

(pictured on page 66)

½ *cup margarine, softened*
½ *cup sugar*
2 *tablespoons water*
1 *cup quick-cooking oats,*
uncooked
½ *cup whole wheat flour*
½ *cup oat bran*
1 *teaspoon baking powder*
1 *teaspoon ground cinnamon*
½ *teaspoon ground nutmeg*
Dash of salt

Cream margarine in a large bowl; gradually add sugar, beating at medium speed of an electric mixer until light and fluffy. Add water; beat well. Combine oats and remaining ingredients; stir well. Gradually add to creamed mixture, beating well.

Drop dough by rounded teaspoonfuls 2 inches apart onto cookie sheets lined with parchment paper. Bake at 350° for 12 minutes or until cookies are lightly browned. Remove from cookie sheets, and cool. Yield: 46 cookies (50 calories each).

PROTEIN 0.9 / FAT 2.4 / CARBOHYDRATE 6.4 / CHOLESTEROL 0 / IRON 0.3 / SODIUM 33 / CALCIUM 9

Oatmeal Lace Cookies

½ *cup margarine, softened*
½ *cup firmly packed brown sugar*
¼ *cup sugar*
1 *egg white*
½ *teaspoon almond extract*
½ *teaspoon vanilla extract*
1 *cup quick-cooking oats,*
uncooked
2 *tablespoons all-purpose flour*
¼ *teaspoon baking soda*

Cream margarine in a large mixing bowl; gradually add sugars, beating well at medium speed of an electric mixer. Add egg white and flavorings; beat until smooth. Stir in oats and remaining ingredients.

Drop dough by level teaspoonfuls 3 inches apart onto cookie sheets lined with parchment paper. Flatten cookies into a 2-inch circle, using a teaspoon dipped in water. Bake at 325° for 6 to 8 minutes or until edges are lightly browned. Cool on cookie sheets. Remove from parchment paper; store in airtight containers. Yield: 68 cookies (33 calories each).

PROTEIN 0.5 / FAT 1.5 / CARBOHYDRATE 4.3 / CHOLESTEROL 0 / IRON 0.2 / SODIUM 20 / CALCIUM 4

For precise measuring, use 2 level teaspoonfuls of dough instead of a rounded teaspoonful to achieve the correct yield on *Light Dessert* cookie recipes. Or, use a small scoop (#70 or smaller) to portion the dough. These scoops are available at restaurant supply stores or in cookware shops.

Fill Wafer Cup Cookies with ice milk, sherbet, or fresh fruit for a quick and easy dessert.

Wafer Cup Cookies

⅓ *cup sugar*

2 *egg whites*

2 *tablespoons all-purpose flour*

1 *tablespoon unsalted margarine, melted*

Vegetable cooking spray

Vanilla ice milk (optional)

Chocolate garnish (optional)

Combine first 4 ingredients in a medium bowl; stir well.

Bake only 2 cookies at a time on a cookie sheet that has been coated with cooking spray. Spoon 2 level teaspoonfuls of batter per cookie on each half of cookie sheet. Spread each portion of batter evenly with a spatula into a 4-inch circle. Bake at 400° for 4 to 5 minutes or until edges are golden.

Let cookies cool 20 seconds. Loosen cookies with a metal spatula. Place each cookie over the top of a small narrow jar. (If cookies become too stiff before placing over jar, return cookie sheet to oven briefly to soften them.) Continue with remaining batter. If desired, fill with ¼ cup ice milk, and garnish with chocolate. Yield: 1 dozen cookies (40 calories each).

PROTEIN 0.7 / FAT 1.2 / CARBOHYDRATE 6.7 / CHOLESTEROL 0 / IRON 0.0 / SODIUM 9 / CALCIUM 1

Pineapple-Walnut Cookies

(pictured on page 66)

1 (8-ounce) can unsweetened
  crushed pineapple, undrained
⅓ cup margarine, softened
⅔ cup firmly packed brown sugar
1 egg white
½ teaspoon coconut extract
1¼ cups all-purpose flour
½ teaspoon baking soda
¼ cup chopped walnuts
2 tablespoons sugar
1 tablespoon margarine
½ cup sifted powdered sugar

Drain pineapple, reserving 1 tablespoon plus 1½ teaspoons juice for glaze. Pat pineapple with paper towels to remove excess moisture. Set aside.

Cream ⅓ cup margarine in a medium bowl; gradually add brown sugar, beating well at medium speed of an electric mixer. Add egg white and coconut extract, beating well.

Combine flour and soda; gradually add to creamed mixture, beating at medium speed of electric mixer until well blended. Stir in drained pineapple and walnuts.

Drop dough by rounded teaspoonfuls 2 inches apart onto ungreased cookie sheets. Bake at 350° for 10 to 12 minutes or until lightly browned. Remove from cookie sheets, and cool completely on wire racks.

Combine 2 tablespoons sugar and 1 tablespoon margarine in a small saucepan. Cook over low heat, stirring constantly, until margarine melts. Add reserved pineapple juice; bring to a boil, stirring constantly. Remove from heat. Add powdered sugar, stirring until smooth. Cool. Spread glaze evenly over tops of cookies. Let stand at room temperature until glaze is set. Yield: 3½ dozen cookies (59 calories each).

PROTEIN 0.7 / FAT 2.1 / CARBOHYDRATE 9.4 / CHOLESTEROL 0 / IRON 0.3 / SODIUM 32 / CALCIUM 8

Meringue Kisses

(pictured on pages 62 and 63)

3 egg whites
1 teaspoon vanilla extract
⅛ teaspoon salt
1 cup sugar
Vegetable cooking spray

Beat egg whites (at room temperature) in a large bowl at high speed of an electric mixer until foamy. Sprinkle vanilla and salt over egg whites; beat until soft peaks form. Gradually add sugar, 1 tablespoon at a time, beating until stiff peaks form.

Drop meringue by 2 level teaspoonfuls per cookie or pipe, using a No. 7 star tip, 1 inch apart onto cookie sheets that have been coated with cooking spray. Bake at 200° for 2 hours and 15 minutes or until dry. Cool slightly on cookie sheets; remove from cookie sheets, and cool completely on wire racks. Store in an airtight container. Yield: 6½ dozen cookies (11 calories each).

PROTEIN 0.1 / FAT 0.0 / CARBOHYDRATE 2.6 / CHOLESTEROL 0 / IRON 0.0 / SODIUM 6 / CALCIUM 0

Pecan Icebox Cookies

(pictured on pages 62 and 63)

½ cup margarine, softened
¾ cup firmly packed brown sugar
1 egg white
1 teaspoon vanilla extract
2 cups all-purpose flour
½ teaspoon baking soda
¼ cup chopped pecans

Cream margarine; gradually add sugar, beating well at medium speed of an electric mixer. Add egg white and vanilla, mixing well.

Combine flour and soda; stir well. Gradually add flour mixture to creamed mixture, mixing well. Stir in pecans. Shape dough into two 8-inch rolls; wrap in heavy-duty plastic wrap, and chill at least 8 hours.

Unwrap rolls, and cut into ¼-inch slices; place 2 inches apart on ungreased cookie sheets. Bake at 350° for 8 to 10 minutes or until lightly browned. Remove from cookie sheets, and cool completely on wire racks. Yield: 64 cookies (41 calories each).

PROTEIN 0.6 / FAT 1.8 / CARBOHYDRATE 5.9 / CHOLESTEROL 0 / IRON 0.2 / SODIUM 25 / CALCIUM 5

Italian Cookie Rusks

(pictured on pages 62 and 63)

½ cup margarine, softened
½ cup sugar
2 egg whites
2 tablespoons anise seeds
2 tablespoons anisette or other
  anise-flavored liqueur
1 teaspoon water
1 teaspoon almond extract
1 teaspoon vanilla extract
½ teaspoon black walnut-flavored
  extract
2½ cups all-purpose flour
1½ teaspoons baking powder
¼ cup finely chopped almonds
Vegetable cooking spray

Cream margarine in a medium bowl; gradually add sugar, beating well at medium speed of an electric mixer. Add egg whites and next 6 ingredients, mixing well.

Combine flour and baking powder; gradually add to creamed mixture, mixing well. Stir in chopped almonds. Cover and chill 8 hours.

Shape dough into two 16-inch rolls. Place rolls 4 inches apart on a cookie sheet that has been coated with cooking spray. Flatten rolls to ¾-inch thickness.

Bake at 375° for 15 minutes. Remove from oven, and cool slightly. Cut rolls into ½-inch diagonal slices, and return to cookie sheets cut side down. Bake at 375° for an additional 8 to 10 minutes or until lightly browned. Cool on wire racks. Yield: 64 cookies (44 calories each).

PROTEIN 0.8 / FAT 1.8 / CARBOHYDRATE 6.0 / CHOLESTEROL 0 / IRON 0.3 / SODIUM 26 / CALCIUM 8

When cookies are baked on parchment paper, there is no need to transfer them to a cooling rack. Simply slide the cookies, paper and all, off onto a counter or rack, and cool.

Molasses Crinkles

⅔ cup margarine, softened
½ cup firmly packed brown sugar
1 egg white
¼ cup molasses
2¼ cups all-purpose flour
1 teaspoon baking soda
1 teaspoon ground cinnamon
1 teaspoon ground ginger
½ teaspoon ground cloves
¼ teaspoon salt
1 tablespoon sugar, divided
Vegetable cooking spray

Cream margarine and brown sugar, beating well at medium speed of an electric mixer. Add egg white, beating until smooth. Stir in molasses.

Combine flour and next 5 ingredients; add to creamed mixture, beating well. Cover and chill at least 8 hours.

Divide dough in half; store 1 portion in refrigerator. Shape half of dough into 1-inch balls; dip tops in 1½ teaspoons sugar. Place 2 inches apart on cookie sheets that have been coated with cooking spray. Bake at 375° for 10 to 12 minutes. (Tops will crack.) Cool on wire racks. Repeat with remaining dough and sugar. Yield: 4 dozen cookies (60 calories each).

PROTEIN 0.8 / FAT 2.6 / CARBOHYDRATE 8.5 / CHOLESTEROL 0 / IRON 0.4 / SODIUM 62 / CALCIUM 13

Peanut Butter Cookies

½ cup margarine, softened
½ cup crunchy peanut butter
½ cup firmly packed brown sugar
1 egg white
1½ cups all-purpose flour
¼ teaspoon baking soda
⅛ teaspoon salt
1 teaspoon vanilla extract

Cream margarine and peanut butter; add brown sugar, beating well at medium speed of an electric mixer. Add egg white, beating well. Combine flour, soda, and salt. Stir flour mixture and vanilla into peanut butter mixture.

Shape dough into 1-inch balls. Place 2 inches apart on ungreased cookie sheets, and flatten with a fork. Bake at 375° for 8 to 10 minutes. Remove from cookie sheets, and cool. Yield: 62 cookies (45 calories each).

PROTEIN 1.0 / FAT 2.5 / CARBOHYDRATE 4.6 / CHOLESTEROL 0 / IRON 0.2 / SODIUM 36 / CALCIUM 4

Brown Sugar Cookies

½ cup margarine, softened
¼ cup vegetable oil
½ cup firmly packed brown sugar
1 egg white
1 teaspoon vanilla extract
2¼ cups all-purpose flour
½ teaspoon baking soda
Dash of salt
1 tablespoon sugar

Cream margarine and oil in a large bowl; gradually add brown sugar, beating at medium speed of an electric mixer until light and fluffy. Add egg white and vanilla, beating well.

Combine flour, soda, and salt; stir well. Gradually add to creamed mixture, beating well. Chill dough at least 30 minutes.

Divide dough in half; store 1 portion in refrigerator. Shape half of dough, 2 level teaspoonfuls at a time, into 1-inch balls. Place 2 inches apart on cookie sheets lined with parchment paper. Flatten each ball to ¼-inch thickness with bottom of glass that has been moistened with water and dipped in sugar. Bake at 350° for 9 minutes or until lightly browned. Remove from cookie sheets, and cool completely on wire racks. Repeat procedure with remaining dough. Yield: 53 cookies (55 calories each).

PROTEIN 0.7 / FAT 2.8 / CARBOHYDRATE 6.7 / CHOLESTEROL 0 / IRON 0.2 / SODIUM 32 / CALCIUM 5

Sugar Cookies

(pictured on pages 62 and 63)

½ *cup margarine, softened*
¼ *cup sugar*
¼ *cup sifted powdered sugar*
1 *egg white*
1 *teaspoon vanilla extract*
2¼ *cups all-purpose flour*
½ *teaspoon baking soda*
½ *teaspoon cream of tartar*
⅛ *teaspoon salt*
Vegetable cooking spray
1 *tablespoon sugar*

Cream margarine in a medium bowl; gradually add ¼ cup sugar and powdered sugar, beating at medium speed of an electric mixer until light and fluffy. Add egg white and vanilla; beat well.

Combine flour, soda, cream of tartar, and salt; add to creamed mixture, beating at low speed of an electric mixer until well blended. Shape dough into a ball; wrap in wax paper, and chill 1 hour.

Divide dough in half. Shape each half into 23 balls. Flatten to 2½-inch circles on cookie sheets that have been coated with cooking spray. Sprinkle cookies with 1 tablespoon sugar. Bake at 375° for 8 minutes or until lightly browned. Cool on wire racks. Yield: 46 cookies (51 calories each).

PROTEIN 0.8 / FAT 2.1 / CARBOHYDRATE 7.2 / CHOLESTEROL 0 / IRON 0.2 / SODIUM 42 / CALCIUM 4

Snickerdoodles

¾ *cup margarine, softened*
¾ *cup sugar*
1 *egg white*
2 *cups all-purpose flour*
2 *teaspoons cream of tartar*
1 *teaspoon baking soda*
⅛ *teaspoon salt*
1 *tablespoon sugar*
1 *teaspoon ground cinnamon*
Vegetable cooking spray

Cream margarine and ¾ cup sugar, beating well at medium speed of an electric mixer. Add egg white, beating well.

Combine flour, cream of tartar, soda, and salt. Add flour mixture to creamed mixture, stirring well. Chill at least 30 minutes.

Combine 1 tablespoon sugar and cinnamon in a small bowl, stirring well; set aside.

Shape dough into 1-inch balls; dip tops in cinnamon-sugar mixture. Place on cookie sheets that have been coated with cooking spray. Bake at 400° for 8 to 10 minutes or until lightly browned. Remove from cookie sheets, and cool on wire racks. Yield: 4 dozen cookies (60 calories each).

PROTEIN 0.7 / FAT 2.9 / CARBOHYDRATE 7.8 / CHOLESTEROL 0 / IRON 0.2 / SODIUM 66 / CALCIUM 6

Frozen Desserts

Few of us can resist the tempting refreshment of a frozen dessert, and with these healthful versions, we don't need to! These flavorful ices and sorbets are simple to prepare and owe their taste to fresh fruits.

Instant nonfat dry milk powder provides the richness traditionally given by the egg yolks and whole milk found in ice cream. The smooth and creamy texture can be attributed to the milk powder and proper freezing of the mixture.

For best results, make ice milks, sherbets, ices, and sorbets in an ice cream freezer using continuous agitation. Either a hand-operated or electric freezer may be used, and the freezing medium is typically crushed ice and rock salt. Allow the dessert to ripen in the freezer for one to two hours. You'll be pleased with the refreshing results!

To cool off on a hot summer day, bring out the freezer and crank up: (clockwise from front) Fresh Pineapple Sorbet, Pink Grapefruit Sorbet, and Cantaloupe Sorbet (page 92).

Almond Tortoni

⅓ cup cold water

1 egg white

¼ cup plus 1 tablespoon sifted powdered sugar

½ cup instant nonfat dry milk powder

½ teaspoon almond extract

½ teaspoon rum extract

2 tablespoons chopped almonds, toasted

2 tablespoons sliced almonds, toasted

Edible flowers (optional)

Place water in a small, narrow glass or stainless steel bowl; freeze 25 minutes or until a ⅛-inch-thick layer of ice forms on surface.

Beat egg white (at room temperature) in a large glass or stainless steel bowl at high speed of an electric mixer until soft peaks form. Gradually add powdered sugar, 1 tablespoon at a time, beating until stiff peaks form. (Do not overbeat.)

Add milk powder to partially frozen water; beat at high speed of an electric mixer 5 minutes or until stiff peaks form. Stir in flavorings. Gently fold milk mixture into egg white mixture.

Sprinkle chopped almonds in 6 paper-lined muffin pans. Divide whipped mixture evenly among cups. Arrange sliced almonds on top to resemble flower petals. Freeze at least 8 hours. Garnish with edible flowers, if desired. Yield: 6 servings (93 calories per serving).

PROTEIN 5.1 / FAT 2.5 / CARBOHYDRATE 12.4 / CHOLESTEROL 2 / IRON 0.2 / SODIUM 62 / CALCIUM 139

Chunky Banana Ice Milk

½ cup sugar

2 tablespoons instant nonfat dry milk powder

1 cup skim milk

2 eggs, separated

1½ teaspoons vanilla extract

¾ cup mashed, ripe banana

2 teaspoons lime juice

1 (12-ounce) can evaporated skimmed milk

Combine sugar and milk powder in a medium saucepan; stir in skim milk and egg yolks. Cook over medium heat, stirring constantly, until mixture is smooth and slightly thickened (do not boil). Remove mixture from heat; stir in vanilla. Cover and chill thoroughly.

Combine banana and lime juice; stir well. Set aside. Beat egg whites (at room temperature) in a small bowl at high speed of an electric mixer until stiff peaks form. Gently fold into chilled milk mixture. Stir in banana mixture and evaporated milk. Pour into freezer can of a 2-quart hand-turned or electric freezer. Freeze according to manufacturer's instructions. Let ripen 1 hour, if desired. Scoop ice milk into individual dessert bowls, and serve immediately. Yield: 10 servings (115 calories per ½-cup serving).

PROTEIN 5.4 / FAT 1.3 / CARBOHYDRATE 20.7 / CHOLESTEROL 57 / IRON 0.4 / SODIUM 74 / CALCIUM 155

Dress up individual servings of Almond Tortoni by freezing them in paper liners and adding sliced almonds and edible flowers as the perfect garnish.

Amaretto-Peach Ice Milk

(pictured on pages 88 and 89)

1 cup skim milk
2 tablespoons instant nonfat dry
  milk powder
1 egg, beaten
⅓ cup sugar
2 tablespoons amaretto
1 teaspoon vanilla extract
½ teaspoon almond extract
2 cups peeled, sliced ripe peaches
1 tablespoon lemon juice

Combine milk, milk powder, egg, and sugar in a medium saucepan. Cook over medium heat, stirring constantly, until mixture is slightly thickened. Cover and chill thoroughly. Stir in amaretto, vanilla, and almond extract.

Position knife blade in food processor bowl; add peach slices. Top with cover, and process until smooth. Stir lemon juice into peaches.

Combine peach mixture and chilled custard; stir well. Pour into freezer can of a 2-quart hand-turned or electric freezer. Freeze according to manufacturer's instructions. Let ripen at least 1 hour. Scoop ice milk into individual dessert bowls, and serve immediately. Yield: 8 servings (111 calories per ½-cup serving).

PROTEIN 3.1 / FAT 0.9 / CARBOHYDRATE 21.7 / CHOLESTEROL 35 / IRON 0.2 / SODIUM 35 / CALCIUM 69

Cappuccino Ice Milk

(pictured on pages 88 and 89)

1½ cups skim milk
¾ cup sugar
⅓ cup instant nonfat dry milk
  powder
2 teaspoons unsweetened cocoa
½ teaspoon ground cinnamon
1 egg white, lightly beaten
1 (12-ounce) can evaporated
  skimmed milk
1 tablespoon Kahlúa or other
  coffee-flavored liqueur

Combine first 5 ingredients in a 2-quart saucepan; stir well with a wire whisk. Cook mixture over medium heat until sugar and milk powder dissolve. Gradually stir about one-fourth of hot mixture into egg white; add to remaining hot mixture, stirring constantly. Cook over low heat 1 minute, stirring constantly. Remove from heat. Stir in evaporated milk. Cover and chill. Stir in liqueur.

Pour mixture into freezer can of a 2-quart hand-turned or electric freezer. Freeze according to manufacturer's instructions. Let ripen 1 hour, if desired. Scoop ice milk into individual dessert bowls, and serve immediately. Yield: 12 servings (100 calories per ½-cup serving).

PROTEIN 4.8 / FAT 0.2 / CARBOHYDRATE 19.5 / CHOLESTEROL 2 / IRON 0.2 / SODIUM 71 / CALCIUM 164

Easy Buttermilk Ice Milk

4 ounces light process cream
    cheese product
1/3 cup honey
2¾ cups nonfat buttermilk
½ cup unsweetened pineapple
    juice
1 teaspoon vanilla extract

Combine all ingredients in container of an electric blender. Top with cover, and process until smooth. Pour into freezer can of a 2-quart hand-turned or electric freezer. Freeze according to manufacturer's instructions. Let ripen 1 hour. Scoop ice milk into individual dessert bowls, and serve immediately. Yield: 10 servings (91 calories per ½-cup serving).

PROTEIN 3.7 / FAT 2.3 / CARBOHYDRATE 15.3 / CHOLESTEROL 0 / IRON 0.1 / SODIUM 134.2 / CALCIUM 19

Caramel Ice Milk

1/3 cup sugar
1 (12-ounce) can evaporated
    skimmed milk
2 cups skim milk
1/3 cup instant nonfat dry milk
    powder
3 tablespoons sugar
Dash of salt
2 eggs, lightly beaten
1 teaspoon vanilla extract

Sprinkle ⅓ cup sugar in a heavy skillet. Cook over medium heat until sugar melts and becomes golden, stirring constantly (about 10 minutes). Add evaporated milk, stirring constantly. Remove from heat. Set aside.

Combine skim milk, milk powder, 3 tablespoons sugar, and salt in a medium saucepan. Bring to a boil over medium heat, stirring constantly. Gradually stir about one-fourth of hot mixture into beaten eggs. Add to remaining hot mixture, stirring constantly. Cook over low heat, stirring constantly, until mixture coats a metal spoon. Remove from heat. Stir in vanilla and caramelized sugar mixture. Cover and chill.

Pour mixture into freezer can of a 2-quart hand-turned or electric freezer. Freeze according to manufacturer's instructions. Let ripen 1 hour, if desired. Scoop ice milk into individual dessert bowls, and serve immediately. Yield: 10 servings (116 calories per ½-cup serving).

PROTEIN 6.9 / FAT 1.3 / CARBOHYDRATE 18.9 / CHOLESTEROL 58 / IRON 0.3 / SODIUM 115 / CALCIUM 215

Adding instant nonfat dry milk powder to ice milk mixtures will add a rich creaminess to the dessert. The milk powder also contributes protein and calcium, without adding additional fat to the recipe.

(Left to right): Vanilla Ice Milk (page 86), Strawberry Ice Milk (page 87), and Chocolate Ice Milk are lightened versions of all-time favorites.

Chocolate Ice Milk

⅔ *cup sugar*

⅔ *cup instant nonfat dry milk powder*

¼ *cup unsweetened cocoa*

1 tablespoon cornstarch

4 cups skim milk, divided

1 egg yolk, lightly beaten

1 tablespoon vanilla extract

½ *teaspoon chocolate extract*

Combine first 4 ingredients in a medium saucepan; stir well. Stir in 2 cups skim milk. Cook over medium heat, stirring constantly, until mixture is smooth and coats a metal spoon (do not boil). Gradually stir about one-fourth of hot mixture into beaten egg yolk; add to remaining hot mixture, stirring constantly. Cook over low heat 1 minute, stirring constantly, until mixture is slightly thickened (do not boil). Remove from heat; stir in remaining 2 cups milk, and vanilla and chocolate flavorings. Cover and chill thoroughly.

Pour mixture into freezer can of a 2-quart hand-turned or electric freezer. Freeze according to manufacturer's instructions. Let ripen 1 hour, if desired. Scoop ice milk into individual dessert bowls, and serve immediately. Yield: 12 servings (115 calories per ½-cup serving).

PROTEIN 5.9 / FAT 0.9 / CARBOHYDRATE 20.3 / CHOLESTEROL 26 / IRON 0.4 / SODIUM 79 / CALCIUM 189

Cinnamon Ice Milk

⅔ cup sugar

⅔ cup instant nonfat dry milk powder

1 tablespoon cornstarch

1½ teaspoons ground cinnamon

3⅔ cups skim milk, divided

1 egg white, lightly beaten

½ teaspoon vanilla extract

Combine first 4 ingredients in a medium saucepan; stir well. Stir in 2 cups skim milk. Cook over medium heat, stirring constantly, until mixture is smooth and coats a metal spoon (do not boil). Gradually stir about one-fourth of hot mixture into egg white; add to remaining hot mixture, stirring constantly. Cook over low heat 1 minute, stirring constantly (do not boil). Remove from heat; stir in remaining 1⅔ cups milk and vanilla. Cover and chill thoroughly.

Pour mixture into freezer can of a 2-quart hand-turned or electric freezer. Freeze according to manufacturer's instructions. Let ripen 1 hour, if desired. Scoop ice milk into individual dessert bowls, and serve immediately. Yield: 12 servings (98 calories per ½-cup serving).

PROTEIN 5.2 / FAT 0.2 / CARBOHYDRATE 19.1 / CHOLESTEROL 3 / IRON 0.2 / SODIUM 79 / CALCIUM 180

Fresh Ginger Ice Milk

4 cups skim milk, divided

1 (1-inch) piece fresh gingerroot, peeled

⅔ cup instant nonfat dry milk powder

⅔ cup sugar

1 tablespoon cornstarch

1 egg white, lightly beaten

Combine 1 cup skim milk and gingerroot in a medium saucepan. Bring to a boil. Remove from heat; cover, and let stand 30 minutes. Pour mixture into container of an electric blender. Top with cover, and process until gingerroot is crushed. Strain mixture, discarding gingerroot pieces. Set strained mixture aside.

Combine 1 cup skim milk, milk powder, sugar, and cornstarch in a medium saucepan; stir well. Bring mixture to a boil, stirring constantly. Reduce heat, and simmer, uncovered, 2 minutes. Remove from heat. Gradually stir about one-fourth of hot mixture into beaten egg white. Add to remaining hot mixture, stirring constantly. Cook 1 minute over low heat. Remove from heat. Stir in reserved strained milk and remaining 2 cups skim milk. Cover and chill 1 to 2 hours.

Pour mixture into freezer can of a 1-gallon hand-turned or electric freezer. Freeze according to manufacturer's instructions. Let ripen 1 hour, if desired. Scoop ice milk into individual dessert bowls, and serve immediately. Yield: 14 servings (85 calories per ½-cup serving).

PROTEIN 4.7 / FAT 0.2 / CARBOHYDRATE 16.4 / CHOLESTEROL 3 / IRON 0.0 / SODIUM 71 / CALCIUM 158

Honey-Vanilla Malt Ice Milk

2¼ cups cold water
2 cups instant nonfat dry milk
   powder
¼ cup honey
2 tablespoons instant malted milk
   powder
1 tablespoon vanilla extract

Combine all ingredients in container of an electric blender; top with cover, and process until smooth.

Pour mixture into freezer can of a 2-quart hand-turned or electric freezer. Freeze according to manufacturer's instructions. Let ripen 1 hour, if desired. Scoop ice milk into individual dessert bowls, and serve immediately. Yield: 8 servings (170 calories per ½-cup serving).

PROTEIN 11.5 / FAT 0.7 / CARBOHYDRATE 28.8 / CHOLESTEROL 6 / IRON 0.2 / SODIUM 185 / CALCIUM 393

Tropical Mango Ice Milk

1 egg, lightly beaten
½ cup sugar
2 cups skim milk
¼ cup instant nonfat dry milk
   powder
1 cup chopped mango
¼ cup lime juice
1 (12-ounce) can evaporated
   skimmed milk
½ teaspoon coconut extract

Combine egg, sugar, skim milk, and milk powder in a medium saucepan. Cook over medium-low heat, stirring constantly with a wire whisk, until mixture is slightly thickened. Remove from heat; chill custard in refrigerator 30 minutes.

Place chopped mango in container of an electric blender or food processor; top with cover, and process until smooth. Add lime juice, and process until mixture is well blended. Chill mixture 15 minutes.

Combine custard, mango mixture, evaporated milk, and coconut extract in a large bowl; stir well. Strain mixture into freezer can of a 1-gallon hand-turned or electric freezer. Discard pulp. Freeze according to manufacturer's instructions. Let ripen 1 hour. Scoop ice milk into individual dessert bowls, and serve immediately. Yield: 14 servings (85 calories per ½-cup serving).

PROTEIN 4.3 / FAT 0.6 / CARBOHYDRATE 16.2 / CHOLESTEROL 22 / IRON 0.2 / SODIUM 63 / CALCIUM 145

To prepare frozen desserts without a hand-turned or electric freezer, pour mixture into an 8-inch square pan, and freeze until almost firm. Break mixture into large pieces, and place in food processor bowl; top with cover, and process several seconds or until fluffy but not thawed. Return to freezer tray, and refreeze until firm.

Fall flavor prevails in Pumpkin-Maple Ice Milk.

Pumpkin-Maple Ice Milk

1½ cups skim milk
½ cup reduced-calorie maple
  syrup
2 egg yolks, beaten
1 cup canned pumpkin
½ cup evaporated skimmed milk
1½ teaspoons pumpkin pie spice
2 teaspoons vanilla extract

Combine skim milk and syrup in a medium saucepan; stir well. Cook over medium heat until thoroughly heated (do not boil). Gradually stir about one-fourth of hot mixture into egg yolks; add to remaining hot mixture, stirring constantly. Reduce heat to medium low and cook, stirring constantly, until mixture coats a metal spoon. Remove from heat.

Combine remaining ingredients, and gradually stir into warm milk mixture. Cover and chill thoroughly.

Pour mixture into freezer can of a 2-quart hand-turned or electric freezer. Freeze according to manufacturer's instructions. Let ripen 1 hour, if desired. Scoop ice milk into individual dessert bowls, and serve immediately. Yield: 8 servings (66 calories per ½-cup serving).

PROTEIN 3.8 / FAT 1.6 / CARBOHYDRATE 9.1 / CHOLESTEROL 70 / IRON 0.8 / SODIUM 50 / CALCIUM 120

Peanut Ice Milk

½ cup sugar
2 tablespoons instant nonfat dry milk powder
1 cup skim milk
2 eggs, separated
1½ teaspoons vanilla extract
1 (12-ounce) can evaporated skimmed milk
¼ cup finely chopped, unsalted, dry-roasted peanuts

Combine sugar and milk powder in a medium saucepan; stir in skim milk and egg yolks. Cook over medium heat, stirring constantly, until mixture is smooth and slightly thickened (do not boil). Remove mixture from heat, and stir in vanilla. Cover and chill thoroughly.

Beat egg whites (at room temperature) in a small bowl at high speed of an electric mixer until stiff peaks form. Gently fold into chilled milk mixture. Stir in evaporated milk and peanuts.

Pour mixture into freezer can of a 2-quart hand-turned or electric freezer. Freeze according to manufacturer's instructions. Let ripen 1 hour, if desired. Scoop ice milk into individual dessert bowls, and serve immediately. Yield: 8 servings (142 calories per ½-cup serving).

PROTEIN 7.4 / FAT 3.3 / CARBOHYDRATE 20.8 / CHOLESTEROL 71 / IRON 0.5 / SODIUM 93 / CALCIUM 195

Vanilla Ice Milk

(pictured on page 82)

4 cups skim milk, divided
⅔ cup instant nonfat dry milk powder
⅔ cup sugar
2 tablespoons cornstarch
1 egg white, lightly beaten
2 teaspoons vanilla extract

Combine 1 cup skim milk, milk powder, sugar, and cornstarch in a medium saucepan; stir well. Cook over low heat, stirring constantly, until mixture comes to a boil. Cook 1 minute or until thickened, stirring constantly. Reduce heat to low. Gradually stir about one-fourth of hot mixture into egg white; add to remaining hot mixture, stirring constantly. Cook an additional minute, stirring constantly. Remove from heat; stir in remaining milk and vanilla. Cover and chill thoroughly

Pour mixture into freezer can of a 2-quart hand-turned or electric freezer. Freeze according to manufacturer's instructions. Let ripen 1 hour, if desired. Scoop ice milk into individual dessert bowls, and serve immediately. Yield: 10 servings (125 calories per ½-cup serving).

PROTEIN 6.6 / FAT 0.2 / CARBOHYDRATE 23.9 / CHOLESTEROL 4 / IRON 0.1 / SODIUM 99 / CALCIUM 221

Strawberry Ice Milk

(pictured on page 82)

3 cups ripe strawberries, hulled
½ cup sugar
½ teaspoon grated lemon rind
1 cup instant nonfat dry milk
   powder
1½ cups water
1 teaspoon lemon juice
Whole strawberries (optional)

*P*lace first 3 ingredients in container of an electric blender or food processor; top with cover, and process until smooth. Add milk powder, water, and lemon juice; process until well blended.

Pour mixture into freezer can of a 2-quart hand-turned or electric freezer. Freeze according to manufacturer's instructions. Let ripen 1 hour, if desired. Scoop ice milk into individual dessert bowls, and serve immediately. Garnish with whole strawberries, if desired. Yield: 8 servings (117 calories per ½-cup serving).

PROTEIN 5.7 / FAT 0.3 / CARBOHYDRATE 23.7 / CHOLESTEROL 3 / IRON 0.2 / SODIUM 81 / CALCIUM 195

Minted Grape Sorbet

(pictured on pages 88 and 89)

1 cup water
½ cup sugar
2 cups unsweetened concord grape
   juice, divided
2 fresh mint sprigs

*C*ombine water, sugar, and ½ cup grape juice in a medium saucepan. Bring to a boil. Boil 3 minutes. Add mint sprigs. Remove from heat. Cover and let stand 5 minutes. Transfer to a small bowl, and chill thoroughly. Remove and discard mint. Stir in remaining 1½ cups grape juice.

Pour mixture into freezer can of a 2-quart hand-turned or electric freezer. Freeze according to manufacturer's instructions. Let ripen 1 hour, if desired. Scoop sorbet into individual dessert bowls, and serve immediately. Or spoon into a 4-cup mold, and freeze overnight. Unmold and serve immediately. Yield: 8 servings (90 calories per ½-cup serving).

PROTEIN 0.0 / FAT 0.0 / CARBOHYDRATE 23.2 / CHOLESTEROL 0 / IRON 0.2 / SODIUM 3 / CALCIUM 8

Overleaf: *Scoop or mold frozen desserts into special treats: (clockwise from right) Amaretto-Peach Ice Milk (page 80), Cappuccino Ice Milk (page 80),* **and** *Minted Grape Sorbet.*

Raspberry Sorbet

1/2 cup sugar
1/2 cup water
4 cups unsweetened frozen
  raspberries, thawed
1/2 cup water
1 teaspoon lemon juice

Combine sugar and 1/2 cup water in a small saucepan; bring to a boil over low heat. Increase heat to high, and boil 5 minutes. Chill thoroughly.

Place raspberries in container of an electric blender or food processor; top with cover, and process until smooth. Press raspberry puree through a sieve; discard seeds.

Combine chilled sugar mixture, raspberry puree, 1/2 cup water, and lemon juice; stir well.

Pour mixture into freezer can of a 2-quart hand-turned or electric freezer. Freeze according to manufacturer's instructions. Let ripen 1 hour, if desired. Scoop sorbet into individual dessert bowls, and serve immediately. Yield: 6 servings (104 calories per 1/2-cup serving).

PROTEIN 0.7 / FAT 0.4 / CARBOHYDRATE 25.9 / CHOLESTEROL 0 / IRON 0.5 / SODIUM 0 / CALCIUM 18

Orange Alaskas

4 medium oranges
1 cup water
1/2 cup sugar, divided
2 egg whites
1/2 teaspoon cream of tartar
Orange curls (optional)

Cut a small slice from top of each orange. Clip membranes; carefully remove pulp (do not puncture bottom). Set shells aside. Place pulp in container of an electric blender; top with cover, and process 30 seconds. Strain pulp, reserving juice.

Combine water and 1/4 cup sugar in a medium saucepan. Bring to a boil; reduce heat, and simmer 5 minutes. Cool; stir in reserved orange juice. Pour mixture into freezer trays; freeze until almost firm. Spoon mixture into orange shells. Place shells on a baking sheet; freeze 4 hours or until mixture is firm.

Beat egg whites (at room temperature) and cream of tartar at high speed of an electric mixer until foamy. Gradually add remaining 1/4 cup sugar, 1 tablespoon at a time, beating until stiff peaks form.

Spread meringue over top of each orange shell; seal to edges of shells. Freeze until ready to serve.

Broil orange shells 6 inches from heat 1 to 2 minutes or until golden. Garnish with orange curls, if desired. Serve immediately. Yield: 4 servings (140 calories per serving).

PROTEIN 2.2 / FAT 0.0 / CARBOHYDRATE 33.5 / CHOLESTEROL 0 / IRON 0.1 / SODIUM 52 / CALCIUM 9

Orange cups are scooped out and used as the base for Orange Alaskas.

Cantaloupe Sorbet

(pictured on pages 76 and 77)

1 ripe cantaloupe (about 1
  pound)
1 cup unsweetened orange juice
½ cup sugar
1 tablespoon lemon juice

Cut melon in half; remove seeds into a sieve, catching juice in a bowl. Discard seeds. Add water to cantaloupe juice to make 1 cup.

Combine cantaloupe juice, orange juice, and sugar in a nonaluminum saucepan. Bring to a boil, and boil until sugar dissolves, stirring occasionally. Remove from heat, and let cool to room temperature.

Scoop pulp from cantaloupe; place in container of an electric blender or food processor. Add cantaloupe juice mixture and lemon juice; top with cover, and process until smooth.

Pour mixture into freezer can of a 2-quart hand-turned or electric freezer. Freeze according to manufacturer's instructions. Let ripen 1 hour, if desired. Scoop sorbet into individual dessert bowls, using a small scoop, and serve immediately. Yield: 8 servings (77 calories per ½-cup serving).

PROTEIN 0.6 / FAT 0.1 / CARBOHYDRATE 19.5 / CHOLESTEROL 0 / IRON 0.1 / SODIUM 4 / CALCIUM 8

Pink Grapefruit Sorbet

(pictured on pages 76 and 77)

4 cups unsweetened pink
  grapefruit juice
½ cup sugar
¼ cup corn syrup

Combine all ingredients in freezer can of a 2-quart hand-turned or electric freezer; stir well. Freeze according to manufacturer's instructions. Let ripen 1 hour, if desired. Scoop sorbet into individual dessert bowls, and serve immediately. Yield: 10 servings (100 calories per ½-cup serving).

PROTEIN 0.5 / FAT 0.1 / CARBOHYDRATE 24.8 / CHOLESTEROL 0 / IRON 2.0 / SODIUM 11 / CALCIUM 7

Fresh Pineapple Sorbet

(pictured on pages 76 and 77)

2 ripe pineapples (about 4
  pounds)
⅓ cup sugar

Cut each pineapple into six wedges; scoop out pulp and reserve shell. Place pulp and sugar in container of an electric blender or food processor; top with cover, and process until smooth. Press pineapple mixture through a sieve; discard pulp.

Pour mixture into freezer can of a 2-quart hand-turned or electric freezer. Freeze according to manufacturer's instructions.

Let ripen 1 hour, if desired. Place frozen mixture into a pastry bag fitted with a No. 6 star tip. Pipe ½ cup mixture into each wedge. Serve immediately. Yield: 12 servings (53 calories per ½-cup serving).

PROTEIN 0.2 / FAT 0.3 / CARBOHYDRATE 13.6 / CHOLESTEROL 0 / IRON 0.2 / SODIUM 1 / CALCIUM 5

Papaya Sorbet

⅔ *cup sugar, divided*
⅔ *cup water*
¼ *cup lime juice*
1½ *cups chopped papaya*
1 *egg white*

*R*eserve 1 tablespoon sugar. Combine remaining sugar and water in a small saucepan. Cook over medium heat, stirring occasionally, until sugar dissolves. Remove from heat; let syrup mixture cool.

Combine syrup mixture, lime juice, and papaya in container of an electric blender; top with cover, and process until smooth. Transfer to a large bowl.

Beat egg white (at room temperature) in a small bowl at high speed of an electric mixer until soft peaks form; add reserved 1 tablespoon sugar, beating until stiff peaks form. Gently fold beaten egg white into papaya mixture.

Pour mixture into freezer can of a 2-quart hand-turned or electric freezer. Freeze according to manufacturer's instructions. Let ripen at least 1 hour. Scoop sorbet into individual dessert bowls, and serve immediately. Yield: 8 servings (85 calories per ½-cup serving).

PROTEIN 0.7 / FAT 0.1 / CARBOHYDRATE 21.5 / CHOLESTEROL 0 / IRON 0.1 / SODIUM 8 / CALCIUM 11

Pear and White Grape Sorbet

5 *cups peeled, chopped pear*
⅓ *cup sugar*
1 *cup unsweetened white grape juice*
3 *tablespoons lime juice*
½ *teaspoon grated fresh gingerroot*

*C*ombine first 4 ingredients in a 2-quart saucepan; bring to a boil. Reduce heat, and simmer 10 minutes or until pears are tender. Remove from heat. Stir in gingerroot. Chill.

Pour mixture into freezer can of a 2-quart hand-turned or electric freezer. Freeze according to manufacturer's instructions. Let ripen 1 hour, if desired. Scoop sorbet into individual dessert bowls, and serve immediately. Yield: 14 servings (65 calories per ½-cup serving).

PROTEIN 0.2 / FAT 0.2 / CARBOHYDRATE 16.7 / CHOLESTEROL 0 / IRON 0.2 / SODIUM 1 / CALCIUM 9

Offer Lime Sherbet for a simple but refreshing dessert.

Lime Sherbet

2 cups skim milk
¾ cup sugar
⅓ cup lime juice
2 tablespoons instant nonfat dry
  milk powder
Scalloped lemon cups (optional)
Fresh mint sprigs (optional)
Lime twists (optional)

Combine first 4 ingredients, stirring well. Pour mixture into freezer can of a 2-quart hand-turned or electric freezer. Freeze according to manufacturer's instructions. Let ripen 1 hour, if desired. Scoop sherbet into individual dessert bowls or, if desired, into lemon cups. If desired, garnish with mint sprigs and lime twists. Serve immediately. Yield: 6 servings (138 calories per ½-cup serving).

PROTEIN 3.7 / FAT 0.2 / CARBOHYDRATE 31.4 / CHOLESTEROL 2 / IRON 0.1 / SODIUM 56 / CALCIUM 133

Pineapple-Buttermilk Sherbet

1 fresh pineapple (about 2
  pounds)
1 quart nonfat buttermilk
½ cup honey

Peel and trim eyes from pineapple; remove core. Cut pineapple into wedges.

Place pineapple and buttermilk in container of an electric blender. Top with cover, and process until smooth. With blender on high, gradually add honey in a slow, steady stream. Blend about 30 seconds.

Strain mixture into freezer can of a 1-gallon hand-turned or electric freezer. Discard pulp. Freeze according to manufacturer's instructions. Let ripen 1 hour. Scoop sherbet into individual dessert bowls, and serve immediately. Yield: 14 servings (78 calories per ½-cup serving).

PROTEIN 2.7 / FAT 0.4 / CARBOHYDRATE 17.4 / CHOLESTEROL 0 / IRON 0.2 / SODIUM 74 / CALCIUM 3

Strawberry-Buttermilk Sherbet

2 cups sliced fresh strawberries, divided
1 cup nonfat buttermilk
1 egg
¼ cup sugar
1 teaspoon vanilla extract
⅛ teaspoon salt

*P*lace 1½ cups strawberries and remaining ingredients in container of an electric blender or food processor; top with cover, and process until smooth.

Pour strawberry mixture into freezer can of a 2-quart hand-turned or electric freezer. Freeze according to manufacturer's instructions. Stir in remaining ½ cup strawberries before mixture is completely frozen. Freeze until mixture is firm. Let ripen 1 hour, if desired. Scoop sherbet into individual dessert bowls, and serve immediately. Yield: 6 servings (80 calories per ½-cup serving).

PROTEIN 2.9 / FAT 1.3 / CARBOHYDRATE 12.6 / CHOLESTEROL 46 / IRON 0.4 / SODIUM 61 / CALCIUM 13

Sugarless Fruit Sherbet

1 quart fresh strawberries, hulled
2 cups diced banana (about 3 medium)
½ cup low-fat sour cream
2 tablespoons instant nonfat dry milk powder
1 (6-ounce) can unsweetened frozen pineapple juice concentrate, thawed and undiluted
½ cup unsweetened white grape juice
2 teaspoons vanilla extract

*P*lace first 4 ingredients in container of an electric blender or food processor; top with cover, and process until smooth. Transfer mixture to a large bowl. Stir in pineapple juice, grape juice, and vanilla.

Pour mixture into freezer can of a 2-quart hand-turned or electric freezer. Freeze according to manufacturer's instructions. Let ripen 1 hour, if desired. Scoop sherbet into individual dessert bowls, and serve immediately. Yield: 12 servings (93 calories per ½-cup serving).

PROTEIN 1.5 / FAT 1.5 / CARBOHYDRATE 19.3 / CHOLESTEROL 4 / IRON 0.4 / SODIUM 12 / CALCIUM 41

Vanilla Tofutti

2 (10½-ounce) packages soft tofu,
  drained
1½ cups plain nonfat yogurt
¾ cup sugar
¼ cup instant nonfat dry milk
  powder
2 teaspoons grated lemon rind
1 tablespoon vanilla extract

Combine all ingredients in container of an electric blender or food processor; top with cover, and process until smooth.

Pour mixture into freezer can of a 2-quart hand-turned or electric freezer. Freeze according to manufacturer's instructions. Let ripen 1 hour, if desired. Scoop tofutti into individual dessert bowls, and serve immediately. Yield: 10 servings (126 calories per ½-cup serving).

PROTEIN 6.2 / FAT 2.2 / CARBOHYDRATE 20.7 / CHOLESTEROL 1 / IRON 0.8 / SODIUM 43 / CALCIUM 207

Blueberry Frozen Yogurt

2 cups fresh or frozen
  unsweetened blueberries, thawed
1 cup water
½ cup instant nonfat dry milk
  powder
2 (8-ounce) cartons plain nonfat
  yogurt
¼ cup plus 2 tablespoons honey

Place blueberries and water in container of an electric blender; top with cover, and process until smooth. Press puree through a sieve to remove seeds, catching juice in a bowl. Discard seeds. Stir remaining ingredients into juice in bowl.

Pour mixture into freezer can of a 2-quart hand-turned or electric freezer. Freeze according to manufacturer's instructions. Let ripen 1 hour, if desired. Scoop yogurt into individual dessert bowls, and serve immediately. Yield: 10 servings (83 calories per ½-cup serving).

PROTEIN 4.1 / FAT 0.2 / CARBOHYDRATE 17.2 / CHOLESTEROL 2 / IRON 0.1 / SODIUM 57 / CALCIUM 140

Banana-Strawberry Frozen Yogurt

1 large banana, peeled and sliced
½ cup halved fresh strawberries
½ cup plain nonfat yogurt
¼ cup unsweetened pineapple
  juice
2 tablespoons instant nonfat dry
  milk powder
2 tablespoons honey

Combine all ingredients in container of an electric blender; top with cover, and process until smooth.

Pour mixture into freezer can of a 2-quart hand-turned or electric freezer. Freeze according to manufacturer's instructions. Let ripen 1 hour, if desired. Scoop yogurt into individual dessert bowls, and serve immediately. Yield: 4 servings (114 calories per ½-cup serving).

PROTEIN 3.6 / FAT 0.4 / CARBOHYDRATE 26.0 / CHOLESTEROL 1 / IRON 0.3 / SODIUM 43 / CALCIUM 113

(Clockwise from right): Vanilla Tofutti, Banana-Strawberry Frozen Yogurt, Strawberry-Raspberry Frozen Yogurt (page 99), Banana-Lime Frozen Yogurt (page 98), and Blueberry Frozen Yogurt.

Banana-Lime Frozen Yogurt

(pictured on page 96)

1 envelope unflavored gelatin
1 cup cold water, divided
2 (8-ounce) cartons plain nonfat yogurt
1 (6-ounce) can frozen limeade concentrate, thawed and undiluted
⅓ cup sugar
¾ cup chopped banana
2 tablespoons light rum

*S*often gelatin in ¼ cup cold water in a small saucepan; let stand 1 minute. Cook over medium heat, stirring constantly, until gelatin dissolves.

Combine gelatin mixture, remaining ¾ cup cold water, and remaining ingredients in container of an electric blender or food processor; top with cover, and process until smooth.

Pour banana-lime mixture into freezer can of a 2-quart hand-turned or electric freezer. Freeze according to manufacturer's instructions. Let ripen 1 hour, if desired. Scoop yogurt into individual dessert bowls, and serve immediately. Yield: 11 servings (102 calories per ½-cup serving).

PROTEIN 3.1 / FAT 0.2 / CARBOHYDRATE 21.1 / CHOLESTEROL 1 / IRON 0.2 / SODIUM 32 / CALCIUM 84

Frozen Berry Yogurt

1 cup fresh raspberries
1 cup fresh strawberries, hulled
⅔ cup instant nonfat dry milk powder
2 cups plain nonfat yogurt
½ cup sugar
1 envelope unflavored gelatin
1 cup cold water
1 tablespoon Grand Marnier or other orange-flavored liqueur

*P*lace berries in container of an electric blender; top with cover, and process at high speed 10 to 15 seconds. Press puree through a sieve to remove seeds. Discard seeds; return puree to container of electric blender, and add milk powder, yogurt, and sugar. Top with cover, and process until smooth.

Sprinkle gelatin over 1 cup cold water in a small saucepan; let stand 1 minute. Cook over low heat, stirring until gelatin dissolves.

Add gelatin mixture and liqueur slowly to mixture in blender; blend until smooth.

Pour mixture into freezer can of a 2-quart hand-turned or electric freezer. Freeze according to manufacturer's instructions. Let ripen at least 1 hour before serving. Scoop yogurt into individual dessert bowls, and serve immediately. Yield: 8 servings (139 calories per ½-cup serving).

PROTEIN 7.9 / FAT 0.3 / CARBOHYDRATE 25.7 / CHOLESTEROL 3 / IRON 0.2 / SODIUM 98 / CALCIUM 245

Cheesecake Frozen Yogurt

2 cups plain low-fat yogurt
⅔ cup instant nonfat dry milk
 powder
½ cup light process cream cheese
 product
⅓ cup sugar
1 tablespoon honey
1 envelope unflavored gelatin
1 cup cold water, divided
2 tablespoons vanilla extract
2 teaspoons grated lemon rind
⅛ teaspoon ground nutmeg

Combine first 5 ingredients in container of an electric blender. Top with cover, and process until smooth. Soften gelatin in ¼ cup cold water, and add remaining ¾ cup cold water to blender. Place gelatin mixture in a small saucepan. Cook over medium heat, stirring frequently, until gelatin dissolves. Remove from heat, and add to yogurt mixture. Add vanilla, lemon rind, and nutmeg. Top with cover, and process until blended.

Pour mixture into freezer can of a 2-quart hand-turned or electric freezer. Freeze according to manufacturer's instructions. Let ripen 1 hour, if desired. Scoop yogurt into individual dessert bowls, and serve immediately. Yield: 12 servings (104 calories per ½-cup serving).

PROTEIN 5.9 / FAT 2.3 / CARBOHYDRATE 14.6 / CHOLESTEROL 4 / IRON 0.1 / SODIUM 115 / CALCIUM 167

Strawberry-Raspberry Frozen Yogurt
(pictured on page 96)

2 cups frozen whole raspberries,
 thawed
2 cups frozen whole strawberries,
 thawed
2 cups plain nonfat yogurt
⅓ cup sugar
1 tablespoon Grand Marnier or
 other orange-flavored liqueur
¼ teaspoon grated orange rind

Place berries in container of an electric blender; top with cover, and process until smooth. Press puree through a sieve to remove seeds. Discard seeds. Combine puree and remaining ingredients; stir well.

Pour mixture into freezer can of a 2-quart hand-turned or electric freezer. Freeze according to manufacturer's instructions. Let ripen 1 hour, if desired. Scoop yogurt into individual dessert bowls, and serve immediately. Yield: 8 servings (97 calories per ½-cup serving).

PROTEIN 3.7 / FAT 0.3 / CARBOHYDRATE 20.0 / CHOLESTEROL 1 / IRON 0.5 / SODIUM 44 / CALCIUM 125

Frozen yogurts are simple to make and several sizes of small ice cream freezers are available today for making them, ranging from single serving yields to one quart. Freeze fruit yogurts to make a wide variety of "soft serve" flavors that the whole family will love.

Fruit Desserts

No food offers more in color, texture, and flavor than fresh fruit. First, select fresh fruits ripe with flavor. This is the key to the sweetness of most fruit desserts. Judge the quality and ripeness by appearance, softness, and fragrance. Peaches and apricots should look velvety, feel firm but not hard, have a rosy blush, and have a sweet aroma. A pineapple should have a tangy aroma, feel heavy in relation to its size, and yield to light pressure.

Berries, peaches, and cherries are among the fruits that have a definite season, but when frozen while at their peak, these fruits can be used with success throughout the year.

The recipes that follow are based on simple techniques for sautéing, poaching, broiling, and baking fruits. These techniques will yield a variety of dishes from fruit soups and crisps to brûlées and compotes.

(Left to right): Prepare Baked Apples With Cinnamon Filling (page 102) and Raspberries Brûlée (page 123) and enjoy the freshness of a fruit dessert.

Baked Apples With Cinnamon Filling

(pictured on pages 100 and 101)

6 medium cooking apples (about
    1½ pounds)
¼ cup firmly packed brown sugar
2 tablespoons finely chopped
    walnuts
1 tablespoon margarine, softened
2 teaspoons all-purpose flour
½ teaspoon ground cinnamon
⅓ cup unsweetened apple juice

Cut a 1-inch cap from the top of each apple. Core apple, cutting to but not through the bottom.

Combine brown sugar, walnuts, margarine, flour, and cinnamon; stir well. Spoon 1 tablespoon mixture into cavity of each apple; place top of apple on bottom half and place in a 10- x 6- x 2-inch baking dish.

Pour apple juice into baking dish. Cover and bake at 375° for 50 minutes to 1 hour or until apples are tender, basting occasionally with apple juice. Yield: 6 servings (182 calories per serving).

PROTEIN 1.0 / FAT 3.9 / CARBOHYDRATE 39.0 / CHOLESTEROL 0 / IRON 0.8 / SODIUM 26 / CALCIUM 26

Sautéed Apples With Apricot-Rum Sauce

1 tablespoon margarine
8 Golden Delicious apples, peeled,
    cored, and thinly sliced (about
    2 pounds)
¼ cup raisins
¼ cup sugar
1 teaspoon grated lemon
    rind
½ teaspoon ground cinnamon
¼ teaspoon grated nutmeg
Apricot-Rum Sauce

Melt margarine in a large nonstick skillet over medium heat; stir in apples. Cook 2 minutes or until apples are warm, stirring occasionally. Stir in raisins, sugar, lemon rind, and cinnamon. Sauté 8 to 10 minutes or until apples are tender. Stir in nutmeg. Serve warm with chilled Apricot-Rum Sauce. Yield: 8 servings (164 calories per serving).

Apricot-Rum Sauce

1 (12-ounce) can apricot
    nectar
2 tablespoons sugar
1 tablespoon cornstarch
3 tablespoons dark rum
2 teaspoons vanilla extract

Bring apricot nectar to a boil in a large, heavy skillet. Boil 3 minutes or until reduced to 1 cup. Reduce heat to medium. Combine remaining ingredients; add to apricot nectar. Stir with a wire whisk until mixture thickens. Remove from heat. Cover and chill thoroughly. Yield: 1¼ cups.

PROTEIN 0.5 / FAT 1.8 / CARBOHYDRATE 35.3 / CHOLESTEROL 0 / IRON 0.4 / SODIUM 19 / CALCIUM 12

Apple Crisp

4 medium cooking apples, peeled, cored, and sliced (about 1 pound)
1 tablespoon lemon juice
1/8 teaspoon ground nutmeg
2 tablespoons all-purpose flour
1/4 cup regular oats, uncooked
2 tablespoons corn oil
1/4 cup firmly packed brown sugar
1 teaspoon ground cinnamon

Arrange apples in a shallow 1-quart baking dish. Sprinkle with lemon juice and nutmeg.

Combine flour, oats, oil, brown sugar, and cinnamon until mixture resembles coarse meal; sprinkle over apples. Bake at 350° for 40 minutes or until browned. Yield: 4 servings (199 calories per serving).

PROTEIN 1.5 / FAT 7.5 / CARBOHYDRATE 33.5 / CHOLESTEROL 0 / IRON 1.1 / SODIUM 4 / CALCIUM 26

Streusel Apples With Bourbon Sauce

5 medium cooking apples, peeled, cored, and thinly sliced (about 1 1/4 pounds)
Vegetable cooking spray
3 tablespoons unsweetened apple cider
1 tablespoon bourbon
2 tablespoons margarine
1/4 cup quick-cooking oats, uncooked
1/4 cup chopped pecans
1/2 teaspoon ground cinnamon
1/8 teaspoon ground cloves
1/8 teaspoon ground allspice
2 tablespoons brown sugar
Bourbon Sauce

Arrange apple slices, mounding slightly, in a 9-inch square baking pan that has been coated with cooking spray. Sprinkle with apple cider and bourbon.

Combine margarine, oats, and pecans in a small skillet. Cook over medium heat until lightly browned, stirring constantly. Stir in cinnamon, cloves, allspice, and brown sugar. Sprinkle over apple mixture. Bake at 375° for 35 minutes. Spoon into individual serving dishes; spoon Bourbon Sauce evenly over servings. Yield: 6 servings (179 calories per serving).

Bourbon Sauce

1/2 cup vanilla ice milk
2 teaspoons bourbon
2 teaspoons reduced-calorie maple syrup
1/8 teaspoon freshly ground nutmeg

Let ice milk stand at room temperature 5 minutes or until softened; stir in bourbon, syrup, and nutmeg. Yield: 1/2 cup.

PROTEIN 1.5 / FAT 8.2 / CARBOHYDRATE 26.5 / CHOLESTEROL 2 / IRON 0.6 / SODIUM 55 / CALCIUM 30

Apricots With Ricotta

1 cup part-skim ricotta cheese
¼ cup sifted powdered sugar
1 teaspoon grated orange rind
3 tablespoons amaretto, divided
1 teaspoon vanilla extract
2 (16-ounce) cans unsweetened
 apricot halves, drained and
 divided
Fresh mint sprigs (optional)

Combine ricotta cheese, powdered sugar, orange rind, 2 tablespoons amaretto, and vanilla in container of an electric blender or food processor; top with cover, and process until smooth. Transfer to a bowl, and set aside.

Place half of drained apricot halves and remaining 1 tablespoon amaretto in container of an electric blender or food processor; top with cover, and process until smooth. Spoon apricot mixture evenly into 6 stemmed glasses. Spoon ricotta mixture over apricot mixture. Top with remaining apricot halves. Garnish with fresh mint sprigs, if desired. Yield: 6 servings (136 calories per serving).

PROTEIN 5.7 / FAT 3.3 / CARBOHYDRATE 17.9 / CHOLESTEROL 13 / IRON 1.0 / SODIUM 68 / CALCIUM 124

Blueberry Crisp

1 (16-ounce) package frozen
 unsweetened blueberries, thawed
1 tablespoon plus 2 teaspoons
 cornstarch
1 tablespoon plus 1½ teaspoons
 lemon juice
2 teaspoons water
⅛ teaspoon ground nutmeg
½ cup regular oats, uncooked
¼ cup firmly packed brown sugar
2 tablespoons plus 1½ teaspoons
 all-purpose flour
¾ teaspoon ground cinnamon
2 tablespoons margarine

Place blueberries in a shallow 1-quart baking dish. Combine cornstarch, lemon juice, water, and nutmeg; stir well. Pour over blueberries, stirring gently to coat.

Combine oats, brown sugar, flour, and cinnamon in a small bowl; cut in margarine with a pastry blender until mixture resembles coarse meal. Sprinkle mixture evenly over blueberries. Bake at 375° for 30 minutes or until bubbly. Spoon into individual serving bowls, and serve warm. Yield: 6 servings (155 calories per serving).

PROTEIN 1.8 / FAT 4.8 / CARBOHYDRATE 27.8 / CHOLESTEROL 0 / IRON 0.9 / SODIUM 48 / CALCIUM 23

Serve Apricots With Ricotta in stemmed glasses; garnish with fresh mint sprigs for a formal touch.

Chilled fruit soups are an attractive addition to almost any meal; (from top) Merry Berry Soup (page 123) and Blueberry Kissel are sure to please.

Blueberry Kissel

2 pints fresh blueberries
1½ cups water
¼ cup sugar
2 tablespoons cornstarch
2 tablespoons lemon juice
2 tablespoons honey
3 tablespoons orange-flavored
   liqueur
½ cup low-fat sour cream

*P*lace blueberries in container of an electric blender; add water. Top with cover, and process until smooth. Press puree through a sieve into a medium saucepan. Discard skins and seeds.

Add sugar, cornstarch, lemon juice, and honey to strained blueberry puree in saucepan, stirring well. Cook over medium heat, stirring constantly, until mixture comes to a boil; stir in liqueur. Cook an additional minute, stirring constantly. Remove mixture from heat.

Pour into 8 individual dessert dishes. Cover and chill thoroughly. To serve, pipe 1 tablespoon sour cream over each serving; draw a wooden pick through sour cream to create a pattern. Yield: 8 servings (113 calories per serving).

PROTEIN 0.9 / FAT 2.0 / CARBOHYDRATE 23.0 / CHOLESTEROL 6 / IRON 0.1 / SODIUM 10 / CALCIUM 20

Glazed Baked Bananas

2 large, firm bananas, peeled,
   split lengthwise, and halved
1 tablespoon plus 1 teaspoon
   margarine, melted
¼ cup firmly packed brown sugar
¼ cup unsweetened orange juice
¼ cup dark rum

*P*lace bananas in a 10- x 6- x 2-inch baking dish, and brush with margarine. Combine sugar, orange juice, and rum; stir well. Pour juice mixture over bananas. Bake at 450° for 6 to 8 minutes or until bubbly. (Do not overbake.)

To serve, place bananas on individual serving dishes. Spoon glaze mixture evenly over bananas. Serve immediately. Yield: 4 servings (153 calories per serving).

PROTEIN 0.8 / FAT 4.1 / CARBOHYDRATE 30.3 / CHOLESTEROL 0 / IRON 0.7 / SODIUM 49 / CALCIUM 18

Scandinavian Fruit Soup

4 cups water
1½ cups dried fruit bits
1 (3-inch) stick cinnamon
¼ cup sugar
2 tablespoons cornstarch
2 tablespoons water

*C*ombine first 4 ingredients in a large saucepan. Bring mixture to a boil; cover, reduce heat, and simmer 30 minutes or until fruit is tender. Discard cinnamon stick. Combine cornstarch and 2 tablespoons water; stir well. Add to fruit mixture; cook, stirring constantly, until mixture is slightly thickened. Remove from heat. Pour into a bowl; cover and chill thoroughly. Yield: 4 cups (197 calories per 1-cup serving).

PROTEIN 1.9 / FAT 0.0 / CARBOHYDRATE 44.7 / CHOLESTEROL 0 / IRON 0.7 / SODIUM 35 / CALCIUM 0

Bing Cherries in Burgundy Wine

1 (16-ounce) package frozen
   unsweetened dark sweet cherries,
   thawed
1½ cups Burgundy or other dry
   red wine
¼ cup sugar
1 (3-inch) stick cinnamon
1 orange slice

*C*ombine all ingredients in a medium saucepan; bring to a boil. Reduce heat and simmer 10 minutes. Remove cherries using a slotted spoon; set aside. Remove and discard cinnamon stick and orange slice. Boil wine mixture over medium heat for 5 minutes. Remove from heat; pour over reserved cherries. Cover and chill thoroughly. Spoon into individual dessert dishes. Yield: 6 servings (81 calories per serving).

PROTEIN 0.7 / FAT 0.0 / CARBOHYDRATE 19.3 / CHOLESTEROL 0 / IRON 1.2 / SODIUM 10 / CALCIUM 5

Cherry Crisp

1 (16-ounce) package frozen
   unsweetened cherries, thawed
1 tablespoon cornstarch
1 tablespoon plus 1½ teaspoons
   lemon juice
2 teaspoons water
⅛ teaspoon ground nutmeg
½ cup regular oats, uncooked
¼ cup firmly packed brown
   sugar
2 tablespoons all-purpose flour
2 tablespoons margarine

Place cherries in a shallow 1-quart baking dish. Combine cornstarch, lemon juice, water, and nutmeg; stir well. Pour over cherries, stirring gently to coat.

Combine oats, brown sugar, and flour in a small bowl; cut in margarine with a pastry blender until mixture resembles coarse meal. Sprinkle mixture evenly over cherries. Bake at 375° for 30 minutes or until fruit is bubbly. Spoon into individual serving bowls, and serve warm. Yield: 6 servings (165 calories per serving).

PROTEIN 2.3 / FAT 5.0 / CARBOHYDRATE 29.5 / CHOLESTEROL 0 / IRON 1.0 / SODIUM 47 / CALCIUM 25

Flaming Cherries Jubilee

½ cup unsweetened orange juice
¼ cup sugar
2 tablespoons grated orange rind
1 teaspoon cornstarch
1 (16-ounce) package frozen
   unsweetened dark sweet cherries,
   thawed
⅓ cup light rum
2 cups vanilla ice milk

Combine first 4 ingredients in a large skillet, stirring well. Place over medium heat and bring to a boil, stirring constantly. Reduce heat, and simmer 2 to 3 minutes or until thickened. Remove from heat; stir in cherries.

Place rum in a small, long-handled pan; heat just until warm. Ignite with a long match, and pour over cherry mixture. Stir gently until flame dies down. Serve immediately over ⅓-cup portions of ice milk. Yield: 6 servings (182 calories per serving).

PROTEIN 2.6 / FAT 1.9 / CARBOHYDRATE 29.7 / CHOLESTEROL 6 / IRON 1.0 / SODIUM 42 / CALCIUM 64

Serve Flaming Cherries Jubilee over ice milk for an impressive finale to a gala meal.

Grapes Brûlée

2 cups seedless green grapes
3 ounces Neufchâtel cheese,
   softened
¼ cup low-fat sour cream
½ teaspoon vanilla extract
¼ cup firmly packed brown sugar

*P*lace grapes in six 6-ounce custard cups.

Beat Neufchâtel cheese and sour cream in a small bowl at medium speed of an electric mixer until smooth. Stir in vanilla. Spread cheese mixture evenly over grapes.

Sprinkle brown sugar evenly over cheese mixture. Broil 4 inches from heat 2 minutes or until sugar melts. Serve immediately. Yield: 6 servings (126 calories per serving).

PROTEIN 2.1 / FAT 4.8 / CARBOHYDRATE 19.9 / CHOLESTEROL 15 / IRON 0.5 / SODIUM 64 / CALCIUM 35

Fruit and Pumpkin Crisp

1½ cups shredded fresh pumpkin,
   divided
Vegetable cooking spray
⅓ cup dried apricots, chopped
⅓ cup pitted prunes, chopped
1 medium apple, peeled, cored,
   and diced
¼ cup honey, divided
1 cup low-fat cottage cheese
1 egg
1 teaspoon pumpkin pie spice
⅓ cup old-fashioned oats,
   uncooked
3 tablespoons brown sugar
2 tablespoons vegetable oil

*S*pread 1 cup shredded pumpkin in bottom of a 9-inch square baking pan that has been coated with cooking spray. Combine apricots, prunes, and diced apple in a small bowl; sprinkle evenly over pumpkin. Drizzle with 2 tablespoons honey.

Position knife blade in food processor bowl; add remaining 2 tablespoons honey, cottage cheese, egg, and pumpkin pie spice. Top with cover, and process until smooth. Spread mixture evenly over fruit. Top with remaining ½ cup shredded pumpkin.

Combine oats, brown sugar, and oil in a small bowl; stir well. Sprinkle over pumpkin. Bake at 375° for 45 minutes. Yield: 9 servings (154 calories per serving).

PROTEIN 5.2 / FAT 4.7 / CARBOHYDRATE 24.6 / CHOLESTEROL 32 / IRON 1.1 / SODIUM 115 / CALCIUM 36

Orange Sections in Spiced Wine Sauce

3 medium navel oranges
½ cup sugar
2 cups Chablis or other dry white
   wine
3 whole cloves
1 vanilla bean
Fresh mint sprigs (optional)

*R*emove rind from oranges with a paring knife, being careful not to include the white pith. Cut rind into very narrow, hair-like strips. Reserve oranges.

Combine orange strips, sugar, wine, cloves, and vanilla bean in a heavy saucepan; bring to a boil. Reduce heat and simmer 10 minutes or until liquid is reduced by half. Remove from heat.

Orange Sections in Spiced Wine Sauce
(Continued)

Peel and section reserved oranges over a medium bowl, collecting juice. Add orange sections to juice. Pour orange strip mixture over orange sections. Cover; chill at least 8 hours.

To serve, arrange orange sections in pinwheel patterns in 6 individual bowls. Spoon syrup over orange sections. Top with orange strips, and garnish each serving with a mint sprig, if desired. Yield: 6 servings (139 calories per serving).

PROTEIN 0.6 / FAT 0.0 / CARBOHYDRATE 22.8 / CHOLESTEROL 0 / IRON 0.5 / SODIUM 4 / CALCIUM 27

Peach Melba

1 cup water
1/4 cup sugar
1 (1½-inch) piece vanilla bean
1 teaspoon lemon juice
2 medium peaches, peeled and
   halved
1 teaspoon vanilla extract
1⅓ cups vanilla ice milk
Raspberry Sauce

*C*ombine water, sugar, vanilla bean, and lemon juice in a medium saucepan; bring to a boil over medium heat, stirring until sugar dissolves. Add peach halves; cover, reduce heat, and simmer 10 to 12 minutes or until peaches are tender. Stir in vanilla extract. Transfer peaches and liquid to a medium bowl; cover and chill thoroughly.

To serve, spoon ⅓ cup ice milk onto each of 4 dessert plates, and top each with a drained peach half, round side up; top with 2 tablespoons Raspberry Sauce. Serve immediately. Yield: 4 servings (187 calories per serving).

Raspberry Sauce

1½ cups frozen unsweetened
   raspberries, thawed
2 teaspoons sugar
1 teaspoon cornstarch
1 tablespoon Chambord or other
   raspberry-flavored liqueur

*P*lace raspberries in container of an electric blender; top with cover, and process until smooth. Press puree through a sieve to yield ½ cup juice; discard seeds.

Combine raspberry juice, sugar, and cornstarch in a small saucepan; stir well. Cook over medium heat, stirring constantly, until mixture thickens. Stir in liqueur, and cook an additional minute. Remove from heat, and cool. Yield: ½ cup.

PROTEIN 2.6 / FAT 2.1 / CARBOHYDRATE 39.2 / CHOLESTEROL 6 / IRON 0.4 / SODIUM 35 / CALCIUM 70

There is an endless combination for fruit crisps. Combine either fresh, frozen, or canned fruit with spices, top with a crumble topping, and bake in an ovenproof dish.

Summer Fruit Crumble

4 medium-size ripe peaches,
    peeled and sliced (about 1
    pound)
1 cup fresh or frozen raspberries,
    thawed
1 cup fresh or frozen blueberries,
    thawed
½ cup firmly packed brown sugar
1 tablespoon cornstarch
½ cup all-purpose flour
¼ cup sugar
¼ teaspoon ground nutmeg
2 tablespoons corn oil

Combine first 5 ingredients in a large bowl, and toss gently. Spoon fruit mixture into a shallow 1½-quart baking dish. Set dish aside.

Combine flour, sugar, and nutmeg in a small bowl. Add oil; stir with a fork until dry ingredients are moistened and mixture is crumbly. Sprinkle topping over fruit mixture. Bake at 400° for 40 minutes or until topping is lightly browned. Yield: 8 servings (180 calories per serving).

PROTEIN 1.5 / FAT 3.7 / CARBOHYDRATE 36.7 / CHOLESTEROL 0 / IRON 0.9 / SODIUM 6 / CALCIUM 21

Prune-Stuffed Peaches With Almond Cream

6 dried pitted prunes
⅓ cup Chablis or other dry white
    wine
6 medium-size ripe peaches
    (about 1½ pounds)
1 tablespoon lemon juice
Almond Cream
Fresh mint sprigs (optional)

Combine prunes and wine in a small saucepan. Bring to a boil; cook, uncovered, over medium heat 3 minutes or until liquid is absorbed.

Peel peaches; cut in half lengthwise. Remove pits and replace each with a prune. Place peach halves together with prunes enclosed. Brush with lemon juice to prevent browning.

Spoon 2 tablespoons Almond Cream into each of 6 individual compotes. Top each serving with 1 peach. Garnish with fresh mint sprigs, if desired. Yield: 6 servings (120 calories per serving).

Almond Cream

¾ cup skim milk
2 tablespoons sugar
1 teaspoon cornstarch
1 egg yolk, lightly beaten
1 tablespoon peach-flavored
    schnapps
½ teaspoon almond extract

Combine first 4 ingredients in a medium saucepan, stirring well. Cook over medium heat, stirring constantly, until mixture thickens. Remove from heat; stir in peach-flavored schnapps and almond extract. Yield: ¾ cup.

PROTEIN 2.5 / FAT 1.3 / CARBOHYDRATE 25.0 / CHOLESTEROL 46 / IRON 0.5 / SODIUM 22 / CALCIUM 52

Meringue Peaches

3 egg whites
⅛ teaspoon salt
⅛ teaspoon cream of tartar
1 teaspoon vanilla extract
3 tablespoons sugar
1 tablespoon cornstarch
3 large ripe peaches, peeled and halved (about 1½ pounds)
2 tablespoons finely chopped walnuts

*B*eat egg whites (at room temperature) in a large bowl at high speed of an electric mixer until foamy. Sprinkle salt, cream of tartar, and vanilla over egg whites; continue beating until soft peaks form. Gradually add sugar, 1 tablespoon at a time, and cornstarch, beating until stiff peaks form.

Place peach halves, cut side down, in six 10-ounce custard cups. Spread peaches evenly with meringue. Sprinkle with walnuts. Bake at 375° for 10 minutes or until golden brown. Serve immediately. Yield: 6 servings (103 calories per serving).

PROTEIN 3.0 / FAT 1.4 / CARBOHYDRATE 20.7 / CHOLESTEROL 0 / IRON 0.2 / SODIUM 78 / CALCIUM 9

Peach-Almond Crisp
(*pictured on pages 114 and 115*)

6 medium-size ripe peaches, peeled and sliced (about 1½ pounds)
¼ cup plus 1½ teaspoons sugar
1 tablespoon all-purpose flour
⅛ teaspoon ground nutmeg
⅛ teaspoon almond extract
Vegetable cooking spray
¼ cup plus 1½ teaspoons regular oats, uncooked
3 tablespoons brown sugar
1 tablespoon plus 1½ teaspoons all-purpose flour
⅛ teaspoon salt
⅛ teaspoon ground cinnamon
1 tablespoon unsalted margarine
3 tablespoons toasted almonds, chopped
Sliced fresh peaches (optional)
Fresh mint sprigs (optional)

*C*ombine first 5 ingredients in a large bowl; toss gently. Place peach mixture in a 1-quart baking dish that has been coated with cooking spray.

Combine oats and next 4 ingredients, stirring well. Cut in margarine with a pastry blender until mixture resembles coarse meal. Add almonds. Sprinkle mixture evenly over peach mixture. Bake at 375° for 20 to 25 minutes or until golden and bubbly. If desired, garnish with sliced peaches and fresh mint sprigs. Yield: 6 servings (166 calories per serving).

PROTEIN 2.5 / FAT 4.5 / CARBOHYDRATE 30.8 / CHOLESTEROL 0 / IRON 0.7 / SODIUM 51 / CALCIUM 22

Overleaf: *(left to right) Strawberries Romanoff (page 124), Peach-Almond Crisp, and Pears Poached in Red Wine (page 118) offer a variety of summertime fruits.*

Peaches With Sabayon Sauce

1 tablespoon lemon juice
6 medium-size ripe peaches,
    peeled and sliced (about 1½
    pounds)
1 egg
¼ cup sugar
⅓ cup Sauterne or other sweet
    white wine

Sprinkle lemon juice over peaches; cover and chill.

Combine egg and sugar in top of a large double boiler. Place over simmering water. Beat at low speed of an electric mixer for 2 minutes or until smooth. Gradually add wine; continue beating for 5 minutes or until mixture has thickened and doubled in volume. Remove from heat.

Spoon chilled peaches and any juice into 6 individual dessert dishes. Spoon 3 tablespoons sauce over each serving. Serve immediately. Yield: 6 servings (115 calories per serving).

PROTEIN 2.0 / FAT 1.0 / CARBOHYDRATE 24.1 / CHOLESTEROL 46 / IRON 0.4 / SODIUM 13 / CALCIUM 13

Pear Crumble With Rum Cream Sauce

3 large pears, peeled, cored, and
    sliced (about 1½ pounds)
Vegetable cooking spray
2 tablespoons dark rum
2 tablespoons margarine
¼ cup quick-cooking oats,
    uncooked
¼ cup chopped pecans
2 tablespoons brown sugar
½ teaspoon ground cinnamon
⅛ teaspoon ground allspice
⅛ teaspoon ground cloves
Rum Cream Sauce

Rum Cream Sauce

½ cup vanilla ice milk, softened
2 teaspoons dark rum
⅛ teaspoon ground nutmeg

Place pear slices in a 9-inch round or square baking pan that has been coated with cooking spray. Sprinkle rum over pear slices. Set aside.

Combine margarine, oats, and pecans in a small skillet. Cook over medium heat until lightly browned. Stir in brown sugar, cinnamon, allspice, and cloves. Sprinkle topping over pear slices. Bake at 375° for 35 minutes or until pears are tender. Spoon mixture into 6 individual dessert dishes. Top each with 1 tablespoon Rum Cream Sauce. Serve warm. Yield: 6 servings (178 calories per serving).

Combine all ingredients; stir well. Yield: ¼ cup plus 2 tablespoons.

PROTEIN 2.2 / FAT 8.6 / CARBOHYDRATE 24.4 / CHOLESTEROL 2 / IRON 0.9 / SODIUM 55 / CALCIUM 37

Poached Pears in Raspberry Sauce

1 (16-ounce) package frozen
  unsweetened raspberries, thawed
2 tablespoons sugar
2 medium-size ripe pears, peeled,
  halved, and cored (about ¾
  pound)
1 tablespoon plus 1 teaspoon
  unsweetened grated coconut,
  toasted

*P*lace raspberries in container of an electric blender; top with cover, and process until smooth. Press puree through a sieve to remove seeds; discard seeds.

Place puree in a medium saucepan. Stir in sugar. Bring to a boil over medium heat, stirring until sugar dissolves. Add pears. Reduce heat, and simmer 15 minutes or just until pears are tender. Place pears in 4 individual dessert dishes.

Cook raspberry sauce over medium heat 5 minutes or until reduced to ¾ cup. Spoon 3 tablespoons sauce over each pear half. Sprinkle each with 1 teaspoon coconut. Yield: 4 servings (137 calories per serving).

PROTEIN 1.4 / FAT 2.0 / CARBOHYDRATE 31.5 / CHOLESTEROL 0 / IRON 0.9 / SODIUM 1 / CALCIUM 34

Wine-Poached Pears With Vanilla Cream

4 medium-size ripe pears (about
  1½ pounds)
2 tablespoons lemon juice
1 quart Burgundy or other dry
  red wine
½ cup sugar
2 tablespoons lemon juice
1 vanilla bean, split
1 (2½-inch) stick cinnamon
3 whole cloves
Vanilla Cream

*P*eel and core pears, leaving stem end intact. Slice in half lengthwise, leaving stem intact on one side. Brush pears with lemon juice to prevent browning.

Combine Burgundy and next 5 ingredients in a Dutch oven; bring to a boil. Place pears in wine mixture. Cover; reduce heat, and simmer 10 minutes or until pears are tender. Remove pears with a slotted spoon. Reserve wine mixture for other uses. Cover and chill pears thoroughly.

Spread Vanilla Cream in a large, shallow baking dish. Place pear halves, cut side down, on a flat cutting surface. Cut 5 to 6 lengthwise slits in each pear half one-third down from the stem end to the base. Arrange fanned pear halves over Vanilla Cream. Broil until thoroughly heated and cream is bubbly. Yield: 8 servings (101 calories per serving).

Vanilla Cream

1½ cups skim milk
3 tablespoons sugar
1 tablespoon cornstarch
1 egg yolk, lightly beaten
1 teaspoon vanilla extract

*C*ombine first 4 ingredients in a medium saucepan, stirring well. Cook over medium heat, stirring constantly, until mixture thickens. Remove mixture from heat, and stir in vanilla. Yield: 1½ cups.

PROTEIN 2.2 / FAT 1.0 / CARBOHYDRATE 21.8 / CHOLESTEROL 35 / IRON 0.4 / SODIUM 26 / CALCIUM 69

Pears Poached in Red Wine

(pictured on pages 114 and 115)

3 large, firm pears (about 1½
   pounds)
1½ cups Burgundy or other dry
   red wine
1 cup water
1 envelope unflavored gelatin
1 lemon, quartered
3 tablespoons sugar
1 whole clove
1 (3-inch) stick cinnamon
Fresh mint sprigs (optional)

Peel and core pears, leaving stem end intact. Slice in half lengthwise, leaving stem intact on one side.

Combine Burgundy and next 6 ingredients in a Dutch oven; bring to a boil. Place pears in wine mixture. Cover; reduce heat, and simmer 15 minutes or until pears are tender. Remove pears with a slotted spoon, and transfer to a bowl; chill thoroughly. Strain wine mixture; discard spices. Chill until the consistency of unbeaten egg whites.

Place pear halves, cut side down, on a flat cutting surface. Cut 5 to 6 lengthwise slits in each pear half one-third down from the stem end to the base. Arrange fanned pear halves on individual serving plates. Spoon ¼ cup wine mixture over each pear half. Chill 1 hour or until gelatin is partially set. Garnish with fresh mint sprigs, if desired. Yield: 6 servings (86 calories per serving).

PROTEIN 1.4 / FAT 0.3 / CARBOHYDRATE 21.0 / CHOLESTEROL 0 / IRON 0.4 / SODIUM 4 / CALCIUM 14

Baked Pears With Caramel Sauce

6 medium-size ripe pears (about
   2¼ pounds)
3 tablespoons finely chopped
   pecans
½ teaspoon grated lemon rind
¼ cup firmly packed brown sugar
3 tablespoons dark corn syrup
¼ cup water
1 teaspoon margarine

Core pears from the bottom, cutting to, but not through, the stem end.

Combine pecans and lemon rind; stir well. Divide mixture evenly, packing mixture into cavity of each pear. Place pears, stem end up, in an ungreased 3-quart baking dish. Pour water into baking dish to a depth of 1 inch. Cover and bake at 350° for 50 minutes or until pears are tender.

Combine brown sugar, corn syrup, ¼ cup water, and margarine in a small saucepan; bring to a boil over medium heat, stirring until sugar dissolves. Boil gently 5 minutes.

Place pears in individual dessert dishes; spoon sauce evenly over warm pears. Yield: 6 servings (196 calories per serving).

PROTEIN 1.0 / FAT 4.5 / CARBOHYDRATE 41.7 / CHOLESTEROL 0 / IRON 1.2 / SODIUM 17 / CALCIUM 32

Brown Sugar Baked Pears

3 large ripe pears, peeled, halved,
  and cored (about 1½ pounds)
2 teaspoons grated orange rind
½ cup unsweetened orange juice
¼ cup firmly packed brown sugar
3 tablespoons all-purpose flour
¼ teaspoon ground nutmeg
2 tablespoons margarine

Slice each pear half crosswise into ¼-inch-thick slices, taking care not to cut all the way through so that pear half remains intact.

Arrange pear halves in a circle, cut side down, in a 9-inch pieplate. Sprinkle with orange rind; pour orange juice over pears.

Combine brown sugar, flour, and nutmeg; stir well. Cut in margarine with a pastry blender until mixture resembles coarse meal; sprinkle over pears.

Bake at 375° for 25 to 30 minutes or until pears are tender. Serve warm. Yield: 6 servings (141 calories per serving).

PROTEIN 0.9 / FAT 4.2 / CARBOHYDRATE 26.7 / CHOLESTEROL 0 / IRON 0.7 / SODIUM 48 / CALCIUM 22

Pears au Gratin

4 large ripe pears (about 2
  pounds)
2 tablespoons Triple Sec or other
  orange-flavored liqueur
¼ cup apricot syrup
10 vanilla wafers, crushed
2 tablespoons ground almonds
1 tablespoon margarine, melted

Peel and core pears; cut into ¼-inch-thick lengthwise slices. Arrange pears in a shallow au gratin dish.

Combine liqueur and syrup; brush over pears.

Combine vanilla wafer crumbs, almonds, and margarine, blending well. Sprinkle over pears. Bake at 400° for 20 to 30 minutes or until pears are tender. Serve hot or cold. Yield: 6 servings (170 calories per serving).

PROTEIN 1.4 / FAT 5.1 / CARBOHYDRATE 29.4 / CHOLESTEROL 0 / IRON 0.6 / SODIUM 50 / CALCIUM 24

To make pears and apples appear whole when serving them, core them from the bottom, cutting to, but not through, the stem end.

Poached Pears With Chocolate Sauce

4 medium pears (about 1½
    pounds)
1 tablespoon lemon juice
4 cups water
Chocolate Sauce
Fresh mint sprigs (optional)

Peel pears and core just from the bottom, cutting to but not through the stem end. Brush pears with lemon juice to prevent browning.

Bring water to a boil in a large saucepan. Place pears in saucepan in an upright position; cover, reduce heat, and simmer 12 to 15 minutes or until tender.

To serve, spoon 1 tablespoon plus 1 teaspoon Chocolate Sauce onto each of 4 dessert dishes; top each with a poached pear. Drizzle 2 teaspoons Chocolate Sauce over each pear. Garnish with fresh mint sprigs, if desired. Yield: 4 servings (159 calories per serving).

Chocolate Sauce

½ cup water
3 tablespoons sugar
2 tablespoons unsweetened cocoa
1 teaspoon cornstarch
1 teaspoon vanilla extract
2 tablespoons Chablis or other dry
    white wine

Combine first 5 ingredients in a medium saucepan, stirring until smooth. Cook over medium heat, stirring constantly, until smooth and thickened. Stir in wine; let cool. Yield: ½ cup.

PROTEIN 1.4 / FAT 1.0 / CARBOHYDRATE 37.9 / CHOLESTEROL 0 / IRON 0.9 / SODIUM 1 / CALCIUM 24

Plum and Blueberry Crisp

8 ripe plums (about 1 pound)
1 pound fresh blueberries
⅓ cup sugar
1 tablespoon cornstarch
1 tablespoon vanilla extract
1 teaspoon ground cinnamon
2 tablespoons sliced almonds
10 vanilla wafers
1 tablespoon margarine, melted

Cut each plum into 8 wedges; discard pits. Combine plums and next 5 ingredients, tossing until fruit is coated with cinnamon mixture. Spoon into an 11- x 7- x 2-inch baking dish. Set aside.

Position knife blade in food processor bowl. Add almonds; top with cover, and process 10 to 15 seconds or until finely chopped. Break vanilla wafers; add to almonds. Cover and process until blended. Pour melted margarine into mixture; process until mixture resembles coarse meal.

Sprinkle crumb mixture evenly over fruit in baking dish. Bake at 400° for 40 minutes or until fruit bubbles and crumb mixture is lightly browned. Serve warm. Yield: 8 servings (158 calories per serving).

PROTEIN 1.6 / FAT 4.6 / CARBOHYDRATE 28.8 / CHOLESTEROL 0 / IRON 0.5 / SODIUM 43 / CALCIUM 19

Poached Pears With Chocolate Sauce is a simple but elegant fruit dessert.

Plum Crisp

12 ripe plums, pitted and
    quartered (about 1½ pounds)
Vegetable cooking spray
2 tablespoons dark rum
2 tablespoons margarine
¼ cup quick-cooking oats,
    uncooked
2 tablespoons chopped walnuts
¼ cup firmly packed brown sugar
1 teaspoon ground cinnamon
½ cup vanilla ice milk
2 teaspoons amaretto

*P*lace plums in an 8-inch square baking dish that has been coated with cooking spray. Drizzle rum over plums, stirring gently to coat.

Melt margarine in a small saucepan; stir in oats and walnuts. Cook mixture over medium heat, stirring constantly, 2 to 3 minutes or until nuts are lightly toasted. Remove from heat, and stir in brown sugar and cinnamon. Sprinkle mixture evenly over plums. Bake at 375° for 35 minutes or until fruit is bubbly.

Combine ice milk and amaretto in a small bowl; stir gently. To serve, spoon fruit mixture into 6 individual serving bowls, and top with 1 tablespoon plus 1 teaspoon ice milk mixture. Serve immediately. Yield: 6 servings (196 calories per serving).

PROTEIN 3.0 / FAT 7.1 / CARBOHYDRATE 31.6 / CHOLESTEROL 2 / IRON 1.0 / SODIUM 56 / CALCIUM 38

Fresh Plum Fool

8 ripe plums, pitted and sliced
    (about 1 pound)
¼ cup sugar
½ cup ruby port wine
2 teaspoons lime juice
1 (8-ounce) carton low-fat sour
    cream
2 tablespoons Chambord or other
    raspberry-flavored liqueur
½ cup cold water
½ cup instant nonfat dry milk
    powder
¼ cup firmly packed brown sugar

*C*ombine first 4 ingredients in a medium saucepan. Bring to a boil. Cover, reduce heat to low, and simmer 1 hour or until sauce thickens, stirring occasionally. Remove from heat.

Position knife blade in food processor bowl; add plum mixture. Top with cover, and pulse 3 times or just until plums are chopped. Pour mixture into a large bowl; cover and chill thoroughly. Stir in sour cream and liqueur.

Place ½ cup water in a small, narrow glass or stainless steel bowl; freeze 25 minutes or until a ⅛-inch-thick layer of ice forms on surface. Add milk powder; beat at high speed of an electric mixer 5 minutes or until stiff peaks form.

Pour whipped milk into plum mixture; fold in slightly, leaving streaks of color. Spoon into 8 individual dessert dishes. Sprinkle with brown sugar. Cover and chill 1 to 2 hours before serving. Yield: 8 servings (161 calories per ¾-cup serving).

PROTEIN 4.0 / FAT 3.8 / CARBOHYDRATE 27.1 / CHOLESTEROL 12 / IRON 0.4 / SODIUM 54 / CALCIUM 133

Plum Rum Soup

8 ripe plums, peeled, pitted, and
  chopped (about 1 pound)
2 cups water
¼ cup sugar
1 (3-inch) stick cinnamon
3 tablespoons dark rum
1 tablespoon plus 2 teaspoons
  cornstarch

Combine first 4 ingredients in a large saucepan. Bring mixture to a boil; cover, reduce heat, and simmer 15 minutes or until plums are tender. Discard cinnamon stick. Combine rum and cornstarch; stir well. Add to plum mixture. Cook, stirring constantly, until mixture is slightly thickened. Remove from heat. Pour into a bowl; cover and chill thoroughly. Yield: 3 cups (78 calories per ½-cup serving).

PROTEIN 0.5 / FAT 0.4 / CARBOHYDRATE 19.1 / CHOLESTEROL 0 / IRON 0.1 / SODIUM 0 / CALCIUM 3

Merry Berry Soup
(pictured on page 106)

2 cups fresh raspberries
2 cups fresh blackberries
4 cups water
½ cup sugar
1 (3-inch) stick cinnamon
3 tablespoons cornstarch
3 tablespoons cold water
2 cups fresh strawberries
Strawberry fans (optional)

Combine raspberries, blackberries, and 4 cups water in a large saucepan. Bring to a boil; remove from heat.

Press berry mixture through a sieve and return to saucepan; discard seeds. Add sugar and cinnamon stick. Combine cornstarch and 3 tablespoons cold water; stir well. Bring strained liquid to a boil. Reduce heat to low; stir in cornstarch mixture. Cook, stirring constantly, until slightly thickened. Remove from heat. Discard cinnamon stick. Stir in strawberries. Chill 6 to 8 hours. Garnish with strawberry fans, if desired. Yield: 6 cups (62 calories per ½-cup serving).

PROTEIN 0.4 / FAT 0.2 / CARBOHYDRATE 15.4 / CHOLESTEROL 0 / IRON 0.3 / SODIUM 0 / CALCIUM 12

Raspberries Brûlée
(pictured on pages 100 and 101)

2 cups fresh raspberries
½ cup low-fat sour cream
¼ cup firmly packed brown sugar

Divide raspberries evenly into four 6-ounce custard cups or ovenproof dessert bowls. Spread sour cream evenly on top of raspberries; sprinkle evenly with brown sugar. Broil 4 inches from heat 2 minutes or until sugar melts. Serve immediately. Yield: 4 servings (132 calories per serving).

PROTEIN 1.6 / FAT 4.0 / CARBOHYDRATE 23.9 / CHOLESTEROL 11 / IRON 0.9 / SODIUM 16 / CALCIUM 61

Warm Berries and Chilled Cream Sauce

3 tablespoons sugar, divided
1 tablespoon cornstarch
1 cup skim milk
1 tablespoon amaretto
1 teaspoon vanilla extract
3 tablespoons low-sugar
  strawberry spread
3 cups fresh strawberries, hulled

Combine 2 tablespoons sugar, cornstarch, and milk in a 2-quart saucepan. Bring mixture to a boil over medium heat, stirring constantly. Boil 1 minute or until slightly thickened. Remove from heat; stir in amaretto and vanilla. Cover and chill thoroughly.

Combine remaining 1 tablespoon sugar and strawberry spread in a large skillet. Cook over medium heat, stirring constantly, until sugar dissolves. Add strawberries, and toss to coat. Cook just until strawberries are warm, stirring frequently.

To serve, spoon strawberries into 6 individual dessert dishes. Spoon chilled sauce evenly over berries. Serve immediately. Yield: 6 servings (78 calories per serving).

PROTEIN 1.8 / FAT 0.3 / CARBOHYDRATE 16.2 / CHOLESTEROL 1 / IRON 0.2 / SODIUM 22 / CALCIUM 59

Strawberries Romanoff

(pictured on pages 114 and 115)

⅓ cup unsweetened orange juice
1 quart fresh strawberries, hulled
3 tablespoons Grand Marnier or
  other orange-flavored liqueur,
  divided
⅓ cup instant nonfat dry milk
  powder
½ cup low-fat sour cream
2 tablespoons sugar
1 teaspoon lemon juice
Black currants (optional)

Place orange juice in a small, narrow glass or stainless steel bowl; freeze 25 minutes or until a ⅛-inch-thick layer of ice forms on surface.

Combine strawberries and 2 tablespoons liqueur in a medium bowl; stirring well to coat. Divide strawberries among 6 individual dessert dishes; set aside.

Add milk powder to partially frozen orange juice. Beat at high speed of an electric mixer 5 minutes or until stiff peaks form. Combine sour cream, sugar, lemon juice, and remaining 1 table-spoon liqueur; stir well. Gradually add sour cream mixture to whipped orange mixture, beating at low speed of an electric mixer just until blended.

To serve, spoon whipped mixture evenly over strawberries. Garnish with black currants, if desired. Serve immediately. Yield: 6 servings (132 calories per serving).

PROTEIN 3.8 / FAT 2.9 / CARBOHYDRATE 20.2 / CHOLESTEROL 9 / IRON 0.5 / SODIUM 45 / CALCIUM 122

Rhubarb-Strawberry Crumble

4 cups rhubarb, trimmed and cut
  into 1-inch pieces
2 cups fresh strawberries, hulled
  and sliced
2/3 cup sugar, divided
1/3 cup all-purpose flour
1/2 teaspoon baking powder
1/8 teaspoon salt
2 tablespoons margarine

Combine rhubarb, strawberries, and 1/3 cup sugar; stir well. Pour into an 11- x 7- x 2-inch baking dish.

Combine remaining 1/3 cup sugar, flour, baking powder, and salt; cut in margarine with a pastry blender until mixture resembles coarse meal. Sprinkle over fruit. Bake at 350° for 20 to 30 minutes or until lightly browned. Yield: 6 servings (178 calories per serving).

PROTEIN 1.7 / FAT 4.2 / CARBOHYDRATE 34.9 / CHOLESTEROL 0 / IRON 0.6 / SODIUM 122 / CALCIUM 91

Strawberry-Peach Sabayon

1/2 cup sugar
2 eggs
2/3 cup Sauterne
1 teaspoon grated lemon rind
2 cups sliced fresh or frozen
  peaches, thawed
2 cups fresh strawberries, hulled
  and halved
2 oranges, peeled and sectioned

Combine first 3 ingredients in top of a large double boiler. Place over simmering water. Beat with a wire whisk until frothy. Continue beating for 10 minutes or until mixture has doubled in volume. Remove from heat, and stir in lemon rind. Set mixture aside.

Arrange fruit in a 13- x 9- x 2-inch baking dish. Spoon sauce over fruit.

Broil 4 inches from heat 15 to 20 seconds or until sauce is glazed and lightly browned. Serve immediately. Yield: 8 servings (129 calories per serving).

PROTEIN 2.4 / FAT 1.6 / CARBOHYDRATE 24.4 / CHOLESTEROL 69 / IRON 0.6 / SODIUM 20 / CALCIUM 31

Strawberry-Topped Strawberries

1/2 (8-ounce) package Neufchâtel
  cheese, softened
2 tablespoons strawberry schnapps
1 tablespoon sugar
1 teaspoon skim milk
1 pint fresh strawberries, hulled
  and sliced

Combine Neufchâtel, schnapps, sugar, and milk in a medium bowl. Beat at low speed of an electric mixer until smooth. Cover and chill.

To serve, divide sliced strawberries evenly among 4 dessert dishes. Dollop chilled cheese mixture evenly over strawberries. Yield: 4 servings (139 calories per serving).

PROTEIN 3.5 / FAT 7.0 / CARBOHYDRATE 12.9 / CHOLESTEROL 22 / IRON 0.4 / SODIUM 115 / CALCIUM 36

Pies and Pastries

Ahh—the aroma of freshly baked pastry— an irresistible temptation. Look to our light recipes for a delectable version of cream puffs, pies, tarts, and pastries. They are sure to please family and friends alike.

Like pies, tarts can be filled with creamy custards, fresh fruits, or a combination of the two, but tarts may vary from the standard size to individual tartlets.

For easy-to-follow techniques for making pastry shells, see page 11; handling the dough lightly will help ensure a tender, flaky crust.

Nothing can match the sweet aroma and rich-tasting goodness of freshly baked pastries: (clockwise from top) Cherry Cobbler (page 147), Almond-Peach Tart (page 164), and Danish Almond Pastry (page 174).

Low-Fat Pastry Shells

2 cups all-purpose flour
½ teaspoon salt
⅓ cup vegetable oil
1 tablespoon cider vinegar
2 to 3 tablespoons cold water
Vegetable cooking spray

Combine flour and salt in a medium bowl. Combine oil and vinegar. Add to flour mixture, stirring until crumbly. Sprinkle cold water, 1 tablespoon at a time, evenly over surface; stir with a fork until dry ingredients are moistened. Divide dough in half; set half of dough aside.

Gently press half of dough between 2 sheets of heavy-duty plastic wrap into a 4-inch circle. Chill 15 minutes. Roll dough into a 12-inch circle. Place in freezer 5 minutes or until plastic wrap can be removed easily. Remove bottom sheet of plastic wrap; fit dough into a 9-inch pieplate that has been coated with cooking spray, and remove top sheet of plastic wrap. Fold edges under and flute, if desired. Repeat procedure with remaining half of dough.

For baked pastry shells, prick bottom of pastry lightly with a fork. Bake at 425° for 10 to 15 minutes or until golden brown. Yield: 16 servings (103 calories per serving).

PROTEIN 1.8 / FAT 4.8 / CARBOHYDRATE 13.1 / CHOLESTEROL 0 / IRON 0.5 / SODIUM 74 / CALCIUM 3

Egg Pastry

1 egg, beaten
¼ cup plus 1½ teaspoons
   vegetable oil
¾ teaspoon vinegar
2 cups sifted cake flour
¼ teaspoon salt
1 to 2 tablespoons cold water

Combine egg, oil, and vinegar; stir well. Set aside.

Combine flour and salt in a medium bowl. Add egg mixture and 1 tablespoon cold water, stirring until dry ingredients are moistened; stir in remaining water, if needed. Divide dough in half; shape each half into a ball. Set one aside.

Gently press dough between 2 sheets of heavy-duty plastic wrap into a 4-inch circle. Chill 15 minutes. Roll dough into a 12-inch circle. Place in freezer 5 minutes or until plastic wrap can be removed easily. Remove bottom sheet of plastic wrap; fit into a 9-inch pieplate, and remove top sheet of plastic wrap. Fold edges under and flute, if desired. Repeat with remaining dough.

For baked pastry shells, prick bottom and sides of pastry generously with a fork. Bake at 400° for 10 to 15 minutes or until golden brown. Yield: 16 servings (83 calories per serving).

PROTEIN 1.3 / FAT 4.3 / CARBOHYDRATE 9.6 / CHOLESTEROL 17 / IRON 0.1 / SODIUM 41 / CALCIUM 4

Richer Single Crust

¾ *cup all-purpose flour*
¼ *teaspoon salt*
3 *tablespoons vegetable oil*
1 *tablespoon cold water*
2 *teaspoons lemon juice*

Combine flour and salt; stir well. Combine oil, cold water, and lemon juice, stirring well with a wire whisk. Add to dry ingredients, stirring with a fork until dry ingredients are moistened. Shape into a ball; chill.

Roll dough to ⅛-inch thickness between 2 sheets of heavy-duty plastic wrap. Place in freezer 5 minutes or until plastic wrap can be removed easily. Remove bottom sheet of plastic wrap; fit dough into a 9-inch pieplate, and remove top sheet of plastic wrap. Fold edges under and flute, if desired.

For baked pastry shell, prick bottom of pastry lightly with a fork. Bake at 400° for 10 to 15 minutes or until golden brown. Yield: 8 servings (92 calories per serving).

PROTEIN 1.4 / FAT 5.2 / CARBOHYDRATE 9.9 / CHOLESTEROL 0 / IRON 0.4 / SODIUM 74 / CALCIUM 3

Easy Press-In Pastry

¾ *cup all-purpose flour*
1 *tablespoon brown sugar*
¼ *teaspoon salt*
3 *tablespoons vegetable oil*
1 *tablespoon cold water*

Combine flour, sugar, and salt in a medium bowl. Add oil, and stir with a fork until mixture is crumbly. Add cold water, and stir with a fork until dry ingredients are moistened. Press dough evenly over bottom and up sides of a 9-inch pieplate.

For baked pastry shell, bake at 350° for 15 minutes or until golden brown. Yield: 8 servings (96 calories per serving).

PROTEIN 1.3 / FAT 5.2 / CARBOHYDRATE 10.9 / CHOLESTEROL 0 / IRON 0.4 / SODIUM 74 / CALCIUM 3

Nutty Press-In Pie Shell

¾ *cup all-purpose flour*
2 *tablespoons ground almonds*
1 *tablespoon brown sugar*
2 *tablespoons cold margarine*
1 *to 2 tablespoons cold water*

Combine flour, almonds, and sugar in a medium bowl, blending well. Cut in margarine with a pastry blender until mixture resembles coarse meal. Sprinkle cold water, 1 tablespoon at a time, evenly over surface. Stir with a fork until mixture resembles texture of cottage cheese. Press into a 9-inch pieplate.

For baked pastry shell, bake at 350° for 20 minutes or until golden brown. Yield: 8 servings (87 calories per serving).

PROTEIN 1.8 / FAT 3.9 / CARBOHYDRATE 11.1 / CHOLESTEROL 0 / IRON 0.5 / SODIUM 34 / CALCIUM 8

Coconut Pie Shell

¾ cup all-purpose flour
2 tablespoons unsweetened grated
   coconut, toasted
2 tablespoons margarine, melted
1 to 2 tablespoons cold water
Vegetable cooking spray

Combine first 3 ingredients in a medium bowl; stir well. Sprinkle cold water, 1 tablespoon at a time, evenly over surface of mixture; stir with a fork until dry ingredients are moistened. Shape into a ball.

Roll dough between 2 sheets of heavy-duty plastic wrap into a 12-inch circle. Remove bottom sheet of plastic wrap; fit dough into a 9-inch pieplate that has been coated with cooking spray, and remove top sheet of plastic wrap. Fold edges of shell under and flute, if desired. Bake at 325° for 15 to 17 minutes or until coconut is toasted. Cool completely on a wire rack. Yield: 8 servings (84 calories per serving).

PROTEIN 1.5 / FAT 4.2 / CARBOHYDRATE 10.2 / CHOLESTEROL 0 / IRON 0.4 / SODIUM 34 / CALCIUM 4

Crumb Pie Crust

1 cup graham cracker crumbs
¼ cup margarine, melted
¼ teaspoon ground cinnamon

Combine all ingredients, stirring well. Firmly press crumb mixture evenly into bottom and up sides of a 9-inch pieplate. Bake at 375° for 5 to 7 minutes. Yield: 8 servings (104 calories per serving).

PROTEIN 0.8 / FAT 7.0 / CARBOHYDRATE 9.6 / CHOLESTEROL 0 / IRON 0.5 / SODIUM 147 / CALCIUM 7

Crisp Cornflake Crust

1 cup cornflake crumbs
3 tablespoons reduced-calorie
   margarine, melted
2 teaspoons sugar

Combine cornflake crumbs, margarine, and sugar; stir well. Press mixture into bottom and up sides of a 9-inch pieplate. Bake at 350° for 10 to 15 minutes or until toasted and crisp. Cool. Yield: 8 servings (82 calories per serving).

PROTEIN 1.1 / FAT 2.8 / CARBOHYDRATE 13.2 / CHOLESTEROL 0 / IRON 0.9 / SODIUM 217 / CALCIUM 0

Scotch Shortcake

1 cup sifted cake flour
1 tablespoon sugar
1 teaspoon baking powder
⅛ teaspoon salt
3 tablespoons cold margarine
1 teaspoon vanilla extract
2 to 4 tablespoons cold water
Vegetable cooking spray
1 teaspoon sugar

Combine first 4 ingredients in a medium bowl. Cut in margarine with a pastry blender until mixture resembles coarse meal. Sprinkle vanilla and cold water, 1 tablespoon at a time, evenly over surface of mixture; stir with a fork until dry ingredients are thoroughly moistened. Shape mixture into a ball.

Gently press dough between 2 sheets of heavy-duty plastic wrap into a 4-inch circle. Chill 15 minutes. Roll dough to a 6-inch circle about ½-inch thick. Place dough in freezer 5 minutes or until plastic wrap can be removed easily.

Remove plastic wrap. Place dough on a baking sheet that has been coated with cooking spray; sprinkle with 1 teaspoon sugar. Cut into 6 wedges; pierce with a fork. Bake at 400° for 10 minutes or until lightly browned. Serve with fresh fruit. Yield: 6 servings (123 calories per serving).

PROTEIN 1.3 / FAT 5.8 / CARBOHYDRATE 15.9 / CHOLESTEROL 0 / IRON 0.1 / SODIUM 166 / CALCIUM 37

Meringue Shells

3 egg whites
¼ teaspoon cream of tartar
¼ teaspoon vanilla extract
⅔ cup sugar

Beat egg whites (at room temperature) in a large bowl at high speed of an electric mixer until foamy. Sprinkle cream of tartar and vanilla over egg whites; continue beating until soft peaks form. Gradually add sugar, 1 tablespoon at a time, beating until stiff peaks form and sugar dissolves (2 to 4 minutes).

Pipe or spread meringue in 12 equal portions onto baking sheets lined with parchment paper. Using the back of a spoon, shape meringues into 4-inch circles, shaping each circle into a shell. (Sides should be about 1 inch high.) Bake at 275° for 1 hour. Turn oven off, and cool shells in oven 2 hours. Carefully peel paper from shells, and cool completely on wire racks. Store in an airtight container, at room temperature, up to 2 days or freeze for several weeks. Yield: 12 shells (48 calories each).

PROTEIN 0.8 / FAT 0.0 / CARBOHYDRATE 11.2 / CHOLESTEROL 0 / IRON 0.0 / SODIUM 17 / CALCIUM 1

Apple Pie

(pictured on pages 134 and 135)

1 unbaked 9-inch Easy Press-In
  Pastry (page 129)
5 cups peeled, sliced cooking
  apples
3 tablespoons lemon juice
⅓ cup sugar
2 tablespoons all-purpose flour
½ teaspoon ground cinnamon
¼ teaspoon ground nutmeg
1 tablespoon margarine
2 tablespoons chopped walnuts

Prepare Easy Press-In Pastry; set aside.

Combine apples and lemon juice in a large bowl, tossing gently to coat. Combine sugar, flour, cinnamon, and nutmeg; stir well. Spoon over apple mixture, tossing gently to coat. Spoon filling evenly into pastry shell, and dot with margarine. Sprinkle walnuts evenly over top of pie. Cover pie with an aluminum foil tent. Bake at 375° for 50 minutes to 1 hour or until golden. Yield: 8 servings (198 calories per serving).

PROTEIN 2.2 / FAT 8.0 / CARBOHYDRATE 30.8 / CHOLESTEROL 0 / IRON 0.6 / SODIUM 91 / CALCIUM 10

Five-Minute Blueberry Pie

1 baked 9-inch Crumb Pie Crust
  (page 130)
½ cup water
½ cup sugar
2 tablespoons cornstarch
4 cups fresh or frozen
  unsweetened blueberries, thawed

Prepare Crumb Pie Crust; set aside.

Combine water, sugar, and cornstarch in a medium saucepan, stirring well. Cook over medium heat, stirring constantly, until smooth and thickened. Add blueberries; simmer, stirring gently, until thickened and transparent. Pour mixture into crust; cover and chill thoroughly. Yield: 8 servings (198 calories per serving).

PROTEIN 1.3 / FAT 7.2 / CARBOHYDRATE 33.6 / CHOLESTEROL 0 / IRON 0.6 / SODIUM 151 / CALCIUM 12

Lemon-Blueberry Pie

1 unbaked 9-inch Richer Single
  Crust (page 129)
1 (16-ounce) package frozen
  unsweetened blueberries, thawed
3 tablespoons cornstarch
1 tablespoon lemon juice
¼ cup plus 2 tablespoons sugar
½ teaspoon grated lemon rind
¼ teaspoon salt

Prepare Richer Single Crust; set aside.

Combine blueberries and remaining ingredients in a medium bowl; stir gently. Pour into prepared pastry shell. Bake at 400° for 10 minutes; reduce heat to 325°, and bake an additional 25 to 30 minutes or until crust is brown and filling is bubbly. Cool completely. Yield: 8 servings (169 calories per serving).

PROTEIN 1.6 / FAT 5.6 / CARBOHYDRATE 28.9 / CHOLESTEROL 0 / IRON 0.5 / SODIUM 147 / CALCIUM 8

Old-Fashioned Custard Pie

1 unbaked 9-inch Egg Pastry
  (page 128)
3 egg whites, lightly beaten
1 egg, lightly beaten
½ cup sugar
1 teaspoon vanilla extract
⅛ teaspoon salt
2 cups skim milk
⅛ teaspoon ground nutmeg

Prepare Egg Pastry; prick bottom and sides with a fork. Bake at 400° for 3 minutes; remove from oven. Set aside.

Combine beaten egg whites, egg, sugar, vanilla, and salt in a medium bowl; stir well with a wire whisk. Gradually stir in milk. Pour filling into prepared pastry shell; sprinkle ground nutmeg over top of pie.

Bake at 350° for 40 minutes or until a knife inserted in center comes out clean. Cool to room temperature before serving. Store in refrigerator. Yield: 8 servings (170 calories per serving).

PROTEIN 5.4 / FAT 5.1 / CARBOHYDRATE 25.4 / CHOLESTEROL 53 / IRON 0.3 / SODIUM 137 / CALCIUM 85

Pumpkin Custard Pie

(pictured on pages 134 and 135)

½ recipe Egg Pastry (page 128)
Vegetable cooking spray
½ cup sugar
1 egg
1 egg white
1 tablespoon cornstarch
2 teaspoons ground cinnamon
1 teaspoon vanilla extract
½ teaspoon ground ginger
¼ teaspoon ground cloves
⅛ teaspoon salt
1 (16-ounce) can pumpkin
½ cup instant nonfat dry milk
  powder
½ cup water

Prepare Egg Pastry. Gently press dough between 2 sheets of heavy-duty plastic wrap into a 4-inch circle; chill 15 minutes. Roll dough between plastic wrap to ⅛-inch thickness. Place in freezer 5 minutes or until plastic wrap can be removed easily. Cut leaf shapes in pastry, making vein markings with the back of the knife. Arrange leaves around edge of a 9-inch pieplate. Chill 15 minutes. Spray bottom of pieplate with cooking spray.

Combine sugar and remaining ingredients in a large mixing bowl. Mix well at medium speed of an electric mixer. Pour pumpkin mixture into prepared pieplate. Bake at 425° for 15 minutes; reduce heat to 350°, and bake 45 minutes or until a knife inserted in center comes out clean. Cool completely. Yield: 8 servings (197 calories per serving).

PROTEIN 5.8 / FAT 5.2 / CARBOHYDRATE 32.2 / CHOLESTEROL 53 / IRON 1.3 / SODIUM 136 / CALCIUM 125

Overleaf: *Simple pies become fancy with decorative crusts and fillings; (left to right) Banana Yogurt Pie (page 136), Pumpkin Custard Pie, and Apple Pie (page 132) are mouth-watering delights.*

Banana Yogurt Pie

(pictured on pages 134 and 135)

1 baked 9-inch Crumb Pie Crust
(page 130)
1 envelope unflavored gelatin
¼ cup cold water
1 (8-ounce) carton banana
low-fat yogurt
⅛ teaspoon salt
2 tablespoons lemon juice
3 egg whites
1 teaspoon vanilla extract
¼ cup sugar
1 medium banana, peeled and
sliced
1 tablespoon unsweetened orange
juice
1 teaspoon graham cracker
crumbs
3 banana slices, diagonally sliced
(optional)
Fresh mint sprigs (optional)
2 orange curls (optional)

Prepare Crumb Pie Crust; set aside.

Sprinkle gelatin over cold water in a small saucepan; let stand 1 minute. Cook over medium-low heat, stirring constantly, until gelatin dissolves. Remove from heat; set aside.

Combine yogurt, salt, and lemon juice in a medium bowl; stir well. Add gelatin mixture, stirring well. Chill mixture 8 to 10 minutes or until the consistency of unbeaten egg white.

Beat egg whites (at room temperature) and vanilla in a large bowl at high speed of an electric mixer until soft peaks form. Gradually add sugar, 1 tablespoon at a time, beating until stiff peaks form. Fold egg whites into chilled yogurt mixture. Combine banana slices and orange juice; stir gently to coat. Gently spoon 2 cups egg mixture into baked crumb crust. Arrange banana slices over filling; spread remaining filling over banana layer. Sprinkle graham cracker crumbs over top of pie. Chill at least 4 hours. If desired, garnish with additional banana slices, mint sprigs, and orange curls. Yield: 8 servings (187 calories per serving).

PROTEIN 4.2 / FAT 7.4 / CARBOHYDRATE 26.3 / CHOLESTEROL 1 / IRON 0.6 / SODIUM 220 / CALCIUM 50

Mocha Chiffon Pie

1 baked 9-inch Crisp Cornflake
Crust (page 130)
⅓ cup cold water
1 envelope unflavored gelatin
1 tablespoon cold water
2 teaspoons instant coffee granules
¾ cup skim milk
1 egg yolk, lightly beaten
2 egg whites
⅓ cup sugar
1 tablespoon unsweetened cocoa
1 tablespoon crème de cacao
⅓ cup instant nonfat dry milk
powder
Finely grated chocolate (optional)

Prepare Crisp Cornflake Crust. Bake at 350° for 10 to 15 minutes or until toasted and crisp. Set aside.

Place ⅓ cup cold water in a small, narrow glass or stainless steel bowl; freeze 25 minutes or until a ⅛-inch-thick layer of ice forms on surface.

Sprinkle gelatin over 1 tablespoon cold water in a small bowl; let stand 1 minute.

Mix coffee granules and skim milk in a medium saucepan. Cook over medium heat 8 minutes or until mixture simmers. Remove from heat. Add gelatin mixture, stirring until gelatin dissolves.

Add ¼ cup gelatin mixture to beaten egg yolk; beat with a wire whisk until mixture is blended. Add egg yolk mixture to remaining gelatin mixture; cook over low heat 1 minute, stirring constantly. Chill, stirring occasionally, 30 minutes or until mixture mounds from a spoon.

Mocha Chiffon Pie
(CONTINUED)

Beat egg whites (at room temperature) at high speed of an electric mixer until soft peaks form. Gradually add sugar, 1 tablespoon at a time, beating until stiff peaks form. Sift cocoa over egg whites and fold in. Gently fold egg whites into gelatin mixture. Stir in crème de cacao.

Add milk powder to partially frozen water; beat at high speed of an electric mixer 5 minutes or until stiff peaks form. Fold whipped milk into gelatin mixture; spoon mixture into baked crust. Chill 2 to 4 hours or until firm. Garnish with grated chocolate, if desired. Yield: 8 servings (165 calories per serving).

PROTEIN 5.9 / FAT 3.7 / CARBOHYDRATE 26.4 / CHOLESTEROL 36 / IRON 1.2 / SODIUM 270 / CALCIUM 97

Lime Angel Pie

1 baked 9-inch Crisp Cornflake
  Crust (page 130)
½ cup sugar
1 envelope unflavored gelatin
½ cup cold water
⅓ cup lime juice
2 eggs, separated
1 teaspoon grated lime rind
⅓ cup cold water
¼ cup sugar
⅓ cup instant nonfat dry milk
  powder
Lime twists (optional)

*P*repare Crisp Cornflake Crust; set aside.

Combine ½ cup sugar and gelatin in a medium saucepan. Add ½ cup cold water and lime juice; let stand 1 minute. Lightly beat egg yolks in a small bowl. Add yolks to gelatin mixture; stir well. Cook over medium heat, stirring frequently, until mixture comes to a boil. Remove from heat. Stir in lime rind. Cover and chill 45 minutes or until mixture is syrupy.

Place ⅓ cup cold water in a small, narrow glass or stainless steel bowl; freeze 25 minutes or until a ⅛-inch-thick layer of ice forms on surface.

Beat egg whites (at room temperature) at high speed of an electric mixer until soft peaks form. Gradually add ¼ cup sugar, 1 tablespoon at a time, beating until stiff peaks form.

Add milk powder to partially frozen water; beat at high speed of an electric mixer 5 minutes or until stiff peaks form.

Fold egg white mixture and whipped milk into gelatin mixture; spoon into baked crust. Chill 3 hours or until set. Garnish with lime twists, if desired. Yield: 8 servings (198 calories per serving).

PROTEIN 5.3 / FAT 4.2 / CARBOHYDRATE 35.6 / CHOLESTEROL 70 / IRON 1.2 / SODIUM 262 / CALCIUM 72

Lemon Angel Pie

1 baked 9-inch Crumb Pie Crust
  (page 130)
½ cup cold water
¼ cup sugar
2 eggs, beaten
1 tablespoon grated lemon rind
3 tablespoons lemon juice
1 tablespoon water
1 tablespoon margarine
1 teaspoon unflavored gelatin
1 tablespoon cold water
½ cup instant nonfat dry milk
  powder
1 teaspoon vanilla extract

Prepare Crumb Pie Crust; set aside.

Place ½ cup cold water in a small, narrow glass or stainless steel bowl; freeze 25 minutes or until a ⅛-inch-thick layer of ice forms on surface.

Combine sugar and next 4 ingredients in a saucepan. Cook over medium heat until thickened, stirring constantly with a wire whisk. Remove from heat; stir in margarine. Cool.

Sprinkle gelatin over 1 tablespoon cold water in a small saucepan; let stand 1 minute. Cook over low heat, stirring constantly, until gelatin dissolves. Set aside.

Add milk powder and vanilla to partially frozen water; beat at high speed of an electric mixer 5 minutes or until stiff peaks form. Add gelatin mixture, beating well. Fold into lemon mixture. Spoon into prepared piecrust. Cover and chill. Yield: 8 servings (192 calories per serving).

PROTEIN 5.4 / FAT 9.8 / CARBOHYDRATE 20.6 / CHOLESTEROL 70 / IRON 0.8 / SODIUM 221 / CALCIUM 111

Lemon Meringue Pie

1 baked 9-inch Crisp Cornflake
  Crust (page 130)
¾ cup sugar, divided
3 tablespoons cornstarch
¼ teaspoon salt
1½ cups water
2 egg yolks, lightly beaten
2 teaspoons margarine
1½ teaspoons grated lemon rind
¼ cup lemon juice
3 egg whites
¼ teaspoon cream of tartar

Prepare Crisp Cornflake Crust; set aside.

Combine ½ cup sugar, cornstarch, and salt in a nonaluminum saucepan. Gradually add water, stirring until smooth. Cook over medium heat, stirring constantly, until thickened.

Gradually stir about one-fourth of hot mixture into egg yolks; add to remaining hot mixture, stirring constantly. Cook, stirring constantly, 2 minutes or until thickened. Remove from heat; stir in margarine, lemon rind, and juice. Spoon into crust.

Beat egg whites (at room temperature) and cream of tartar in a large mixing bowl at high speed of an electric mixer until foamy. Gradually add remaining ¼ cup sugar, 1 tablespoon at a time, beating until stiff peaks form and sugar dissolves (2 to 4 minutes). Spread meringue over hot filling, sealing to edge of crust. Bake at 400° for 3 to 4 minutes or until golden brown. Cool to room temperature. Chill thoroughly before serving. Yield: 8 servings (197 calories per serving).

PROTEIN 3.1 / FAT 5.1 / CARBOHYDRATE 35.4 / CHOLESTEROL 68 / IRON 1.2 / SODIUM 329 / CALCIUM 10

Lemon Meringue Pie is an appealing light dessert.

Maple-Nut Chiffon Pie

1 baked 9-inch Low-Fat Pastry
  Shell (page 128)
⅓ cup cold water
¾ cup skim milk
⅓ cup reduced-calorie maple
  syrup
2 eggs, separated
Dash of salt
1 envelope unflavored gelatin
¼ cup cold water
1 teaspoon vanilla extract
⅓ cup instant nonfat dry milk
  powder
⅓ cup chopped walnuts

Prepare Low-Fat Pastry Shell; set aside.

Place ⅓ cup cold water in a small, narrow glass or stainless steel bowl; freeze 25 minutes or until a ⅛-inch-thick layer of ice forms on surface.

Combine skim milk, syrup, egg yolks, and salt in a medium saucepan. Cook over medium heat, stirring constantly, until mixture is slightly thickened.

Combine gelatin and ¼ cup cold water. Let stand 1 minute. Add to custard mixture. Cook, stirring constantly, until gelatin dissolves. Remove from heat. Stir in vanilla. Chill until slightly thickened, stirring occasionally.

Add milk powder to partially frozen water; beat at high speed of an electric mixer 5 minutes or until stiff peaks form. Gently fold into chilled custard mixture.

Beat egg whites (at room temperature) in a medium bowl at high speed of an electric mixer until stiff peaks form. Fold in walnuts. Gently fold into custard mixture. Pour mixture into prepared pastry shell. Chill several hours or until set. Yield: 8 servings (190 calories per serving).

PROTEIN 8.0 / FAT 9.2 / CARBOHYDRATE 19.1 / CHOLESTEROL 70 / IRON 0.9 / SODIUM 151 / CALCIUM 105

Pineapple-Coconut Pie

30 vanilla wafers, crushed
1 tablespoon margarine, melted
¼ cup water
Vegetable cooking spray
1 envelope unflavored gelatin
2 tablespoons cold water
¼ cup boiling water
1 cup low-fat cottage cheese
1 teaspoon vanilla extract
1 teaspoon coconut extract
3 tablespoons sugar
1 (15¼-ounce) can unsweetened
  crushed pineapple, undrained
2 tablespoons unsweetened grated
  coconut

Combine vanilla wafers and margarine, stirring well. Add ¼ cup water, 1 tablespoon at a time, mixing just until crumbs are moistened. Press crumb mixture into bottom and up sides of a 9-inch pieplate that has been coated with cooking spray. Bake at 350° for 10 minutes. Cool.

Soften gelatin in 2 tablespoons cold water in a small bowl. Add ¼ cup boiling water, stirring until gelatin dissolves.

Combine gelatin mixture, cottage cheese, and next 3 ingredients in container of an electric blender or food processor; top with cover, and blend until smooth. Add pineapple and coconut; stir well. Pour into cooled crust; chill 4 hours or until firm. Yield: 8 servings (176 calories per serving).

PROTEIN 5.7 / FAT 6.1 / CARBOHYDRATE 24.5 / CHOLESTEROL 2 / IRON 0.5 / SODIUM 198 / CALCIUM 34

Peach-Almond Cream Pie

1 baked 9-inch Nutty Press-In Pie
  Shell (page 129)
1 envelope unflavored gelatin
¼ cup cold water
1 cup low-fat sour cream
2 tablespoons sugar
⅛ teaspoon salt
2 egg whites
¼ teaspoon almond extract
¼ cup sugar
1 cup sliced fresh peaches

Prepare Nutty Press-In Pie Shell; set aside.

Sprinkle gelatin over cold water in a small mixing bowl; let stand 1 minute.

Combine sour cream, 2 tablespoons sugar, and salt in a medium saucepan. Cook over medium heat, stirring constantly, 5 minutes or until sugar dissolves. Add gelatin, stirring to dissolve. Remove from heat, and place over ice water until slightly thickened, stirring occasionally.

Beat egg whites (at room temperature) at medium speed of an electric mixer until foamy. Add almond extract; beat at high speed until soft peaks form. Gradually add ¼ cup sugar, 1 tablespoon at a time, beating until stiff peaks form. Fold into sour cream mixture. Spoon into prepared pie shell. Cover and chill until firm. Top with sliced peaches. Yield: 8 servings (180 calories per serving).

PROTEIN 4.4 / FAT 7.5 / CARBOHYDRATE 24.2 / CHOLESTEROL 11 / IRON 0.6 / SODIUM 96 / CALCIUM 42

Pumpkin Chiffon Pie

1 baked 9-inch Crisp Cornflake
  Crust (page 130)
1 envelope unflavored gelatin
¼ cup cold water
¾ cup sugar, divided
3 tablespoons cornstarch
1 teaspoon ground cinnamon
½ teaspoon ground ginger
¼ teaspoon ground nutmeg
1 cup skim milk
1 cup cooked, mashed pumpkin
4 egg whites

Prepare Crisp Cornflake Crust; set aside.

Sprinkle gelatin over cold water in a small mixing bowl; let stand 1 minute. Set aside.

Combine ¼ cup sugar, cornstarch, cinnamon, ginger, nutmeg, and milk in a medium saucepan. Cook over medium heat, stirring constantly, until mixture is thickened. Add gelatin mixture, stirring until gelatin dissolves. Remove from heat; stir in pumpkin. Chill until partially set.

Beat egg whites (at room temperature) at high speed of an electric mixer until soft peaks form. Gradually add remaining ½ cup sugar, 1 tablespoon at a time, beating until stiff peaks form. Fold in pumpkin mixture. Spoon into prepared crust, and chill until firm. Yield: 8 servings (199 calories per serving).

PROTEIN 5.0 / FAT 3.0 / CARBOHYDRATE 39.0 / CHOLESTEROL 1 / IRON 1.5 / SODIUM 261 / CALCIUM 52

Piña Colada Pie

¾ cup all-purpose flour
2 tablespoons unsweetened grated
  coconut
2 tablespoons margarine, melted
1 to 2 tablespoons cold water
Vegetable cooking spray
1 (15-ounce) can unsweetened
  crushed pineapple, undrained
1 envelope unflavored gelatin
2 (8-ounce) cartons piña colada
  low-fat yogurt
¼ teaspoon coconut extract
¼ teaspoon rum extract
Fresh mint sprigs (optional)

Combine first 3 ingredients in a medium bowl; stir well. Sprinkle cold water, 1 tablespoon at a time, evenly over surface; stir with a fork just until dry ingredients are moistened. Shape into a ball.

Roll dough between 2 sheets of heavy-duty plastic wrap into a 12-inch circle. Remove plastic wrap, and place pastry in a 9-inch pieplate that has been coated with cooking spray; fold edges under and flute. Bake at 325° for 15 to 17 minutes or until coconut is toasted. Cool completely on a wire rack.

Drain pineapple, reserving juice. Set pineapple aside. Add water to juice to make ¾ cup liquid.

Soften gelatin in pineapple juice; let stand 2 minutes. Place gelatin mixture in a small saucepan over low heat, stirring until gelatin dissolves. Remove from heat; chill until consistency of unbeaten egg white. Beat at medium speed of an electric mixer until frothy. Stir in pineapple, yogurt, and flavorings. Pour mixture into cooled crust. Chill until set. Garnish with mint sprigs, if desired. Yield: 8 servings (176 calories per serving).

PROTEIN 4.7 / FAT 4.9 / CARBOHYDRATE 29.1 / CHOLESTEROL 2 / IRON 0.6 / SODIUM 66 / CALCIUM 89

Raspberry Chiffon Pie

⅓ cup water
1 pound frozen unsweetened
  raspberries, thawed
1 envelope unflavored gelatin
½ cup cold water
½ cup sugar
2 tablespoons lemon juice
1 tablespoon cornstarch
1 tablespoon water
⅓ cup instant nonfat dry milk
  powder
1 tablespoon sugar
Vegetable cooking spray
5 chocolate wafer cookies, halved

Place ⅓ cup water in a small, narrow glass or stainless steel bowl; freeze 25 minutes or until a ⅛-inch-thick layer of ice forms on surface.

Place raspberries and juice in container of an electric blender; top with cover, and process until pureed. Strain puree, discarding seeds.

Sprinkle gelatin over ½ cup cold water in a medium saucepan; let stand 1 minute. Add strained raspberries, ½ cup sugar, and lemon juice. Combine cornstarch and 1 tablespoon water. Add to raspberry mixture, stirring well. Cook over medium heat 3 to 5 minutes or until gelatin dissolves and mixture is slightly thickened. Remove from heat, and chill until mixture is syrupy, stirring occasionally.

Add milk powder to partially frozen water; beat at high

Raspberry Chiffon Pie
(CONTINUED)

speed of an electric mixer 5 minutes or until stiff peaks form. Add 1 tablespoon sugar; beat well. Gently fold chilled raspberry mixture into whipped milk mixture.

Coat an 8-inch springform pan with cooking spray. Line side of pan with cookie halves, cut side down. Spoon raspberry mixture into prepared pan. Cover and chill several hours or until firm. Remove sides of springform pan. Slice into 8 wedges to serve. Yield: 8 servings (125 calories per serving).

PROTEIN 3.3 / FAT 1.3 / CARBOHYDRATE 26.2 / CHOLESTEROL 4 / IRON 0.4 / SODIUM 44 / CALCIUM 79

Crustless Strawberry Pie

2 tablespoons frozen lemonade
  concentrate, thawed
¼ cup cold water
¾ cup quick-cooking oats,
  uncooked
1 tablespoon brown sugar
3 tablespoons cold margarine
2½ cups sliced fresh strawberries,
  divided
½ cup sugar
1 envelope unflavored gelatin
½ cup cold water
⅓ cup instant nonfat dry milk
  powder

*P*lace lemonade concentrate and ¼ cup cold water in a small, narrow glass or stainless steel bowl; freeze 25 minutes or until a ⅛-inch-thick layer of ice forms on surface.

Combine oats and brown sugar in a small bowl; stir well. Cut in margarine with a pastry blender until mixture resembles coarse meal. Spread mixture in a 9-inch square baking pan. Bake at 375° for 15 minutes or until lightly toasted.

Place 1½ cups sliced strawberries in container of an electric blender; top with cover, and process until smooth.

Combine strawberry puree with ½ cup sugar in a small saucepan; cook over medium-low heat, stirring constantly, until sugar dissolves.

Sprinkle gelatin over ½ cup cold water; let stand 1 minute. Add to hot strawberry mixture; cook over medium heat, stirring until gelatin dissolves. Chill until consistency of unbeaten egg white.

Add milk powder to partially frozen lemonade mixture; beat at high speed of an electric mixer 5 minutes or until stiff peaks form.

Combine remaining 1 cup sliced strawberries and chilled strawberry mixture. Fold in whipped milk mixture.

Pour into an ungreased 9-inch pieplate; sprinkle toasted oat mixture over top of pie. Chill at least 4 hours or until set. Yield: 8 servings (160 calories per serving).

PROTEIN 4.1 / FAT 5.1 / CARBOHYDRATE 25.4 / CHOLESTEROL 1 / IRON 0.6 / SODIUM 79 / CALCIUM 76

Everyone is sure to enjoy the lightness of Strawberry Daiquiri Pie.

Strawberry Daiquiri Pie

1 baked 9-inch Nutty Press-In Pie
 Shell (page 129)
1 envelope unflavored gelatin
¼ cup cold water
½ cup skim milk
2 egg yolks
1 (6-ounce) can frozen strawberry
 daiquiri fruit juice concentrate,
 undiluted
4 egg whites
⅛ teaspoon salt
¼ cup sugar
Fresh strawberries (optional)

Prepare Nutty Press-In Pie Shell; set aside.

Sprinkle gelatin over ¼ cup cold water in a medium saucepan; let stand 1 minute. Add milk and egg yolks, mixing well. Cook over medium heat, stirring constantly with a wire whisk, until mixture comes to a boil. Remove from heat, and stir in frozen juice concentrate. Cover and chill until mixture mounds from a spoon.

Beat egg whites (at room temperature) at medium speed of an electric mixer until foamy. Add salt; beat at high speed until soft peaks form. Gradually add sugar, 1 tablespoon at a time, beating until stiff peaks form. Fold into strawberry daiquiri mixture. Spoon into prepared pie shell. Chill until set. Garnish with fresh strawberries, if desired. Yield: 8 servings (196 calories per serving).

PROTEIN 5.5 / FAT 5.3 / CARBOHYDRATE 31.5 / CHOLESTEROL 68 / IRON 0.8 / SODIUM 107 / CALCIUM 36

Apple-Raspberry Cobbler

2 cups frozen unsweetened
  raspberries, thawed and
  undrained
¼ cup sugar
1 tablespoon plus 1 teaspoon
  cornstarch
2 tablespoons water
2 medium-size cooking apples,
  peeled, cored, and cut into thin
  wedges (about ¾ pound)
1 cup all-purpose flour
1 teaspoon baking powder
¼ teaspoon salt
¼ cup vegetable oil
¼ cup water
1 tablespoon sugar

Combine first 4 ingredients in a medium saucepan; stir well. Cook over medium heat, stirring constantly, until mixture comes to a boil. Cook 1 minute or until thickened, stirring constantly. Add apples, stirring well; cover and cook, stirring occasionally, until apples are tender. Spoon apple mixture into a 9-inch pieplate.

Combine flour, baking powder, and salt in a medium bowl. Add oil and water; stir with a fork until mixture forms a dough. (Dough will be sticky.)

Roll dough between 2 sheets of heavy-duty plastic wrap into a 7-inch circle. Place dough in freezer for 5 minutes or until top sheet of plastic wrap can be removed easily. Cut dough into 8 equal wedges. Sprinkle with 1 tablespoon sugar. Remove from plastic wrap. Place wedges over apple mixture to form a circle, leaving space between wedges. Bake at 400° for 20 minutes or until crust is golden and filling is bubbly. Yield: 8 servings (192 calories per serving).

PROTEIN 2.2 / FAT 7.3 / CARBOHYDRATE 30.6 / CHOLESTEROL 0 / IRON 0.7 / SODIUM 111 / CALCIUM 36

Deep-Dish Apple and Pear Cobbler

1 9-inch unbaked Richer Single
  Crust (page 129)
3 medium-size tart apples, peeled,
  cored, and sliced (about 1
  pound)
3 medium-size firm pears, peeled,
  cored, and sliced (about 1¼
  pounds)
⅓ cup sugar
2 tablespoons quick-cooking
  tapioca, uncooked
½ teaspoon ground allspice
½ teaspoon ground cinnamon
¼ teaspoon salt
1 tablespoon lemon juice
1 teaspoon vanilla extract
2 teaspoons skim milk

Prepare Richer Single Crust. Roll pastry between 2 sheets of heavy-duty plastic wrap into a 10-inch circle or large enough to fit the top of a shallow 1½-quart baking dish. Set aside.

Combine apples and next 8 ingredients in a large bowl; toss gently. Spoon into baking dish.

Remove plastic wrap from pastry. Place pastry over fruit; tuck in around edges. Brush pastry with milk. Prick with a fork. Bake at 375° for 50 to 60 minutes or until golden. Yield: 8 servings (192 calories per serving).

PROTEIN 1.7 / FAT 5.6 / CARBOHYDRATE 35.2 / CHOLESTEROL 0 / IRON 0.6 / SODIUM 148 / CALCIUM 15

Individual Blueberry Cobblers

4 cups fresh or frozen blueberries,
thawed
3 tablespoons honey
2 tablespoons lemon juice
1 tablespoon plus 1 teaspoon
cornstarch
Vegetable cooking spray
¾ cup all-purpose flour
1 teaspoon baking powder
¼ teaspoon salt
2 tablespoons vegetable oil
3 tablespoons water
1 teaspoon sugar

Combine first 4 ingredients in a large saucepan. Cook over medium heat, stirring constantly, until mixture is thickened. Remove from heat. Pour blueberry mixture into six 6-ounce custard cups that have been coated with cooking spray.

Combine flour, baking powder, and salt in a medium bowl. Add oil and water. Stir with a fork until all ingredients are moistened. Shape into a ball.

Roll dough to ⅛-inch thickness on a lightly floured surface. Cut out six 5-inch circles. Place a pastry circle over each custard cup, pressing firmly to sides of cup to seal edges. Sprinkle evenly with sugar. Bake at 425° for 20 to 25 minutes or until browned. Yield: 6 servings (199 calories per serving).

PROTEIN 2.3 / FAT 5.6 / CARBOHYDRATE 36.6 / CHOLESTEROL 0 / IRON 0.7 / SODIUM 150 / CALCIUM 44

Blueberry-Peach Cobbler

3 cups peeled, sliced ripe peaches
1 cup fresh blueberries
1 tablespoon lemon juice
½ teaspoon almond extract
¼ cup firmly packed brown sugar
1½ teaspoons cornstarch
Vegetable cooking spray
1 cup sifted cake flour
1 teaspoon baking powder
2 tablespoons cold margarine
2 to 3 tablespoons cold water
1 tablespoon sugar

Combine first 6 ingredients; toss gently. Spoon into a 9-inch pieplate that has been coated with cooking spray.

Combine flour and baking powder in a small bowl. Cut in margarine with a pastry blender until mixture resembles coarse meal. Sprinkle cold water, 1 tablespoon at a time, evenly over surface; stir with a fork until dry ingredients are moistened. Shape dough into a ball.

Roll dough between 2 sheets of heavy-duty plastic wrap into an 8-inch circle. Chill 15 minutes. Remove plastic wrap and cut into 8 equal wedges. Press a small cookie cutter into each wedge, making a cut but leaving cutout in place. Place wedges over fruit in baking dish. Sprinkle with sugar.

Bake at 375° for 35 to 40 minutes or until crust is lightly browned and peaches are bubbly. Yield: 8 servings (137 calories per serving).

PROTEIN 1.4 / FAT 3.2 / CARBOHYDRATE 26.7 / CHOLESTEROL 0 / IRON 0.4 / SODIUM 75 / CALCIUM 36

Cherry Cobbler

(pictured on pages 126 and 127)

½ recipe Egg Pastry (page 128)
2 (16-ounce) packages frozen
  unsweetened cherries, thawed
1 teaspoon almond extract
⅓ cup plus 1½ teaspoons sugar
2 tablespoons cornstarch

*P*repare Egg Pastry; roll pastry between 2 sheets of heavy-duty plastic wrap to fit an 8-inch square baking dish. Remove top layer of plastic wrap; gently cut pastry into ¾-inch-wide strips with a sharp knife or pastry wheel. Cover strips with plastic wrap. Place in freezer 5 minutes.

Combine cherries and almond extract in a large bowl. Combine sugar and cornstarch; stir well. Sprinkle sugar mixture over cherries; stir gently to coat. Spoon cherry mixture into an 8-inch square baking dish.

Remove pastry from freezer; remove plastic wrap, and place pastry strips over fruit mixture to make a lattice. Bake at 425° for 45 to 50 minutes or until pastry is golden and cherries are bubbly. Serve warm. Yield: 9 servings (194 calories per serving).

PROTEIN 2.5 / FAT 5.2 / CARBOHYDRATE 35.9 / CHOLESTEROL 17 / IRON 0.5 / SODIUM 41 / CALCIUM 19

Lattice-Topped Peach Cobbler

4 cups peeled, sliced fresh peaches
¼ cup firmly packed brown sugar
1 tablespoon lemon juice
½ teaspoon almond extract
1 cup sifted cake flour
1 teaspoon baking powder
3 tablespoons cold margarine
2 to 3 tablespoons cold water
1 tablespoon sugar

*P*lace peaches in a shallow 1½-quart baking dish. Combine brown sugar, lemon juice, and almond extract; stir well. Drizzle mixture over peaches; stir to coat. Set aside.

Combine flour and baking powder in a medium bowl; cut in margarine with a pastry blender until mixture resembles coarse meal. Sprinkle cold water, 1 tablespoon at a time, evenly over surface; stir with a fork until dry ingredients are moistened and mixture is crumbly.

Gently press dough between 2 sheets of heavy-duty plastic wrap into a 4-inch circle; chill 15 minutes. Roll dough into a 10-inch circle or large enough to fit the top of a 1½-quart baking dish. Place dough in freezer for 5 minutes or until plastic wrap can be removed easily. Remove plastic wrap, and cut pastry into ½-inch-wide strips with a sharp knife or pastry wheel; arrange strips in lattice design over peaches. Sprinkle with 1 tablespoon sugar. Bake at 375° for 40 to 50 minutes or until crust is golden and peaches are bubbly. Yield: 8 servings (149 calories per serving).

PROTEIN 1.5 / FAT 4.5 / CARBOHYDRATE 26.7 / CHOLESTEROL 0 / IRON 0.4 / SODIUM 90 / CALCIUM 37

Gingered Summer Cobbler promises a taste of spicy peaches and plums along with a biscuit pastry.

Gingered Summer Cobbler

¼ cup firmly packed brown sugar

1 tablespoon cornstarch

1 tablespoon finely chopped pecans

½ teaspoon ground cinnamon

⅛ teaspoon ground nutmeg

3 cups peeled, sliced fresh peaches

1¼ cups sliced fresh plums

2 tablespoons lemon juice

2 tablespoons amaretto

½ teaspoon grated fresh gingerroot

¾ cup all-purpose flour

2 tablespoons sugar

¾ teaspoon baking powder

⅛ teaspoon salt

3 tablespoons cold margarine

½ teaspoon vanilla extract

1 to 2 tablespoons cold water

Combine first 5 ingredients; stir well. Set aside.

Combine peaches, plums, lemon juice, amaretto, and gingerroot in a large saucepan. Stir in brown sugar mixture, tossing gently to coat fruit. Bring mixture to a boil over medium heat; reduce heat and simmer 1 minute. Remove from heat, and spoon fruit mixture into a 9-inch square baking dish. Set aside.

Combine flour, 2 tablespoons sugar, baking powder, and salt; cut in margarine with a pastry blender until mixture resembles coarse meal. Sprinkle vanilla and cold water, 1 tablespoon at a time, evenly over surface; stir with a fork until dry ingredients are moistened. Shape into a ball.

Roll dough between 2 sheets of heavy-duty plastic wrap to ¼-inch thickness. Remove plastic wrap. Cut pastry into decorative shapes. Place pastry cutouts on top of fruit mixture. Bake at 425° for 30 minutes or until pastry is lightly browned and filling is bubbly. Yield: 8 servings (199 calories per serving).

PROTEIN 2.6 / FAT 5.3 / CARBOHYDRATE 36.0 / CHOLESTEROL 0 / IRON 0.9 / SODIUM 127 / CALCIUM 41

Minty Mango Cobbler

2 cups peeled, sliced fresh peaches
1 cup peeled, cubed mango
¾ cup fresh blueberries
2 tablespoons lemon juice
3 tablespoons cornstarch
¼ cup sugar
1½ teaspoons minced fresh mint
Vegetable cooking spray
½ cup all-purpose flour
⅛ teaspoon salt
2 tablespoons plus 1½ teaspoons
  cold margarine
1 tablespoon plus 1 teaspoon cold
  water

Combine first 7 ingredients in a large bowl; toss well. Let stand 15 minutes. Spoon fruit mixture into a 10- x 6- x 2-inch baking dish that has been coated with cooking spray. Set aside.

Combine flour and salt in a medium bowl; cut in margarine with a pastry blender until mixture resembles coarse meal. Sprinkle cold water evenly over surface; stir with a fork until dry ingredients are moistened. Shape into a ball; chill.

Roll pastry to ⅛-inch thickness between 2 sheets of heavy-duty plastic wrap. Remove plastic wrap, and cut into decorative shapes. Place pastry cutouts on top of fruit mixture. Bake at 425° for 10 minutes. Reduce heat to 350°, and bake for 25 minutes or until pastry is lightly browned and fruit is tender. Yield: 8 servings (141 calories per serving).

PROTEIN 1.5 / FAT 3.9 / CARBOHYDRATE 26.5 / CHOLESTEROL 0 / IRON 0.4 / SODIUM 80 / CALCIUM 9

Upside-Down Apple Tart

1 cup all-purpose flour
¼ cup cold unsalted margarine
2 to 3 tablespoons cold water
Vegetable cooking spray
½ cup sugar
4 medium-size Golden Delicious
  apples, peeled, cored, and sliced
  (about 1¼ pounds)
½ teaspoon ground cinnamon
2 teaspoons powdered sugar

Place flour in a large bowl; cut in margarine with a pastry blender until mixture resembles coarse meal. Sprinkle cold water, 1 tablespoon at a time, evenly over surface; stir with a fork until dry ingredients are moistened. Shape into a ball.

Gently press dough between 2 sheets of heavy-duty plastic wrap into a 4-inch circle. Chill 15 minutes. Roll dough into a 10-inch circle. Place in freezer 5 minutes or until plastic wrap can be removed easily.

Coat a 9-inch cast-iron skillet with cooking spray. Add sugar; place over medium heat and cook, stirring constantly, until sugar melts and syrup is light golden brown.

Arrange apple slices over melted sugar. Sprinkle with cinnamon. Cook over low heat 5 minutes. Remove from heat.

Remove plastic wrap from pastry. Cover apples with pastry, tucking edges of pastry around apples. Prick with a fork. Bake at 350° for 45 to 55 minutes or until pastry is lightly browned. Remove from oven; cool 15 minutes. Invert onto a serving platter. Sprinkle with powdered sugar. Yield: 8 servings (196 calories per serving).

PROTEIN 1.9 / FAT 6.1 / CARBOHYDRATE 34.6 / CHOLESTEROL 0 / IRON 0.6 / SODIUM 1 / CALCIUM 8

Phyllo-Crusted Apple-Pear Tarts

2 tablespoons unsalted margarine, divided
2 Granny Smith apples, peeled, cored, and chopped (about ¾ pound)
2 medium-size ripe pears, peeled, cored, and chopped (about ¾ pound)
2 tablespoons brown sugar
1 teaspoon ground cinnamon
⅛ teaspoon ground cloves
⅛ teaspoon ground nutmeg
1 tablespoon lemon juice
2 tablespoons slivered almonds
2 tablespoons amaretto
3 sheets commercial frozen phyllo pastry, thawed
Vegetable cooking spray
1 teaspoon sugar
⅛ teaspoon ground cinnamon

Melt 1 tablespoon margarine in a 10-inch nonstick skillet. Add apples and next 6 ingredients; cook over medium heat 8 to 10 minutes or until fruit is tender, stirring occasionally. Add almonds and amaretto. Bring to a boil. Cook 1 minute; remove from heat. Let cool 15 minutes.

Place one sheet of phyllo on a damp towel (keep remaining phyllo covered). Lightly coat phyllo with cooking spray. Layer second sheet of phyllo on first sheet, lightly coating with cooking spray. Cut stack of phyllo into twelve (approximately 4-inch) squares with kitchen shears. Lightly coat remaining sheet of phyllo with cooking spray. Fold in half crosswise; cut into four (approximately 4-inch) squares. Discard remaining phyllo.

Coat eight 6-ounce custard cups with cooking spray. Press 1 square of layered phyllo into each cup, pressing gently in center to form a pastry shell. Spoon fruit mixture evenly into custard cups. Press another square of layered phyllo on top of fruit mixture, tucking in edges.

Melt remaining margarine; gently brush over tarts. Combine sugar and cinnamon; sprinkle over tarts.

Bake at 375° for 15 minutes or until golden brown. Remove from oven, and cool on a wire rack for 10 minutes. Serve warm. Yield: 8 servings (136 calories per serving).

PROTEIN 1.8 / FAT 5.4 / CARBOHYDRATE 21.7 / CHOLESTEROL 0 / IRON 0.5 / SODIUM 1 / CALCIUM 22

Apricot Tart

1 cup all-purpose flour
1½ teaspoons sugar
¼ cup cold margarine
2 to 3 tablespoons cold water
5 fresh apricots, sliced (about 1 pound)
1 tablespoon sugar
3 tablespoons low-sugar apricot spread, melted
½ teaspoon lemon juice

Combine flour and sugar in a medium bowl; cut in margarine with a pastry blender until mixture resembles coarse meal. Sprinkle cold water, 1 tablespoon at a time, evenly over surface; stir with a fork until dry ingredients are moistened. Shape dough into a ball. Cover and chill 10 minutes.

Roll dough between 2 sheets of heavy-duty plastic wrap into a 10-inch circle. Remove bottom sheet of plastic wrap; place pastry on an ungreased baking sheet. Remove top sheet of plastic wrap. Pinch edges of dough to form a ½-inch rim. (Pastry should be a 9-inch circle.) Chill 10 minutes. Prick with a fork. Bake at

400° for 5 minutes. Let cool.

Arrange apricot slices evenly over pastry. Sprinkle apricots with 1 tablespoon sugar. Combine melted apricot spread and lemon juice; stir well. Drizzle mixture evenly over tart. Bake at 400° for 20 to 30 minutes or until pastry is golden and fruit is tender. Serve warm. Yield: 8 servings (151 calories per serving).

PROTEIN 2.3 / FAT 6.0 / CARBOHYDRATE 22.3 / CHOLESTEROL 0 / IRON 0.7 / SODIUM 74 / CALCIUM 10

Banana Cream Tarts

1 cup sifted cake flour
¼ cup cold margarine
2 to 3 tablespoons cold water
¾ cup plus 2 tablespoons water
⅓ cup instant nonfat dry milk powder
2 tablespoons sugar
1 tablespoon plus 1½ teaspoons cornstarch
⅛ teaspoon salt
2 egg yolks, beaten
1 teaspoon vanilla extract
1 small banana, peeled and thinly sliced
2 teaspoons lemon juice

*P*lace flour in a large bowl; cut in margarine with a pastry blender until mixture resembles coarse meal. Sprinkle cold water, 1 tablespoon at a time, evenly over surface; stir with a fork until dry ingredients are moistened.

Divide dough into 8 equal portions. Gently roll each portion between 2 sheets of heavy-duty plastic wrap into a 4-inch circle. Remove bottom sheet of plastic wrap; fit each pastry round into a 3-inch tart pan, and remove top sheet of plastic wrap. Prick with a fork. Bake at 375° for 15 to 20 minutes or until lightly browned. Cool completely; set aside.

Combine ¾ cup plus 2 tablespoons water, milk powder, sugar, cornstarch, and salt in a medium-size nonaluminum saucepan; stir well. Cook over medium heat, stirring constantly, until slightly thickened. Combine egg yolks and vanilla; stir well. Gradually stir about one-fourth of hot mixture into yolk mixture; add to remaining hot mixture, stirring constantly. Cook over low heat, stirring constantly, 1 to 2 minutes or until mixture is smooth and slightly thickened. Cover and chill thoroughly.

Combine banana slices and lemon juice in a small bowl; stir gently to coat. Place a banana slice in each baked, cooled tart shell. Spoon 2 tablespoons chilled custard mixture over banana slice in each tart shell. Top each tart with a banana slice. Serve immediately. Yield: 8 servings (158 calories per serving).

PROTEIN 3.6 / FAT 7.3 / CARBOHYDRATE 19.4 / CHOLESTEROL 69 / IRON 0.4 / SODIUM 133 / CALCIUM 74

Fresh Cherry-Blueberry Tart

1 cup all-purpose flour
¼ cup cold margarine
2 to 3 tablespoons cold water
2 tablespoons sugar, divided
¾ pound fresh cherries, pitted
  and halved
¼ pound fresh blueberries
¼ cup chopped almonds
¼ cup sifted powdered sugar
½ teaspoon almond extract
1¾ teaspoons hot water

Place flour in a medium bowl; cut in margarine with a pastry blender until mixture resembles coarse meal. Sprinkle cold water, 1 tablespoon at a time, evenly over surface; stir with a fork until dry ingredients are moistened. Shape into a ball; cover and chill 10 minutes.

Roll dough between 2 sheets of heavy-duty plastic wrap into a 10-inch circle. Remove plastic wrap. Fit into an ungreased 9-inch tart pan. Sprinkle with 1 tablespoon sugar. Arrange cherries and blueberries in tart shell. Combine remaining 1 tablespoon sugar and chopped almonds. Sprinkle evenly over fruit. Bake at 400° for 30 to 35 minutes. Cool.

Combine powdered sugar, almond extract, and hot water; stir until smooth. Drizzle over cooled tart. Yield: 8 servings (195 calories per serving).

PROTEIN 3.2 / FAT 8.5 / CARBOHYDRATE 27.5 / CHOLESTEROL 0 / IRON 0.8 / SODIUM 69 / CALCIUM 22

Sweet Bing Cherry Tart

1 cup sifted cake flour
¼ cup cold margarine
2 to 3 tablespoons cold water
¼ cup plus 1 tablespoon sugar,
  divided
1 pound pitted fresh or frozen
  black cherries, thawed
1 egg white
¼ teaspoon cream of tartar

Place flour in a medium bowl; cut in margarine with a pastry blender until mixture resembles coarse meal. Sprinkle cold water, 1 tablespoon at a time, evenly over surface; stir with a fork until dry ingredients are moistened. (Do not form a ball.)

Gently press dough between 2 sheets of heavy-duty plastic wrap into a 4-inch circle. Roll dough into a 10-inch circle. Place in freezer 5 minutes or until plastic wrap can be removed easily. Remove bottom sheet of plastic wrap; fit dough onto a 10-inch ovenproof platter, and remove top sheet of plastic wrap. Fold edges under and flute. Sprinkle 1 tablespoon sugar over pastry. Prick bottom of pastry with a fork. Bake at 400° for 5 minutes.

Arrange cherries over pastry. Sprinkle 1 tablespoon sugar over cherries. Bake an additional 25 minutes or until pastry is lightly browned and cherries are tender.

Beat egg white (at room temperature) and cream of tartar at high speed of an electric mixer 1 minute. Gradually add remaining 3 tablespoons sugar, 1 tablespoon at a time, beating until stiff peaks form and sugar dissolves (2 to 4 minutes). Fill pastry bag fitted with open star tip No. 6B with meringue mixture. Pipe mixture inside the outer edge and in the center of tart. Bake 10 minutes or until meringue peaks are golden brown. Yield: 8 servings (168 calories per serving).

PROTEIN 2.1 / FAT 6.4 / CARBOHYDRATE 26.8 / CHOLESTEROL 0 / IRON 0.3 / SODIUM 80 / CALCIUM 13

Blueberry-Rum Cream Tarts

1 cup sifted cake flour
¼ cup cold margarine
2 to 3 tablespoons cold water
⅓ cup instant nonfat dry milk powder
2 tablespoons sugar
Dash of salt
1 tablespoon plus 1½ teaspoons cornstarch
1 cup water
1 egg, lightly beaten
1 tablespoon light rum
1 cup fresh blueberries
¼ cup reduced-calorie apple jelly, melted

*P*lace flour in a large bowl; cut in margarine with a pastry blender until mixture resembles coarse meal. Sprinkle cold water, 1 tablespoon at a time, evenly over surface; stir with a fork until dry ingredients are moistened. Shape dough into a ball.

Divide dough into 8 equal portions. Gently roll each portion between 2 sheets of heavy-duty plastic wrap into a 3½-inch circle. Remove plastic wrap. Fit circles of dough over inverted muffin cups, and prick with a fork. Bake at 375° for 15 minutes or until lightly browned. Remove from oven, and let cool 5 minutes. Carefully remove pastries from pan to wire rack; cool completely.

Combine milk powder, sugar, salt, cornstarch, and 1 cup water in a medium saucepan; stir well. Cook over medium heat, stirring constantly, until mixture comes to a boil; cook an additional minute, stirring constantly. Reduce heat to low.

Gradually stir about one-fourth of hot mixture into egg; add to remaining hot mixture, stirring constantly. Cook an additional minute. Remove from heat; stir in rum. Cover and chill thoroughly.

Beat chilled custard with a whisk. Spoon custard evenly into individual tart shells. Spoon 2 tablespoons blueberries over each. Gently brush tarts evenly with melted jelly. Serve immediately. Yield: 8 servings (159 calories per serving).

PROTEIN 3.6 / FAT 6.6 / CARBOHYDRATE 20.2 / CHOLESTEROL 35 / IRON 0.2 / SODIUM 122 / CALCIUM 71

Chocolate Cheesecake-Raspberry Tart

1 cup sifted cake flour
2 tablespoons unsweetened cocoa
3 tablespoons cold margarine
1¼ cups cold water, divided
⅔ cup plus 1½ teaspoons light
  process cream cheese product,
  softened
½ cup sugar, divided
½ cup instant nonfat dry milk
  powder, divided
1 egg
2 tablespoons Kahlúa or other
  coffee-flavored liqueur
1 teaspoon vanilla extract
1 teaspoon chocolate extract
1 (16-ounce) package frozen
  unsweetened raspberries, thawed
1 tablespoon Chambord or other
  raspberry-flavored liqueur
1 envelope unflavored gelatin
2 egg whites
1 (1-ounce) square semisweet
  chocolate, melted

Sift together flour and cocoa in a medium bowl; cut in margarine with a pastry blender until mixture resembles coarse meal. Sprinkle ¼ cup cold water, 1 tablespoon at a time, evenly over surface; stir with a fork until dry ingredients are moistened. Shape into a ball.

Gently press dough between 2 sheets of heavy-duty plastic wrap into a 4-inch circle. Chill 15 minutes. Roll dough into a 13-inch circle. Place in freezer 5 minutes or until plastic wrap can be removed easily. Remove bottom sheet of plastic wrap; fit dough into an 11-inch tart pan, and remove top sheet of plastic wrap. Set tart pan aside.

Combine cream cheese and ¼ cup sugar in a medium bowl; beat at medium speed of an electric mixer until fluffy. Add ¼ cup milk powder and ¼ cup cold water; beat until smooth. Add egg, Kahlúa, and vanilla and chocolate flavorings; blend well. Spoon mixture into prepared pastry shell. Bake at 350° for 25 to 30 minutes or until mixture is set. Let cool to room temperature on a wire rack; cover and chill thoroughly.

Place ¼ cup cold water in a small, narrow glass or stainless steel bowl; freeze 25 minutes or until a ⅛-inch-thick layer of ice forms on surface.

Place raspberries in a medium saucepan; bring to a boil over medium heat, stirring constantly. Remove from heat. Press raspberries through a sieve to yield 1¼ cups juice; discard seeds. Stir Chambord into juice; cool completely. Set aside.

Sprinkle gelatin over remaining ½ cup cold water in a small saucepan; let stand 1 minute. Cook over low heat, stirring constantly, until gelatin dissolves. Add to raspberry mixture; stir well. Chill until mixture is consistency of unbeaten egg white.

Add remaining ¼ cup milk powder to partially frozen water; beat at high speed of an electric mixer 5 minutes or until stiff peaks form. Gently fold into raspberry mixture.

Beat egg whites (at room temperature) at high speed of an electric mixer until soft peaks form; gradually add remaining ¼ cup sugar, 1 tablespoon at a time, beating until stiff peaks form. Gently fold egg whites into raspberry mixture. Gently spoon mixture over cheesecake layer. Chill 4 hours or until firm. Drizzle melted chocolate over top of tart. Yield: 12 servings (189 calories per serving).

PROTEIN 6.2 / FAT 7.0 / CARBOHYDRATE 24.7 / CHOLESTEROL 24 / IRON 0.5 / SODIUM 155 / CALCIUM 97

A drizzle of chocolate and a creamy filling make Chocolate Cheesecake-Raspberry Tart perfect for dessert.

Brownie Fruit Tart

1 cup all-purpose flour
²⁄₃ cup sugar
¼ cup unsweetened cocoa
1 teaspoon baking powder
¼ teaspoon baking soda
²⁄₃ cup water
¼ cup margarine, softened
1 teaspoon vanilla extract
3 egg whites
Vegetable cooking spray
1 cup low-fat cottage cheese
1 (8-ounce) package Neufchâtel
  cheese, softened
¼ cup sifted powdered sugar
1 teaspoon vanilla extract
1½ cups sliced fresh strawberries
4 kiwifruit, sliced

Combine first 5 ingredients in a large mixing bowl. Add water, margarine, and vanilla. Beat at low speed of an electric mixer 1 minute. Beat at high speed 2 to 3 minutes or until mixture is smooth.

Beat egg whites (at room temperature) at high speed of an electric mixer until stiff peaks form. Stir ½ cup beaten egg whites into chocolate batter. Fold in remaining egg whites. Spoon batter into a 15- x 10- x 1-inch jellyroll pan that has been coated with cooking spray. Bake at 375° for 15 to 20 minutes or until a wooden pick inserted in center comes out clean. Cool.

Combine cottage cheese, Neufchâtel, powdered sugar, and vanilla in container of an electric blender or food processor; top with cover, and process until smooth. Spread over brownie. Arrange strawberries and kiwifruit on top. Cover and chill. Yield: 16 servings (177 calories per serving).

PROTEIN 5.7 / FAT 7.0 / CARBOHYDRATE 22.7 / CHOLESTEROL 12 / IRON 0.7 / SODIUM 189 / CALCIUM 49

Chocolate-Raspberry Meringue Tarts

3 egg whites
⅛ teaspoon salt
1 teaspoon lemon juice
¾ cup sugar, divided
2 teaspoons unsweetened cocoa
2 cups vanilla ice milk
1 pint fresh raspberries
½ cup Chocolate Sauce (page
  225)

Line a baking sheet with parchment paper; draw 8 (3-inch) circles on paper.

Beat egg whites (at room temperature) in a large bowl at high speed of an electric mixer until foamy. Add salt and lemon juice; beat until soft peaks form. Gradually add ½ cup sugar, 1 tablespoon at a time, beating until stiff peaks form. Combine remaining ¼ cup sugar and cocoa; sift over meringue, and fold in just until blended.

Spoon half of meringue into a pastry bag fitted with a round or star tip. Pipe meringue evenly in 4 circles on prepared baking sheet; smooth meringue with the back of a spoon, working quickly. Pipe meringue around edge of each circle; repeat piping around outer edge of each circle, forming a ½-inch rim. Repeat procedure with remaining half of meringue mixture.

Bake at 200° for 2 hours or until dry. Carefully peel off parchment paper, and cool on wire racks.

To serve, scoop ¼ cup ice milk into each meringue shell. Spoon ¼ cup raspberries and 1 tablespoon Chocolate Sauce over ice milk. Yield: 8 servings (169 calories per serving).

PROTEIN 3.4 / FAT 1.8 / CARBOHYDRATE 35.8 / CHOLESTEROL 5 / IRON 0.6 / SODIUM 82 / CALCIUM 55

Chocolate Meringue Tarts

(pictured on pages 6 and 7)

4 egg whites
½ teaspoon lemon juice
½ teaspoon vanilla extract
¼ cup plus 2 tablespoons sugar
1 tablespoon unsweetened cocoa
Chocolate Filling
Edible flowers (optional)

*L*ine a large baking sheet with parchment paper; draw 8 (3½-inch) circles on paper.

Beat egg whites (at room temperature) in a large bowl at high speed of an electric mixer until foamy. Add lemon juice and vanilla; beat until soft peaks form. Gradually add sugar, 1 tablespoon at a time, beating until stiff peaks form and sugar dissolves (2 to 4 minutes). Sift cocoa over meringue mixture. Beat at high speed until well blended.

Spoon or pipe meringue evenly in 8 circles on prepared baking sheet. Smooth meringue with the back of a spoon, working quickly, and shape into 3½-inch circles. Shape each circle into a shell. (Sides should be about 1 inch high.) Bake at 225° for 2 hours. Let cool. Carefully peel off parchment paper, and cool meringues completely on wire racks.

Spoon 3 tablespoons Chocolate Filling into each meringue shell. Garnish with edible flowers, if desired. Serve immediately. Yield: 8 servings (111 calories per serving).

Chocolate Filling

1½ cups skim milk
¼ cup sugar
1 tablespoon plus 2 teaspoons
  cornstarch
2 tablespoons plus 1½ teaspoons
  unsweetened cocoa, sifted
Dash of salt
1 egg yolk, beaten
1 teaspoon vanilla extract

*C*ombine first 5 ingredients in a medium saucepan; stir well. Cook over medium heat, stirring constantly, until mixture comes to a boil; cook an additional minute, stirring constantly. Reduce heat to low. Gradually stir about one-fourth of hot mixture into egg yolk; add to remaining hot mixture, stirring constantly. Cook an additional minute. Remove from heat; stir in vanilla. Cover and chill thoroughly. Yield: 1½ cups.

PROTEIN 4.3 / FAT 1.1 / CARBOHYDRATE 20.9 / CHOLESTEROL 35 / IRON 0.6 / SODIUM 69 / CALCIUM 65

Fresh Grape Tart

1 cup sifted cake flour
¼ cup cold margarine
3 tablespoons cold water
1 tablespoon sugar
2½ cups seedless red grapes
⅔ cup low-sugar strawberry
   spread, melted

*P*lace flour in a small bowl; cut in margarine with a pastry blender until mixture resembles coarse meal. Sprinkle cold water, 1 tablespoon at a time, evenly over surface; stir with a fork until dry ingredients are moistened. Shape into a ball.

Roll dough into a 10-inch circle on an ungreased baking sheet. Make a rim with fingers, fluting edges. Prick bottom of pastry with a fork. Sprinkle with sugar. Freeze 10 minutes.

Bake at 400° for 15 minutes or until golden. Let cool on baking sheet. Transfer to a serving platter.

Combine grapes and melted strawberry spread; toss gently to coat well. Arrange grapes in an even layer in cooled tart shell. Brush with any remaining strawberry spread. Chill thoroughly. Cut into 8 wedges. Yield: 8 servings (151 calories per serving).

PROTEIN 1.3 / FAT 6.1 / CARBOHYDRATE 23.6 / CHOLESTEROL 0 / IRON 0.2 / SODIUM 68 / CALCIUM 9

Fruit Platter Tart

1 cup sifted cake flour
¼ cup cold margarine
1 to 2 tablespoons cold water
3 tablespoons sugar, divided
½ cup unsweetened orange juice
1½ teaspoons cornstarch
3 fresh apricots, peeled and sliced
   (about ½ pound)
⅓ cup pitted fresh or frozen sweet
   cherries, halved
1 medium banana, peeled and
   sliced
1 kiwifruit, peeled and sliced

*P*lace flour in a medium bowl; cut in margarine with a pastry blender until mixture resembles coarse meal. Sprinkle cold water, 1 tablespoon at a time, evenly over surface; stir with a fork until dry ingredients are moistened. Shape into a ball; cover and chill 10 minutes.

Roll dough into a 10-inch circle on an ungreased baking sheet or pizza pan; flute edges. Prick bottom of pastry with a fork; sprinkle with 1 tablespoon sugar. Bake at 400° for 15 to 20 minutes or until golden brown. Let cool completely.

Combine orange juice, remaining 2 tablespoons sugar, and cornstarch in a medium saucepan. Cook over medium heat, stirring constantly, 5 minutes or until thickened. Cool.

Arrange fruit over tart. Spoon orange glaze over fruit. Cut into 8 wedges, and serve immediately. Yield: 8 servings (151 calories per serving).

PROTEIN 1.6 / FAT 6.1 / CARBOHYDRATE 23.2 / CHOLESTEROL 0 / IRON 0.3 / SODIUM 68 / CALCIUM 13

Glazed Fruit Tart

(pictured on pages 6 and 7)

¾ cup all-purpose flour
Dash of salt
¼ cup cold margarine
1 to 2 tablespoons cold water
3 kiwifruit, peeled and sliced
6 medium-size fresh strawberries,
   hulled and halved lengthwise
1 medium banana, peeled and
   thinly sliced
¼ cup reduced-calorie apple jelly,
   melted
Fresh mint sprigs (optional)

Combine flour and salt; cut in margarine with a pastry blender until mixture resembles coarse meal. Sprinkle cold water, 1 tablespoon at a time, evenly over surface; stir with a fork until dry ingredients are moistened. Shape into a ball.

Roll dough between 2 sheets of heavy-duty plastic wrap into a 9-inch square. Remove bottom sheet of plastic wrap; place pastry on an ungreased baking sheet. Remove top sheet of plastic wrap. Turn edges of pastry up to make a ½-inch rim. Chill 10 minutes. Prick bottom of pastry with a fork. Bake at 400° for 10 to 12 minutes or until golden. Remove from oven; transfer to a wire rack, and let cool completely.

Arrange fruit in tart shell. Brush with melted jelly. Garnish with mint sprigs, if desired. Yield: 6 servings (197 calories per serving).

PROTEIN 2.9 / FAT 8.3 / CARBOHYDRATE 28.3 / CHOLESTEROL 0 / IRON 0.9 / SODIUM 114 / CALCIUM 24

Tropical Fruit Tarts

4 sheets commercial frozen phyllo
   pastry, thawed
Vegetable cooking spray
¼ cup reduced-calorie apple jelly,
   melted, divided
1 fresh ripe mango, peeled,
   seeded, and cubed
1 fresh ripe papaya, peeled,
   seeded, and cubed
1 kiwifruit, peeled, sliced, and
   quartered

Place 1 sheet of phyllo on a damp towel (keep remaining phyllo covered). Lightly coat phyllo with cooking spray. Layer 3 more sheets phyllo on first sheet, lightly coating each with cooking spray. Cut stack of phyllo evenly into 6 pieces.

Lightly coat 6 muffin cups with cooking spray. Fit one piece of layered phyllo into each muffin cup, pressing gently to form a pastry shell. Prick bottom and sides of shell with a fork. Bake at 375° for 12 to 15 minutes or until pastry is golden. Gently remove from pan, and let cool on a wire rack.

Brush inside of cooled shells lightly with 2 tablespoons melted jelly. Spoon fruit evenly into shells. Brush fruit with remaining 2 tablespoons jelly. Serve immediately. Yield: 6 servings (106 calories per serving).

PROTEIN 2.1 / FAT 0.9 / CARBOHYDRATE 23.3 / CHOLESTEROL 0 / IRON 0.1 / SODIUM 2 / CALCIUM 18

Lemon-Kiwifruit Tarts

1 cup sifted cake flour
¼ cup cold margarine
2 to 3 tablespoons cold water
1 cup plus 2 tablespoons water
¼ cup plus 2 tablespoons instant
  nonfat dry milk powder
3 tablespoons sugar
1 tablespoon plus 1½ teaspoons
  cornstarch
3 egg yolks, lightly beaten
¾ teaspoon grated lemon rind
3 tablespoons lemon juice
2 kiwifruit, peeled and sliced
2 tablespoons reduced-calorie
  apple jelly, melted

*P*lace flour in a medium bowl; cut in margarine with a pastry blender until mixture resembles coarse meal. Sprinkle cold water, 1 tablespoon at a time, evenly over surface; stir with a fork until dry ingredients are moistened. Divide dough into 8 balls. Roll each ball between 2 sheets of heavy-duty plastic wrap into a 4-inch circle. Remove plastic wrap, and fit each circle into a 3-inch tart pan. Prick with a fork. Bake at 375° for 15 to 20 minutes or until lightly browned. Cool completely; set aside.

Combine 1 cup plus 2 tablespoons water, milk powder, sugar, and cornstarch in a medium-size nonaluminum saucepan; stir well. Cook over medium heat, stirring constantly, until slightly thickened. Combine egg yolks, lemon rind, and lemon juice; stir well. Gradually stir about one-fourth of hot mixture into yolk mixture; add to remaining hot mixture, stirring constantly. Cook over low heat, stirring constantly, 1 to 2 minutes or until smooth and thickened. Cool slightly. Spoon 2 tablespoons custard mixture into each tart shell. Cover; chill until set.

Top each tart with 2 kiwifruit slices; brush with jelly. Serve immediately. Yield: 8 servings (181 calories per serving).

PROTEIN 4.4 / FAT 8.1 / CARBOHYDRATE 22.8 / CHOLESTEROL 103 / IRON 0.6 / SODIUM 100 / CALCIUM 92

Swedish Nut Tarts

Vegetable cooking spray
1½ teaspoons all-purpose flour
3 egg whites
⅛ teaspoon salt
⅔ cup sugar
¾ cup chopped pecans
¾ cup graham cracker crumbs
1½ cups vanilla ice milk
¼ cup Chocolate Sauce (page
  225)

*C*oat 12 (3-inch) tart molds with cooking spray. Dust with flour. Set aside.

Beat egg whites (at room temperature) and salt at high speed of an electric mixer until soft peaks form. Gradually add sugar, 1 tablespoon at a time, beating until stiff peaks form. Fold in pecans and crumbs. Spoon mixture evenly into tart molds. Make an indentation in center of each meringue with the back of a spoon. Place tarts on a baking sheet. Bake at 350° for 25 minutes or until browned. Let cool slightly. Remove tarts to wire racks to cool completely. Chill before serving. Spoon 2 tablespoons ice milk and 1 teaspoon Chocolate Sauce over each tart. Serve immediately. Yield: 12 servings (176 calories per serving).

PROTEIN 2.8 / FAT 6.7 / CARBOHYDRATE 27.0 / CHOLESTEROL 2 / IRON 0.7 / SODIUM 90 / CALCIUM 30

Try this variety of individual tarts: (clockwise from top) Lemon-Kiwifruit Tarts, Swedish Nut Tarts, and Fruit Tarts With Whole Wheat Pastry (page 166).

Lemon Tart

1 cup all-purpose flour
¼ teaspoon salt
3 tablespoons corn oil
5 egg whites, divided
1 tablespoon lemon juice
½ cup sugar, divided
¼ cup lemon juice
¼ cup water
2 egg yolks
1 teaspoon grated lemon rind
¼ teaspoon cream of tartar
Dash of salt

Combine flour and ¼ teaspoon salt in a medium bowl. Combine oil, 1 egg white, and 1 tablespoon lemon juice; add to flour mixture. Stir with a fork until dry ingredients are moistened. Shape dough into a ball.

Roll dough between 2 sheets of heavy-duty plastic wrap into an 11-inch circle. Remove top sheet of plastic wrap. Invert pastry and fit into a 9-inch tart pan. Remove bottom sheet of plastic wrap. Bake at 375° for 10 minutes. Remove from oven, and cool completely.

Combine ¼ cup sugar, ¼ cup lemon juice, water, and egg yolks in a medium saucepan. Cook over medium-low heat, stirring constantly, until mixture comes to a boil and thickens slightly. Remove from heat, and stir in lemon rind. Cover and refrigerate 15 minutes or until cool.

Beat remaining 4 egg whites (at room temperature), cream of tartar, and dash of salt at high speed of an electric mixer until soft peaks form. Gradually add remaining ¼ cup sugar, 1 tablespoon at a time, beating until stiff peaks form. Fold egg white mixture into cooled lemon mixture. Spoon into cooled tart shell. Bake at 375° for 18 to 20 minutes or until lightly browned. Cool completely. Yield: 8 servings (184 calories per serving).

PROTEIN 4.6 / FAT 6.7 / CARBOHYDRATE 26.6 / CHOLESTEROL 68 / IRON 0.8 / SODIUM 132 / CALCIUM 13

Orange Tart

1 cup sifted cake flour
¼ cup cold margarine
1 to 2 tablespoons cold water
2 tablespoons cornstarch
1⅓ cups unsweetened orange juice
3 tablespoons sugar
4 ounces Neufchâtel cheese, softened
3 tablespoons unsweetened orange juice
3 large oranges

Place flour in a medium bowl; cut in margarine with a pastry blender until mixture resembles coarse meal. Sprinkle cold water, 1 tablespoon at a time, evenly over surface; stir with a fork until dry ingredients are moistened. Shape into a ball.

Roll dough between 2 sheets of heavy-duty plastic wrap into a 10-inch circle. Remove top sheet of plastic wrap. Invert pastry, and fit into a 9-inch tart pan. Remove remaining sheet of plastic wrap. Prick bottom of pastry with a fork. Bake at 425° for 20 minutes or until golden brown.

Combine cornstarch and 1⅓ cups orange juice in a nonaluminum saucepan. Stir in sugar. Cook over medium-low

Orange Tart
(Continued)

heat, stirring constantly, until mixture is smooth and thickened. Remove from heat, and let cool.

Cream Neufchâtel cheese and 3 tablespoons orange juice at medium speed of an electric mixer until smooth. Spread mixture evenly over bottom of tart shell. Remove peel, pith, and seeds from oranges. Separate oranges into sections, and arrange over cheese mixture. Spoon orange juice mixture evenly over orange sections. Chill 3 to 4 hours before serving. Yield: 8 servings (193 calories per serving).

PROTEIN 3.0 / FAT 9.2 / CARBOHYDRATE 25.3 / CHOLESTEROL 11 / IRON 0.2 / SODIUM 124 / CALCIUM 33

Provençal Pear Tart

1 cup all-purpose flour
¼ cup cold margarine
2 to 3 tablespoons cold water
1 egg
2 tablespoons sugar
1 teaspoon almond extract
¼ cup ground almonds
2 tablespoons low-sugar apricot
　spread
1 tablespoon lemon juice
2 medium-size ripe pears, peeled,
　cored, and thinly sliced (about
　1 pound)

Place flour in a medium bowl; cut in margarine with a pastry blender until mixture resembles coarse meal. Sprinkle cold water, 1 tablespoon at a time, evenly over surface; stir with a fork until dry ingredients are moistened. Shape into a ball.

Gently press dough between 2 sheets of heavy-duty plastic wrap into a 4-inch circle. Chill 15 minutes. Roll dough into a 10-inch circle. Place in freezer 5 minutes or until plastic wrap can be removed easily. Remove top sheet of plastic wrap. Invert and fit pastry into a 9-inch tart pan. Remove remaining sheet of plastic wrap. Line pastry with aluminum foil, and fill with pie weights or uncooked dried beans. Bake at 400° for 15 to 20 minutes or until pastry is golden brown on the edges. Remove from oven. Remove pie weights and foil.

Beat egg at high speed of an electric mixer until foamy. Add sugar and almond extract; beat until mixture thickens. Stir in ground almonds. Spread mixture evenly over bottom of baked tart shell. Bake at 400° for 9 to 10 minutes or until filling is set.

Place apricot spread in a small saucepan; cook over low heat until melted. Press through a sieve to strain. Stir lemon juice into strained spread. Brush almond layer with half of apricot glaze. Arrange pear slices over glaze. Brush with remaining apricot glaze. Serve at room temperature. Yield: 8 servings (192 calories per serving).

PROTEIN 3.7 / FAT 8.6 / CARBOHYDRATE 25.7 / CHOLESTEROL 34 / IRON 0.9 / SODIUM 80 / CALCIUM 22

Fresh Peach Tart

1 cup sifted cake flour
¼ cup cold margarine
1 to 2 tablespoons cold water
1 tablespoon sifted cake flour
4 medium-size ripe peaches,
   peeled and sliced (about 1
   pound)
1 tablespoon cornstarch
1 (8-ounce) carton lemon low-fat
   yogurt
¼ cup sugar
1 egg
1 teaspoon vanilla extract
½ teaspoon almond extract
⅛ teaspoon ground nutmeg
Fresh mint sprigs (optional)

*P*lace flour in a medium bowl; cut in margarine with a pastry blender until mixture resembles coarse meal. Sprinkle cold water, 1 tablespoon at a time, evenly over surface; stir with a fork just until dry ingredients are moistened. Shape into a ball; chill.

Sprinkle 1 tablespoon flour evenly over work surface. Roll dough into a 10-inch circle. Fit pastry into a 9-inch tart pan. Prick bottom and sides of pastry with a fork. Bake at 375° for 5 minutes. Cool on a wire rack.

Place peaches in a medium bowl; add cornstarch, and toss to coat. Arrange peaches in cooled tart shell. Combine yogurt, sugar, egg, and flavorings in a medium bowl; stir well. Pour yogurt mixture over peaches. Sprinkle with nutmeg.

Bake at 375° for 45 to 55 minutes or until pastry is golden brown and tart is set. Serve warm or at room temperature. Garnish with mint sprigs, if desired. Yield: 8 servings (196 calories per serving).

PROTEIN 3.2 / FAT 6.8 / CARBOHYDRATE 30.9 / CHOLESTEROL 34 / IRON 0.3 / SODIUM 94 / CALCIUM 46

Almond-Peach Tart
(pictured on pages 126 and 127)

1 cup all-purpose flour
¼ cup cold margarine
2 to 3 tablespoons cold water
2 tablespoons sugar, divided
3 cups peeled, sliced, fresh
   peaches (about 1¼ pounds)
¼ cup sliced almonds, toasted
¼ cup plus 1 tablespoon sifted
   powdered sugar
¼ teaspoon almond extract
¾ teaspoon hot water

*P*lace flour in a large bowl; cut in margarine with a pastry blender until mixture resembles coarse meal. Sprinkle cold water, 1 tablespoon at a time, evenly over surface; stir with a fork just until dry ingredients are moistened. Shape into a ball.

Gently press dough between 2 sheets of heavy-duty plastic wrap into a 4-inch circle. Chill 15 minutes. Roll dough into an 11-inch circle. Place in freezer 5 minutes or until plastic wrap can be removed easily. Remove bottom sheet of plastic wrap; fit into a 9½-inch tart pan. Remove top sheet of plastic wrap. Prick bottom of pastry with a fork. Sprinkle with 1 tablespoon sugar. Bake at 400° for 10 minutes. Remove from oven; cool.

Arrange peaches over tart. Sprinkle with remaining 1

Almond-Peach Tart
(CONTINUED)

tablespoon sugar and almonds. Bake at 400° for 30 to 40 minutes or until crust is golden and peaches are tender. Cool completely.

Combine powdered sugar, almond extract, and hot water; stir until smooth. Drizzle glaze over tart. Cut into 8 wedges, and serve. Yield: 8 servings (187 calories per serving).

PROTEIN 2.8 / FAT 7.3 / CARBOHYDRATE 28.5 / CHOLESTEROL 0 / IRON 0.7 / SODIUM 68 / CALCIUM 15

Peach Meringue Tarts With Strawberry Glaze

3 egg whites
1 teaspoon lemon juice
¾ cup sugar
4 medium-size ripe peaches, peeled and sliced (about 1 pound)
¾ cup sliced fresh strawberries
Strawberry Glaze

*B*eat egg whites (at room temperature) in a large bowl at high speed of an electric mixer until foamy. Add lemon juice; beat until soft peaks form. Gradually add sugar, 1 tablespoon at a time, beating until stiff peaks form.

Spoon meringue into 12 equal portions on baking sheets lined with parchment paper. Shape meringue into circles with the back of a spoon, mounding sides of meringues at least ½-inch higher than centers.

Bake at 300° for 30 minutes. Turn off oven. Cool meringues in oven at least 2 hours before opening oven door. Carefully remove meringue shells from parchment paper.

Arrange sliced fruit evenly in meringue shells. Spoon cooled Strawberry Glaze over fruit. Yield: 12 servings (83 calories per serving).

Strawberry Glaze

1 cup fresh strawberries, hulled
2 tablespoons sugar
2 teaspoons cornstarch

Mash strawberries. Combine mashed strawberries, sugar, and cornstarch in a heavy saucepan; stir well. Cook over medium heat until thickened, stirring constantly. Let cool completely. Yield: ¾ cup.

PROTEIN 1.2 / FAT 0.1 / CARBOHYDRATE 20.2 / CHOLESTEROL 0 / IRON 0.1 / SODIUM 13 / CALCIUM 6

Tarts differ from pies in that they may be larger in diameter, but shallower in depth, holding a thinner layer of filling.

Fruit Tarts With Whole Wheat Pastry

(pictured on page 160)

1 cup whole wheat pastry flour
¼ cup cold margarine
2 to 3 tablespoons cold water
3 ounces Neufchâtel cheese, softened
1 (8-ounce) carton lemon low-fat yogurt
1 tablespoon plus 1 teaspoon powdered sugar
¾ teaspoon grated lemon rind
1½ cups sliced fresh strawberries
⅔ cup fresh blueberries

*P*lace flour in a medium bowl; cut in margarine with a pastry blender until mixture resembles coarse meal. Sprinkle cold water, 1 tablespoon at a time, evenly over surface; stir with a fork just until dry ingredients are moistened. Shape into a ball; cover and chill.

Divide dough into 8 equal portions. Roll each portion between 2 sheets of heavy-duty plastic wrap into a 5-inch circle. Remove plastic wrap. Fit pastry circles into 8 (4-inch) tart pans or shape circles over the bottom of eight muffin cups. Prick pastries with a fork.

Bake at 375° for 18 to 20 minutes or until lightly browned. Let cool 5 minutes; remove from pans, and cool completely on a wire rack.

Beat Neufchâtel cheese at medium speed of an electric mixer until smooth. Stir in yogurt, sugar, and lemon rind. Spoon mixture evenly into cooled tart shells. Spoon strawberries and blueberries evenly over cheese mixture. Serve immediately. Yield: 8 servings (174 calories per serving).

PROTEIN 3.7 / FAT 9.0 / CARBOHYDRATE 20.4 / CHOLESTEROL 9 / IRON 0.3 / SODIUM 142 / CALCIUM 62

Raspberry-Almond Cream Tarts

1 cup sifted cake flour
¼ cup cold margarine
2 to 3 tablespoons cold water
¼ cup instant nonfat dry milk powder
2 tablespoons sugar
1 tablespoon plus 1½ teaspoons cornstarch
¾ cup water
1 egg, lightly beaten
2 tablespoons amaretto
3 tablespoons ground almonds
¼ cup low-sugar raspberry spread
4 cups fresh raspberries

*P*lace flour in a medium bowl; cut in margarine with a pastry blender until mixture resembles coarse meal. Sprinkle cold water, 1 tablespoon at a time, evenly over surface; stir with a fork just until dry ingredients are moistened.

Divide dough into 8 equal portions. Gently press each portion between 2 sheets of heavy-duty plastic wrap into a 4-inch circle. Remove bottom sheet of plastic wrap; fit each portion into a 3-inch tart pan, and remove top sheet of plastic wrap.

Prick bottoms of pastries with a fork. Bake at 375° for 15 to 20 minutes or until lightly browned. Cool in pans 5 minutes. Remove from pans, and cool completely on wire racks.

Combine milk powder and next 3 ingredients in a non-aluminum saucepan; stir with a wire whisk until well blended. Cook over medium heat, stirring constantly, until mixture comes to a boil. Cook an additional minute; remove from heat.

Gradually stir about one-fourth of hot mixture into egg; add to remaining hot mixture, stirring constantly. Cook, stirring constantly, 1 minute or until mixture thickens. Stir in amaretto, and cook an additional minute. Remove from heat; stir in ground almonds. Cover and chill thoroughly.

Cook raspberry spread over low heat until melted. Press through a sieve to strain. Spoon chilled custard mixture evenly into tart shells. Spoon raspberries over custard. Brush strained raspberry spread lightly over raspberries. Serve immediately. Yield: 8 servings (197 calories per serving).

PROTEIN 4.3 / FAT 8.9 / CARBOHYDRATE 25.7 / CHOLESTEROL 35 / IRON 0.7 / SODIUM 124 / CALCIUM 76

Raspberry-Blackberry Tart

½ *cup whole wheat pastry flour*

½ *cup all-purpose flour*

¼ *cup cold margarine*

2 *to 3 tablespoons cold water*

¼ *cup instant nonfat dry milk powder*

2 *tablespoons sugar*

⅛ *teaspoon salt*

1 *tablespoon plus 1½ teaspoons cornstarch*

¾ *cup water*

1 *egg, lightly beaten*

1 *teaspoon almond extract*

¼ *cup low-sugar raspberry spread*

1 *tablespoon Chambord or other raspberry-flavored liqueur*

1 *cup fresh or frozen unsweetened raspberries, thawed*

1 *cup fresh or frozen unsweetened blackberries, thawed*

3 *tablespoons sliced almonds*

Combine flours in a bowl; cut in margarine with a pastry blender until mixture resembles coarse meal. Sprinkle cold water, 1 tablespoon at a time, evenly over surface; stir with a fork just until dry ingredients are moistened. Shape into a ball.

Roll dough between 2 sheets of heavy-duty plastic wrap into a 12-inch circle. Remove plastic wrap; press pastry into bottom and up sides of an 11-inch tart pan. Line pastry with aluminum foil; fill with pie weights or uncooked dried beans. Bake at 425° for 20 minutes or until edges are golden. Remove from oven. Remove weights and foil; cool on a wire rack.

Combine milk powder, sugar, salt, cornstarch, and ¾ cup water in a nonaluminum saucepan; stir with a wire whisk. Cook over medium heat, stirring constantly, until mixture comes to a boil. Remove from heat. Gradually stir about one-fourth of hot mixture into egg; add to remaining hot mixture, stirring constantly. Cook, stirring constantly, 1 minute or until thickened. Remove from heat; stir in almond extract. Cover and chill.

Combine raspberry spread and liqueur in a small saucepan; cook over low heat until melted. Spoon chilled custard mixture into cooled tart. Arrange raspberries and blackberries on cream mixture. Brush melted raspberry mixture over fruit. Sprinkle with almonds. Yield: 8 servings (197 calories per serving).

PROTEIN 4.3 / FAT 8.1 / CARBOHYDRATE 26.0 / CHOLESTEROL 35 / IRON 0.7 / SODIUM 141 / CALCIUM 71

Strawberry-Ricotta Tarts

4 sheets commercial frozen phyllo
  pastry, thawed
Vegetable cooking spray
½ cup part-skim ricotta cheese
3 tablespoons low-sugar
  strawberry spread, divided
1½ cups sliced fresh strawberries

Place 1 sheet of phyllo on a damp towel (keep remaining phyllo covered). Lightly coat phyllo with cooking spray. Layer 3 more sheets of phyllo on first sheet, lightly coating each sheet with cooking spray. Cut stack of phyllo into twelve (approximately 4-inch) squares with kitchen shears.

Coat 4 muffin cups with cooking spray. Layer 3 portions of phyllo in each muffin cup, pressing gently in center to form a pastry shell. Prick bottom of each pastry generously with a fork. Bake at 350° for 8 to 10 minutes or until golden. Gently remove from pan, and let cool on wire racks.

Combine ricotta and 2 tablespoons strawberry spread; stir well. Spoon 2 tablespoons ricotta mixture into each pastry shell. Top each with ¼ cup plus 2 tablespoons strawberries. Melt remaining 1 tablespoon strawberry spread; brush over tarts. Serve immediately. Yield: 4 servings (144 calories per serving).

PROTEIN 6.1 / FAT 3.9 / CARBOHYDRATE 21.7 / CHOLESTEROL 10 / IRON 0.3 /
SODIUM 39 / CALCIUM 92

Danish Strawberry Tart

1 cup all-purpose flour
1 tablespoon sugar
¼ cup cold margarine
1 egg, lightly beaten
1 teaspoon vanilla extract
1 tablespoon sugar
3 tablespoons low-sugar
  strawberry spread, melted
1 quart fresh strawberries, hulled
  and sliced
Fresh mint sprigs (optional)

Combine flour and 1 tablespoon sugar in a medium bowl; stir well. Cut in margarine with a pastry blender until mixture resembles coarse meal. Add egg and vanilla; stir with a fork just until dry ingredients are moistened. Shape into a ball. (Dough will be sticky.)

Gently press dough between 2 sheets of heavy-duty plastic wrap into a 4-inch circle. Chill 15 minutes. Roll dough into an 11-inch circle. Place in freezer 5 minutes or until plastic wrap can be removed easily. Remove bottom sheet of plastic wrap; fit into a 9½-inch tart pan. Remove top sheet of plastic wrap. Prick with a fork. Sprinkle with 1 tablespoon sugar. Bake at 375° for 20 minutes or until lightly browned. Cool completely on a wire rack.

Press strawberry spread through a sieve, reserving syrup; discard seeds. Brush half of syrup over tart shell; arrange strawberries in shell. Brush with remaining syrup. Garnish with mint sprigs, if desired. Yield: 8 servings (159 calories per serving).

PROTEIN 3.0 / FAT 6.8 / CARBOHYDRATE 21.6 / CHOLESTEROL 34 / IRON 0.9 /
SODIUM 77 / CALCIUM 17

Each bite of Danish Strawberry Tart provides a sweet taste of fruit and tender pastry.

Strawberry-Cream Cheese Tart

¾ cup sifted cake flour
3 tablespoons cold margarine
1 tablespoon plus 1 teaspoon cold
  water
1 (8-ounce) carton light process
  cream cheese product
1 tablespoon frozen lemonade
  concentrate, thawed and
  undiluted
1 teaspoon sugar
1 pint fresh strawberries, hulled
  and halved
2 tablespoons reduced-calorie
  apple jelly, melted

Place flour in a large bowl; cut in margarine with a pastry blender until mixture resembles coarse meal. Sprinkle cold water, 1 tablespoon at a time, evenly over surface; stir with a fork just until dry ingredients are moistened. (Do not form a ball.)

Gently press dough between 2 sheets of heavy-duty plastic wrap into a 4-inch circle. Chill 15 minutes. Roll dough into a 10-inch circle. Place in freezer 5 minutes or until plastic wrap can be removed easily. Remove bottom sheet of plastic wrap. Place dough on a 10-inch ovenproof platter, and remove top sheet of plastic wrap. Fold edges under and flute. Prick bottom of pastry with a fork. Bake at 375° for 10 to 12 minutes or until lightly browned; cool completely.

Combine cream cheese, lemonade concentrate, and sugar in a medium bowl. Beat at medium speed of an electric mixer until light and fluffy. Gently spread cream cheese mixture in tart shell. Arrange strawberries over cream cheese mixture. Brush with melted jelly. Cover and chill. Yield: 8 servings (153 calories per serving).

PROTEIN 4.0 / FAT 9.5 / CARBOHYDRATE 14.6 / CHOLESTEROL 0 / IRON 0.2 / SODIUM 210 / CALCIUM 49

Apple Dumplings

4 sheets commercial frozen phyllo
  pastry, thawed
Butter-flavored vegetable cooking
  spray
4 medium-size Golden Delicious
  or other cooking apples, peeled
  and cored (about 1¼ pounds)
2 tablespoons brown sugar
1 teaspoon ground cinnamon
2 teaspoons margarine, divided

Place one sheet of phyllo on a damp towel (keep remaining phyllo covered). Lightly coat phyllo with cooking spray. Fold phyllo in half crosswise.

Place one apple on phyllo square. Combine brown sugar and cinnamon. Place 1¾ teaspoons brown sugar mixture in center of each apple. Place ½ teaspoon margarine on top of brown sugar mixture in each apple. Lightly spray edges of phyllo with cooking spray; bring corners to center, pinching edges to seal. Spray dumpling lightly with cooking spray. Repeat with remaining ingredients, working with one apple at a time.

Place dumplings in a 9-inch square baking pan. Bake at 350° for 30 minutes or until phyllo is lightly browned and apples are tender. Yield: 4 servings (198 calories each).

PROTEIN 2.5 / FAT 4.3 / CARBOHYDRATE 39.8 / CHOLESTEROL 0 / IRON 0.5 / SODIUM 25 / CALCIUM 17

Wrap Golden Delicious apples in phyllo pastry to make easy and attractive Apple Dumplings.

Apple Strudel

4 medium Granny Smith apples,
  peeled, cored, and thinly sliced
  (about 1½ pounds)
¼ cup raisins
¼ cup sugar
½ teaspoon ground cinnamon
¼ teaspoon ground nutmeg
2 tablespoons graham cracker
  crumbs
8 sheets commercial frozen phyllo
  pastry, thawed
Vegetable cooking spray
1 tablespoon skim milk
1 tablespoon powdered sugar

Combine first 6 ingredients in a large mixing bowl, tossing gently; set aside.

Place one sheet of phyllo on a damp towel (keep remaining phyllo covered). Lightly coat phyllo with cooking spray. Layer 3 more sheets phyllo on first sheet, lightly coating each sheet with cooking spray. Cut stack of phyllo into fourths with a sharp knife.

Spoon about ⅔ cup apple mixture into center of each stack of phyllo. Fold sides of phyllo over apple mixture, wrapping filling like a package. Place on a baking sheet that has been coated with cooking spray; repeat with remaining phyllo stacks, using about ⅔ cup filling for each stack.

Brush phyllo packages with milk; prick top of each package two or three times with a sharp knife. Bake at 400° for 25 minutes or until golden. Sprinkle with powdered sugar. Serve warm. Yield: 8 servings (156 calories per serving).

PROTEIN 2.6 / FAT 1.1 / CARBOHYDRATE 35.6 / CHOLESTEROL 0 / IRON 0.3 / SODIUM 13 / CALCIUM 10

Dutch Babies With Apple Filling

½ cup all-purpose flour
½ cup skim milk
2 eggs
¼ teaspoon salt
1 tablespoon plus 2 teaspoons
  margarine, divided
2 medium Granny Smith apples,
  peeled, cored, and sliced (about
  ¾ pound)
1 tablespoon plus 1½ teaspoons
  brown sugar
1 teaspoon ground cinnamon
2 tablespoons water
Vegetable cooking spray
2 teaspoons powdered sugar

Combine first 4 ingredients in a medium bowl; stir with a wire whisk until smooth.

Melt 1 tablespoon margarine in a large nonstick skillet over medium heat. Add apples, brown sugar, and cinnamon. Sauté 10 minutes or until apples are tender, adding water if necessary; set aside, and keep warm.

Place remaining 2 teaspoons margarine in a 10-inch cast-iron skillet that has been coated with cooking spray. Preheat skillet in oven at 425° for 4 minutes or until margarine melts and skillet is hot. Pour batter into hot skillet. Bake at 425° for 15 to 20 minutes or until puffy and browned. Remove skillet from oven; top with sautéed apples, and sprinkle with powdered sugar. Cut into 4 wedges, and serve immediately. Yield: 4 servings (176 calories per serving).

PROTEIN 6.0 / FAT 8.0 / CARBOHYDRATE 19.8 / CHOLESTEROL 138 / IRON 1.4 / SODIUM 254 / CALCIUM 67

Pear Phyllo Turnovers

3 medium-size ripe pears, peeled,
 cored, and coarsely chopped
 (about 1¼ pounds)
2 tablespoons chopped walnuts
2 tablespoons brown sugar
½ teaspoon ground cinnamon
¼ teaspoon ground nutmeg
⅛ teaspoon salt
¼ teaspoon grated lemon rind
6 sheets commercial frozen phyllo
 pastry, thawed
Butter-flavored vegetable cooking
 spray
1 tablespoon powdered sugar

Combine first 7 ingredients, stirring gently; set aside.

Place one sheet of phyllo on a damp towel (keep remaining phyllo covered). Lightly coat phyllo with cooking spray. Fold in half lengthwise and spray again. Place one-sixth of pear mixture at base of phyllo sheet, folding the right bottom corner over filling, making a triangle. Continue folding back and forth into a triangle to end of sheet. Repeat process with remaining phyllo and pear mixture. Keep triangles covered before baking.

Place triangles, seam side down, on a baking sheet lined with parchment paper. Spray each triangle with cooking spray. Bake at 400° for 15 minutes or until golden. Sprinkle with powdered sugar. Serve warm. Yield: 6 servings (155 calories per serving).

PROTEIN 3.1 / FAT 2.4 / CARBOHYDRATE 32.2 / CHOLESTEROL 0 / IRON 0.5 / SODIUM 51 / CALCIUM 17

Strawberry Shortcake

Scotch Shortcake (page 131)
3 cups fresh strawberries, sliced
3 tablespoons sugar
1 teaspoon cornstarch
3 tablespoons cold water
½ teaspoon lemon juice
½ teaspoon vanilla extract
2 tablespoons plus 1½ teaspoons
 instant nonfat dry milk powder
1 tablespoon powdered sugar

Prepare Scotch Shortcake; set aside.

Combine strawberries and 3 tablespoons sugar in a medium bowl. Let stand until syrup forms (about 1 hour). Drain syrup into a small saucepan, reserving strawberries. Add cornstarch to syrup in saucepan. Bring to a boil over medium heat, stirring constantly. Remove from heat, and let cool.

Combine cold water, lemon juice, and vanilla in a small, narrow glass or stainless steel bowl; freeze 25 minutes or until a ⅛-inch-thick layer of ice forms on surface.

Add milk powder and powdered sugar to partially frozen water mixture. Beat at high speed of an electric mixer 5 minutes or until stiff peaks form.

Arrange reserved strawberries on each of 6 Scotch Shortcake wedges. Drizzle with cooled strawberry syrup mixture. Top each serving with whipped milk mixture. Serve immediately. Yield: 6 servings (189 calories per serving).

PROTEIN 2.8 / FAT 6.1 / CARBOHYDRATE 30.8 / CHOLESTEROL 1 / IRON 0.4 / SODIUM 184 / CALCIUM 87

Danish Almond Pastry

(pictured on pages 126 and 127)

1 cup sifted cake flour
¼ cup cold margarine
2 to 3 tablespoons cold water
1 cup water
¼ cup margarine, melted
¼ teaspoon salt
1 cup all-purpose flour
3 eggs
1 cup sifted powdered sugar
1 tablespoon margarine, melted
1 tablespoon plus 1 teaspoon
  water
½ teaspoon almond extract
¼ cup sliced almonds, toasted

*P*lace cake flour in a medium bowl. Cut in ¼ cup margarine with a pastry blender until mixture resembles coarse meal. Sprinkle cold water, 1 tablespoon at a time, evenly over surface; stir with a fork until dry ingredients are moistened. Shape dough into a ball; chill 10 minutes. Divide dough in half.

Roll each half of dough between 2 sheets of heavy-duty plastic wrap into a 12- x 3-inch rectangle. Place dough in freezer 5 minutes or until plastic wrap can be removed easily. Remove plastic wrap. Place rectangles 3 inches apart on an ungreased baking sheet.

Combine 1 cup water, ¼ cup melted margarine, and salt in a saucepan. Bring to a boil. Add flour all at once, stirring vigorously over low heat until mixture leaves sides of pan and forms a smooth ball. Remove from heat, and cool slightly.

Add eggs to flour mixture, one at a time, beating with a wooden spoon after each addition; beat until batter is smooth. Spread or pipe batter evenly over each pastry strip. Bake at 350° for 55 minutes to 1 hour. Let cool.

Combine powdered sugar and next 3 ingredients, stirring until smooth. Drizzle over pastries. Sprinkle with almonds. Yield: 16 servings (165 calories per serving).

PROTEIN 2.9 / FAT 8.5 / CARBOHYDRATE 19.3 / CHOLESTEROL 51 / IRON 0.5 / SODIUM 125 / CALCIUM 15

Crêpes

½ cup all-purpose flour
⅔ cup plus 1 tablespoon skim
  milk
1 egg
⅛ teaspoon salt
Vegetable cooking spray

*C*ombine flour, milk, egg, and salt in container of an electric blender or food processor; top with cover, and process 30 seconds. Scrape sides of container with a rubber spatula; process 30 seconds. Refrigerate batter at least 1 hour. (This allows flour particles to swell and soften so that crêpes are light in texture.)

Coat a 6-inch crêpe pan or heavy skillet with cooking spray; place over medium heat until just hot, not smoking.

Pour 2 tablespoons batter into pan; quickly tilt pan in all directions so batter covers pan in a thin film. Cook 1 minute or

Crêpes
(CONTINUED)

until crêpe is lightly browned.

Lift edge of crêpe to test for doneness. Crêpe is ready for flipping when it can be shaken loose from pan. Flip crêpe, and cook about 30 seconds on other side. (This side is usually spotty brown and is the side on which filling is placed.)

Place crêpes on a towel to cool. Stack crêpes between layers of wax paper to prevent sticking. Repeat until all batter is used. Yield: 10 crêpes (40 calories each).

PROTEIN 1.9 / FAT 0.8 / CARBOHYDRATE 6.1 / CHOLESTEROL 28 / IRON 0.3 / SODIUM 46 / CALCIUM 26

Light Basic Crêpes

¼ cup plus 2 tablespoons
all-purpose flour
3 egg whites
1 cup skim milk
Vegetable cooking spray

Combine flour, egg whites, and milk in container of an electric blender or food processor; top with cover, and process 30 seconds. Scrape sides of container with a rubber spatula; process 30 seconds. Refrigerate batter at least 1 hour. (This allows flour particles to swell and soften so that crêpes are light in texture.)

Coat a 6-inch nonstick skillet with cooking spray; place over medium heat until just hot, not smoking.

Pour 2 tablespoons batter into pan; quickly tilt pan in all directions so batter covers bottom of pan in a thin film. Cook 1 minute or until lightly browned.

Lift edge of crêpe to test for doneness. Crêpe is ready for flipping when it can be shaken loose from pan. Flip crêpe, and cook about 30 seconds on other side. (This side is usually spotty brown and is the side on which filling is placed.)

Place crêpes on a towel to cool. Stack crêpes between layers of wax paper to prevent sticking. Repeat until all batter is used. Yield: 12 crêpes (28 calories each).

PROTEIN 2.0 / FAT 0.2 / CARBOHYDRATE 4.3 / CHOLESTEROL 0 / IRON 0.1 / SODIUM 23 / CALCIUM 27

Crêpes may be made ahead, then wrapped and refrigerated or frozen. Use as many as needed at a time by simply peeling off the crêpes from the stack.

Orange zest and liqueur make Slimmer Crêpes Suzette a light and delicate delight.

Slimmer Crêpes Suzette

1 recipe Light Basic Crêpes (page
  175)
2 tablespoons plus 1 teaspoon
  sugar
2 tablespoons margarine, softened
2 tablespoons Grand Marnier or
  other orange-flavored liqueur
Orange Sauce

Orange Sauce

3 tablespoons sugar
Rind of 1 orange, cut into
  ¼-inch-wide strips
1 cup water
⅓ cup unsweetened orange juice

Prepare Light Basic Crêpes; set aside.

Combine sugar and margarine in a small bowl, stirring well. Spoon ½ teaspoon margarine mixture on each crêpe, spreading to edges. Fold crêpe in half, then in quarters. Arrange 3 crêpes on each of 4 individual dessert plates.

Place Grand Marnier in a small, long-handled saucepan; heat just until warm (do not boil). Remove from heat. Ignite with a long match, and pour evenly over crêpes. Spoon ¼ cup Orange Sauce over each serving of crêpes. Serve immediately. Yield: 4 servings (190 calories per serving).

Combine sugar, orange rind, and water in a small saucepan. Cook over medium heat, stirring occasionally, 10 to 15 minutes or until syrup measures ⅔ cup. Stir in orange juice. Keep warm. Yield: 1 cup.

PROTEIN 4.2 / FAT 6.3 / CARBOHYDRATE 30.2 / CHOLESTEROL 1 / IRON 0.3 / SODIUM 114 / CALCIUM 60

Glazed Apple Crêpes

8 Light Basic Crêpes (page 175)
1 tablespoon margarine
2 large Golden Delicious apples, peeled, cored, and sliced (about 1¼ pounds)
2 tablespoons sugar
1 tablespoon light rum
½ teaspoon ground cinnamon
Vegetable cooking spray
½ cup vanilla low-fat yogurt
1 teaspoon sugar
⅛ teaspoon ground cinnamon

Prepare Light Basic Crêpes; set aside.

Melt margarine in a heavy skillet over medium heat. Add apples; cook 10 minutes, stirring frequently. Add sugar, rum, and ½ teaspoon cinnamon, stirring until sugar dissolves. Cook 10 minutes or until apples are tender, stirring frequently.

Spoon apple mixture evenly over crêpes. Arrange on an ovenproof platter that has been coated with cooking spray.

Broil crêpes 6 inches from heat until lightly browned. Top each crêpe with 1 tablespoon yogurt. Combine sugar and ⅛ teaspoon cinnamon. Lightly sprinkle sugar mixture over crêpes. Yield: 8 servings (96 calories per serving).

PROTEIN 2.8 / FAT 2.1 / CARBOHYDRATE 17.4 / CHOLESTEROL 1 / IRON 0.2 / SODIUM 50 / CALCIUM 55

Hungarian Sweet Crêpes

⅓ cup instant nonfat dry milk powder
2 tablespoons all-purpose flour
2 tablespoons water
1 tablespoon dark rum
3 egg whites
1 teaspoon grated lemon rind
1 teaspoon grated orange rind
Vegetable cooking spray
⅓ cup light process cream cheese product
1 tablespoon unsweetened orange juice
1 (11-ounce) can mandarin orange sections, drained

Combine first 7 ingredients in container of an electric blender; top with cover, and process until smooth. Refrigerate batter 1 hour. (This allows flour particles to swell and soften so that crêpes are light in texture.)

Coat a 6-inch crêpe pan or heavy skillet with cooking spray; place over medium heat until just hot, not smoking.

Pour 2 tablespoons batter into pan; quickly tilt pan in all directions so batter covers pan in a thin film. Cook 1 minute or until lightly browned.

Lift edge of crêpe to test for doneness. Crêpe is ready for flipping when it can be shaken loose from pan. Flip crêpe, and cook about 30 seconds on other side. (This side is usually spotty brown and is the side on which filling is placed.)

Cool crêpes on a towel. Stack crêpes between layers of wax paper to prevent sticking. Repeat until all batter is used.

Combine cream cheese and orange juice; stir well. Spread 1 tablespoon mixture over each crêpe. Spoon orange sections evenly over cream cheese. Fold crêpe in quarters, and place each on a dessert plate. Yield: 6 servings (86 calories per serving).

PROTEIN 5.7 / FAT 2.5 / CARBOHYDRATE 9.1 / CHOLESTEROL 1 / IRON 0.2 / SODIUM 133 / CALCIUM 105

Raspberry-Almond Crêpes

8 Light Basic Crêpes (page 175)
2 egg whites
3 tablespoons sugar
¼ teaspoon almond extract
2 tablespoons toasted almonds,
 ground
Vegetable cooking spray
2 teaspoons margarine, melted
2 teaspoons sugar

Prepare Light Basic Crêpes; set aside.

Beat egg whites (at room temperature) in a large bowl at high speed of an electric mixer until foamy. Gradually add sugar, 1 tablespoon at a time, beating until stiff peaks form. Fold in almond extract and almonds.

Spread egg mixture evenly over 8 crêpes. Roll up, jellyroll fashion. Place crêpes, seam side down, on an ovenproof serving dish that has been coated with cooking spray. Brush top of crêpes with margarine. Sprinkle with sugar.

Bake at 350° for 12 minutes or until lightly browned and puffy. Place 2 crêpes on each dessert plate. Drizzle Raspberry Sauce evenly over crêpes. Serve immediately. Yield: 4 servings (156 calories per serving).

Raspberry Sauce

2 cups frozen unsweetened whole
 raspberries, thawed
1 teaspoon cornstarch
½ teaspoon almond extract

*Place thawed raspberries in a small saucepan, and cook over medium heat 5 minutes. Strain raspberries through a sieve to remove seeds. Discard seeds. Return juice to saucepan; add cornstarch, and cook over medium heat, stirring constantly, until sauce thickens. Stir in almond extract. Drizzle sauce over crêpes. Serve immediately. Yield: ½ cup.

PROTEIN 5.6 / FAT 4.5 / CARBOHYDRATE 24.0 / CHOLESTEROL 1 / IRON 0.6 / SODIUM 79 / CALCIUM 57

Traditional cream puffs are made with a simple cooked mixture of butter, flour, and eggs. For a lighter version, Cream Puff Shells contain margarine and fewer eggs. The baked puffs should have hollow, moist interiors and a crisp outer shell with a lightly browned surface and somewhat irregular shape. If underbaked, they will collapse.

Cream Puff Shells

½ cup water
2 tablespoons margarine
½ cup all-purpose flour
⅛ teaspoon salt
2 eggs
Vegetable cooking spray

Combine water and margarine in a medium saucepan; bring to a boil. Add flour and salt all at once, stirring vigorously over low heat about 1 minute or until mixture leaves sides of pan and forms a smooth ball. Remove mixture from heat, and cool 4 to 5 minutes.

Add eggs to flour mixture, one at a time, beating with a wooden spoon after each addition; beat until dough is smooth.

Divide dough evenly into 6 mounds 3 inches apart on a baking sheet that has been coated with cooking spray. Bake at 450° for 25 to 30 minutes or until golden and puffed. Cut tops off shells; pull out and discard soft dough inside. Fill shells with fruit or pudding; replace tops. Serve immediately or cover and refrigerate. Yield: 6 cream puff shells (104 calories each).

PROTEIN 3.3 / FAT 6.0 / CARBOHYDRATE 8.9 / CHOLESTEROL 91 / IRON 0.7 / SODIUM 117 / CALCIUM 13

Custard-Filled Cream Puffs

6 Cream Puff Shells (above)
⅓ cup instant nonfat dry milk
   powder
2 tablespoons cornstarch
2 tablespoons sugar
⅛ teaspoon salt
¾ cup water
2 eggs, separated
1 teaspoon vanilla extract

Prepare Cream Puff Shells; set aside.

Combine milk powder, cornstarch, sugar, and salt in a medium saucepan; stir well. Stir in water. Cook over medium heat, stirring constantly, until mixture comes to a boil. Cook an additional minute. Beat egg yolks until smooth. Gradually whisk about one-fourth of hot mixture into egg yolks; add to remaining hot mixture, stirring constantly. Cook an additional minute over medium heat, stirring constantly, until mixture is smooth and thickened. Remove from heat, and stir in vanilla.

Beat egg whites (at room temperature) in a small bowl at high speed of an electric mixer until stiff peaks form. Gently fold egg whites into custard mixture. Cook 1 minute over medium heat, stirring constantly (do not boil). Remove from heat; cover and chill thoroughly.

Fill Cream Puff Shells with chilled custard; replace tops. Serve immediately or cover and refrigerate. Yield: 6 servings (183 calories per serving).

PROTEIN 7.8 / FAT 7.9 / CARBOHYDRATE 19.3 / CHOLESTEROL 184 / IRON 1.0 / SODIUM 224 / CALCIUM 106

Cappuccino Cream Puffs

6 Cream Puff Shells (page 179)
½ cup water
⅓ cup instant nonfat dry milk
    powder
1 tablespoon cornstarch
1½ teaspoons instant espresso
    powder
1 teaspoon unflavored gelatin
1 tablespoon Kahlúa or other
    coffee-flavored liqueur
1 teaspoon vanilla extract
1 egg white
3 tablespoons sugar
1½ teaspoons powdered sugar

Prepare Cream Puff Shells; set aside.

Combine water, milk powder, cornstarch, espresso powder, and gelatin in a medium saucepan; stir well. Let stand 5 minutes. Cook over medium heat, stirring constantly with a wire whisk, until mixture thickens and gelatin dissolves. Remove from heat; stir in liqueur and vanilla. Cool 20 minutes.

Beat egg white (at room temperature) at high speed of an electric mixer until soft peaks form. Gradually add sugar, 1 tablespoon at a time, beating until stiff peaks form and sugar dissolves. Gently fold egg white into gelatin mixture. Fill Cream Puff Shells with pudding; replace tops. Sprinkle with powdered sugar. Serve immediately or cover and refrigerate. Yield: 6 servings (175 calories per serving).

PROTEIN 6.7 / FAT 6.1 / CARBOHYDRATE 21.4 / CHOLESTEROL 93 / IRON 0.7 / SODIUM 162 / CALCIUM 98

Chocolate Cream Puffs

6 Cream Puff Shells (page 179)
¼ cup sugar
3 tablespoons Dutch process cocoa
1 tablespoon plus 1½ teaspoons
    cornstarch
1⅓ cups skim milk
1 egg, beaten
½ teaspoon vanilla extract
¼ teaspoon chocolate extract

Prepare Cream Puff Shells; set aside.

Combine sugar, cocoa, and cornstarch in a medium saucepan; stir in milk. Cook over medium heat, stirring constantly, until mixture comes to a boil. Cook 1 minute, stirring constantly.

Gradually stir about one-fourth of hot mixture into egg; add to remaining hot mixture, stirring constantly. Cook 1 minute over medium heat, stirring constantly, until mixture is smooth and thickened. Remove from heat; stir in vanilla and chocolate flavorings. Cover and chill thoroughly.

Fill Cream Puff Shells evenly with chilled pudding; replace tops. Serve immediately or cover and refrigerate. Yield: 6 servings (185 calories per serving).

PROTEIN 6.6 / FAT 7.7 / CARBOHYDRATE 23.0 / CHOLESTEROL 138 / IRON 1.2 / SODIUM 176 / CALCIUM 88

With each bite of Cappuccino Cream Puffs, you'll enjoy the delicate pastry and creamy filling.

Puddings, Mousses, & Soufflés

Here is a variety of rich-tasting treats that belie their simple origins. As alternatives to traditional custards and puddings made with whole milk and egg yolks, these desserts have been created with the use of instant nonfat dry milk powder.

Mousses and baked or chilled soufflés achieve their light and airy volume from beaten egg whites and whipped instant nonfat dry milk powder. Unflavored gelatin is added for stability. Techniques are on page 10.

Presentation is important—serve puddings in stemmed glasses, compote dishes or demi-tasse cups. Custards can be baked in rame-kins, pretty baking dishes, or custard cups. Chilled mousses and soufflés are attractive in any of the above dishes, but look spectacular prepared in festive molds or soufflé dishes.

Two elegant light desserts include (from left) Cold Lemon Soufflé (page 212) and Raspberry-Yogurt Mousse (page 204).

Raisin Bread Pudding

6 slices raisin bread, cubed
2 cups skim milk
2 eggs, lightly beaten
¼ cup firmly packed brown sugar
1 teaspoon ground cinnamon
1 tablespoon vanilla extract
Vegetable cooking spray
4 egg whites
¼ teaspoon cream of tartar
⅓ cup sugar

*P*lace bread in a large bowl. Pour milk over bread; cover and let stand 15 minutes.

Combine beaten eggs, brown sugar, cinnamon, and vanilla; stir well with a wire whisk. Pour egg mixture over bread mixture, stirring gently. Spoon mixture into an 8-inch square baking dish that has been coated with cooking spray. Place baking dish in a larger shallow pan; pour hot water into pan to a depth of 1 inch. Bake at 350° for 35 minutes or until a knife inserted in center comes out clean.

Beat egg whites (at room temperature) and cream of tartar at high speed of an electric mixer until foamy. Gradually add sugar, 1 tablespoon at a time, beating until stiff peaks form. Spread meringue over hot pudding, covering entire surface and sealing edges. Bake at 350° for 10 to 12 minutes or until golden brown. Serve immediately. Yield: 9 servings (145 calories per serving).

PROTEIN 5.8 / FAT 1.8 / CARBOHYDRATE 25.8 / CHOLESTEROL 62 / IRON 0.8 / SODIUM 134 / CALCIUM 95

Whole Wheat Bread Pudding

2 slices whole wheat bread, cubed
Vegetable cooking spray
⅓ cup instant nonfat dry milk
  powder
⅔ cup hot water
¼ cup raisins
⅔ cup instant nonfat dry milk
  powder
½ cup sugar
1¼ cups hot water
4 egg whites, lightly beaten
1 egg
1 teaspoon vanilla extract
½ teaspoon ground cinnamon

*P*lace bread cubes in an 8-inch square baking dish that has been coated with cooking spray. Sprinkle ⅓ cup milk powder over bread. Pour ⅔ cup hot water over milk powder. Sprinkle with raisins.

Combine ⅔ cup milk powder and next 5 ingredients in a medium bowl. Beat at low speed of an electric mixer just until blended. Pour over raisins. Sprinkle with cinnamon. Place dish in a larger shallow pan. Pour hot water into pan to a depth of 1 inch. Bake at 350° for 50 minutes or until a knife inserted in center comes out clean. Remove dish from water. Serve pudding warm or chilled. Yield: 8 servings (161 calories per serving).

PROTEIN 9.0 / FAT 1.2 / CARBOHYDRATE 29.2 / CHOLESTEROL 38 / IRON 0.5 / SODIUM 161 / CALCIUM 207

Baked Light Custard

4 *eggs, lightly beaten*
½ *cup sugar*
¼ *teaspoon salt*
3 *cups skim milk*
2 *tablespoons instant nonfat dry*
  milk powder
1½ *teaspoons vanilla extract*

Combine eggs, sugar, and salt in a large bowl; stir well. Add skim milk, milk powder, and vanilla, stirring well. Pour mixture into six 6-ounce custard cups. Place custard cups in a 13- x 9- x 2-inch baking dish; pour hot water into baking dish to a depth of 1 inch. Bake at 350° for 40 minutes or until a knife inserted halfway between center and edge of custard comes out clean. Remove cups from water; cool to room temperature. Chill thoroughly. Yield: 6 servings (173 calories per serving).

PROTEIN 9.2 / FAT 3.9 / CARBOHYDRATE 24.6 / CHOLESTEROL 186 / IRON 0.8 / SODIUM 221 / CALCIUM 201

Caramel Custards

4 *eggs, lightly beaten*
⅓ *cup sugar*
2 *cups skim milk*
3 *tablespoons instant nonfat dry*
  milk powder
1½ *teaspoons vanilla extract*
Vegetable cooking spray
2 *tablespoons sugar*

Combine first 5 ingredients in a large bowl; stir well. Set mixture aside.

Coat six 6-ounce custard cups with cooking spray. Place sugar in a heavy saucepan. Cook over medium heat, shaking pan occasionally, until sugar melts and turns golden brown. Remove from heat. Pour hot caramelized mixture evenly into custard cups. Let cool. Pour custard mixture evenly into custard cups. Place custard cups in a 12- x 8- x 2-inch baking dish; pour hot water into dish to a depth of 1 inch. Bake at 350° for 35 minutes or until a knife inserted in center comes out clean. Remove cups from water, and cool. To serve, loosen edges of custards with a knife; invert onto individual dessert plates. Yield: 6 servings (159 calories per serving).

PROTEIN 8.2 / FAT 4.1 / CARBOHYDRATE 21.9 / CHOLESTEROL 185 / IRON 0.7 / SODIUM 109 / CALCIUM 166

Custards are mixtures of milk and egg, baked or cooked just until the mixture is set. If a custard is over-cooked, the egg will become rubbery and will water, resulting in a tough texture.

Chocolate-Orange Custard

½ cup instant nonfat dry milk
   powder
¼ cup sugar
¼ cup unsweetened cocoa
2 tablespoons cornstarch
⅛ teaspoon salt
1½ cups water
2 eggs, beaten
1 teaspoon grated orange rind
¼ cup unsweetened orange juice

Combine first 5 ingredients in a medium saucepan; stir well. Add water, and cook over medium-low heat, stirring constantly, until mixture coats a metal spoon.

Gradually stir about one-fourth of hot mixture into eggs; add to remaining hot mixture, stirring constantly. Cook, stirring constantly, 1 minute. Stir in orange rind and juice. Pour into 4 individual dessert dishes. Chill until firm. Yield: 4 servings (187 calories per ½-cup serving).

PROTEIN 10.2 / FAT 3.6 / CARBOHYDRATE 28.5 / CHOLESTEROL 140 / IRON 1.5 / SODIUM 189 / CALCIUM 214

Grand Marnier Custard

1 cup instant nonfat dry milk
   powder
¼ cup sugar
2 tablespoons cornstarch
⅛ teaspoon salt
2 cups cold water
2 eggs, lightly beaten
2 tablespoons Grand Marnier
   liqueur
Orange rind strips (optional)

Combine first 4 ingredients in a medium saucepan, stirring well. Gradually add water, stirring until smooth. Bring to a boil over medium heat, stirring constantly; boil 1 minute.

Gradually stir about one-fourth of hot milk mixture into eggs; add to remaining hot mixture in saucepan. Add liqueur, and cook over low heat, stirring constantly, 1 to 2 minutes. Spoon into 8 individual dessert dishes. Garnish with orange rind strips, if desired. Yield: 8 servings (109 calories per ⅓-cup serving).

PROTEIN 7.0 / FAT 1.5 / CARBOHYDRATE 17.0 / CHOLESTEROL 72 / IRON 0.3 / SODIUM 134 / CALCIUM 196

Maple-Peach Custard

2 eggs
2 egg whites
1 cup skim milk
¼ cup maple syrup
1 teaspoon vanilla extract
2 medium-size ripe peaches,
   peeled and sliced (about ½
   pound)
⅛ teaspoon grated nutmeg

Combine eggs, egg whites, milk, syrup, and vanilla in a large bowl. Beat at medium speed of an electric mixer until mixture is smooth.

Place peaches in four 6-ounce custard cups. Pour egg mixture over peaches, dividing evenly. Sprinkle grated nutmeg over top of egg mixture.

Set custard cups in a 13- x 9- x 2-inch baking pan; pour hot water into pan to a depth of 1 inch. Bake at 350° for 40 to 45 minutes or until a knife inserted in center comes out clean.

Remove custard cups from water. Chill at least 3 hours. Yield: 4 servings (144 calories per serving).

PROTEIN 7.2 / FAT 3.0 / CARBOHYDRATE 22.2 / CHOLESTEROL 138 / IRON 0.8 / SODIUM 93 / CALCIUM 114

Pumpkin Custards

1 (16-ounce) can pumpkin
1 (12-ounce) can evaporated
  skimmed milk
⅔ cup sugar
2 eggs, lightly beaten
1 teaspoon ground cinnamon
½ teaspoon ground ginger
¼ teaspoon salt
¼ teaspoon ground cloves

Combine all ingredients in a medium bowl; stir well. Spoon mixture into eight 6-ounce custard cups. Bake at 350° for 45 to 50 minutes or until a knife inserted in center comes out clean. Serve warm or cold. Yield: 8 servings (138 calories per serving).

PROTEIN 5.4 / FAT 1.7 / CARBOHYDRATE 26.5 / CHOLESTEROL 70 / IRON 1.3 / SODIUM 143 / CALCIUM 150

Rice Custard

1 cup water
½ cup uncooked brown rice
¼ teaspoon salt
⅔ cup instant nonfat dry milk
  powder
½ cup sugar
1½ cups water
1 egg
4 egg whites
1 teaspoon vanilla extract
¼ cup raisins
Vegetable cooking spray
⅛ teaspoon grated nutmeg

Bring 1 cup water to a boil in a medium saucepan. Add rice and salt; cover, reduce heat, and simmer 45 to 50 minutes or until liquid is absorbed. Remove from heat; let stand 5 minutes.

Combine milk powder, sugar, water, egg, egg whites, and vanilla in a large bowl; beat with a wire whisk. Stir in rice and raisins.

Pour mixture into a 10- x 6- x 2-inch baking dish that has been coated with cooking spray. Sprinkle with nutmeg. Place dish in a larger shallow pan. Pour hot water into pan to a depth of 1 inch. Bake, uncovered, at 350° for 45 to 50 minutes or until set. Serve warm or at room temperature. Yield: 8 servings (163 calories per serving).

PROTEIN 7.1 / FAT 1.1 / CARBOHYDRATE 31.3 / CHOLESTEROL 36 / IRON 0.5 / SODIUM 162 / CALCIUM 138

Cranberry Whipped Pudding

2 cups reduced-calorie cranberry
    juice cocktail
¼ cup sugar
¼ cup regular cream of wheat,
    uncooked
Edible flowers (optional)

Combine first 3 ingredients in a medium saucepan; stir well. Bring mixture to a boil over medium heat; reduce heat and cook 8 to 10 minutes or until thickened, stirring constantly. Remove from heat, and let cool 15 minutes. Transfer mixture to a medium bowl; beat at medium speed of an electric mixer until mixture is light and fluffy. Spoon into 8 individual dessert dishes. Cover and chill thoroughly. Garnish with edible flowers, if desired. Yield: 8 servings (55 calories per ½-cup serving).

PROTEIN 0.6 / FAT 0.0 / CARBOHYDRATE 13.2 / CHOLESTEROL 0 / IRON 1.6 / SODIUM 2 / CALCIUM 5

Floating Islands

1 egg white
⅛ teaspoon cream of tartar
¼ cup sugar
2 cups skim milk, divided
¼ cup sugar
¼ teaspoon salt
1 tablespoon cornstarch
2 eggs, lightly beaten
½ teaspoon vanilla extract

Beat egg white (at room temperature) and cream of tartar in a large bowl at high speed of an electric mixer until soft peaks form. Gradually add ¼ cup sugar, 1 tablespoon at a time, beating until stiff peaks form.

Heat 1½ cups milk, ¼ cup sugar, and salt in a medium saucepan to simmering. Drop egg white islands in 4 equal portions, using about ¼ cup for each, into simmering milk mixture. Cook islands 6 to 8 minutes or until slightly firm. Remove from heat. Remove islands with a slotted spoon, and drain on paper towels. Refrigerate until ready to serve.

Combine cornstarch and remaining ½ cup skim milk, stirring until smooth. Add cornstarch mixture to hot milk mixture, stirring with a wire whisk until smooth. Cook over medium-low heat, stirring constantly, until mixture comes to a boil. Remove from heat. Gradually stir about one-fourth of hot mixture into eggs; add to remaining hot mixture. Cook over low heat, stirring constantly, 1 minute or until mixture thickens. Remove from heat. Let cool slightly, and stir in vanilla. Spoon mixture evenly into 4 individual dessert dishes, and top each with an island. Serve warm or chilled. Yield: 4 servings (192 calories per serving).

PROTEIN 8.1 / FAT 3.0 / CARBOHYDRATE 33.2 / CHOLESTEROL 139 / IRON 0.6 / SODIUM 264 / CALCIUM 167

Serve Floating Islands (front) and Cranberry Whipped Pudding in stemmed dishes for desserts that both family and friends will find appealing.

Dutch Chocolate Pudding

⅓ cup sugar
¼ cup Dutch process cocoa
2 tablespoons cornstarch
1¾ cups skim milk
1 egg, beaten
½ teaspoon vanilla extract
½ teaspoon chocolate extract

Combine first 3 ingredients in a medium saucepan; stir in skim milk. Cook over medium heat, stirring constantly, until mixture comes to a boil. Cook 1 minute, stirring constantly.

Gradually stir about one-fourth of hot mixture into egg; add to remaining hot mixture, stirring constantly. Cook 1 minute over medium heat, stirring constantly, until mixture is smooth and thickened. Remove from heat; stir in vanilla and chocolate flavorings. Pour into 6 individual dessert dishes. Cover and chill thoroughly. Yield: 6 servings (103 calories per ⅓-cup serving).

PROTEIN 4.1 / FAT 1.9 / CARBOHYDRATE 18.7 / CHOLESTEROL 47 / IRON 0.6 / SODIUM 74 / CALCIUM 97

Jamocha-Nut Pudding

⅓ cup sugar
3 tablespoons cornstarch
3 tablespoons unsweetened cocoa
1 teaspoon espresso powder
2¾ cups skim milk
1 egg, lightly beaten
½ teaspoon vanilla extract
½ teaspoon chocolate extract
2 tablespoons finely chopped
  pecans, toasted

Combine first 4 ingredients in a nonaluminum saucepan. Add milk and stir until blended. Cook over medium-low heat, stirring constantly with a wire whisk, 10 minutes or until mixture comes to a boil. Cook an additional minute; remove from heat.

Gradually stir about one-fourth of hot mixture into egg; add to remaining hot mixture. Cook over low heat, stirring constantly, 2 to 3 minutes or until mixture thickens (do not boil). Remove from heat; stir in vanilla and chocolate flavorings. Spoon into 6 individual dessert dishes; sprinkle with pecans. Yield: 6 servings (132 calories per ½-cup serving).

PROTEIN 5.8 / FAT 2.3 / CARBOHYDRATE 21.8 / CHOLESTEROL 48 / IRON 0.7 / SODIUM 70 / CALCIUM 148

Maple Pudding

⅓ cup firmly packed brown sugar
2 tablespoons cornstarch
2 cups skim milk
1 egg, beaten
1 teaspoon imitation maple
  flavoring
1 teaspoon margarine

Combine sugar and cornstarch in a medium saucepan; stir in milk. Cook over medium heat, stirring constantly, until mixture comes to a boil. Cook an additional minute, stirring constantly. Remove from heat.

Gradually stir about one-fourth of hot mixture into egg; add to remaining hot mixture, stirring constantly. Cook over low heat, stirring constantly, 2 to 3 minutes or until thickened (do not

Maple Pudding
(CONTINUED)

boil). Remove from heat; stir in maple flavoring and margarine. Pour mixture into four 6-ounce custard cups. Cover with plastic wrap, gently pressing directly on pudding. Chill. Yield: 4 servings (156 calories per ½-cup serving).

PROTEIN 5.7 / FAT 2.6 / CARBOHYDRATE 27.3 / CHOLESTEROL 71 / IRON 0.9 / SODIUM 98 / CALCIUM 174

Rocky Road Pudding

⅓ *cup sugar*
3 *tablespoons quick-cooking tapioca*
2½ *cups skim milk*
1 *egg, beaten*
1 *teaspoon vanilla extract*
½ *cup miniature marshmallows*
¼ *cup chopped walnuts*
2 *tablespoons semisweet chocolate mini-morsels*

Combine sugar and tapioca in a medium saucepan; stir in skim milk. Cook over medium heat, stirring constantly, until mixture comes to a boil. Reduce heat and cook 1 minute, stirring constantly.

Gradually stir about one-fourth of hot mixture into egg; add to remaining hot mixture, stirring constantly. Cook over low heat, stirring constantly, 1 minute or until mixture is smooth and thickened (do not boil). Remove from heat; stir in vanilla. Let mixture cool; stir in marshmallows and remaining ingredients. Pour mixture into 6 individual dessert dishes. Cover and chill thoroughly. Yield: 6 servings (173 calories per ½-cup serving).

PROTEIN 5.9 / FAT 5.0 / CARBOHYDRATE 26.8 / CHOLESTEROL 48 / IRON 0.5 / SODIUM 67 / CALCIUM 135

New York Vanilla Pudding

¼ *cup sugar*
2 *tablespoons cornstarch*
2 *cups skim milk*
1 *egg, beaten*
2 *teaspoons vanilla extract*
1 *teaspoon margarine*

Combine sugar and cornstarch in a medium saucepan; gradually stir in milk. Cook over medium heat, stirring constantly, until mixture comes to a boil. Cook an additional minute, stirring constantly. Remove from heat.

Gradually stir about one-fourth of hot mixture into egg; add to remaining hot mixture, stirring constantly. Cook over low heat, stirring constantly 2 to 3 minutes or until thickened (do not boil). Remove from heat; stir in vanilla and margarine. Pour mixture into four 6-ounce custard cups. Cover with plastic wrap, gently pressing directly on pudding. Chill. Yield: 4 servings (141 calories per ½-cup serving).

PROTEIN 5.7 / FAT 2.6 / CARBOHYDRATE 22.8 / CHOLESTEROL 71 / IRON 0.3 / SODIUM 92 / CALCIUM 158

Vanilla Tapioca

3 tablespoons quick-cooking
  tapioca
2 tablespoons sugar
2 cups skim milk
1 egg, separated
3 tablespoons sugar
1 teaspoon vanilla extract

Combine first 3 ingredients in a medium saucepan; stir well. Let stand 5 minutes. Cook over medium heat, stirring constantly, until mixture comes to a boil. Cook an additional minute, stirring constantly; remove from heat.

Beat egg yolk until thick and lemon colored. Gradually stir about one-fourth of hot mixture into beaten egg yolk; add to remaining hot mixture, stirring constantly. Cook over medium heat, stirring constantly, 1 minute or until mixture thickens. Remove from heat.

Beat egg white (at room temperature) in a large bowl at high speed of an electric mixer until soft peaks form. Gradually add sugar, 1 tablespoon at a time, beating until stiff peaks form. Gradually add hot mixture to beaten egg white, stirring constantly, just until blended. Stir in vanilla. Cool 20 minutes. Stir again. Serve warm or chilled. Yield: 6 servings (101 calories per ½-cup serving).

PROTEIN 3.8 / FAT 1.1 / CARBOHYDRATE 18.8 / CHOLESTEROL 47 / IRON 0.2 / SODIUM 54 / CALCIUM 106

Orange Chiffon

1 envelope unflavored gelatin
¼ cup cold water
1 cup boiling water
¼ cup plus 1 tablespoon sugar,
  divided
1 teaspoon grated orange rind
½ cup unsweetened orange juice
1 tablespoon lemon juice
2 egg whites
Vegetable cooking spray
2 tablespoons Grand Marnier or
  other orange-flavored liqueur
2 tablespoons orange zest

Soften gelatin in cold water. Add boiling water, and stir until gelatin dissolves. Stir in 2 tablespoons sugar and orange rind. Cool. Stir in juices. Chill for 25 minutes or until consistency of unbeaten egg white.

Beat egg whites (at room temperature) at high speed of an electric mixer until soft peaks form. Gradually add remaining 3 tablespoons sugar, 1 tablespoon at a time, beating until stiff peaks form. Fold into chilled gelatin mixture. Spoon mixture into 6 individual dessert molds that have been coated with cooking spray. Cover and chill until set.

To serve, unmold onto serving dishes, and top each with 1 teaspoon liqueur and orange zest. Yield: 6 servings (78 calories per serving).

PROTEIN 2.3 / FAT 0.3 / CARBOHYDRATE 14.8 / CHOLESTEROL 0 / IRON 0.1 / SODIUM 19 / CALCIUM 6

Enjoy the creaminess of Orange Chiffon, a light and luscious dessert.

Banana Coconut Cream

3 tablespoons quick-cooking
  tapioca
¼ cup plus 1 tablespoon sugar,
  divided
2 cups skim milk
1 egg, separated
3 tablespoons light rum
¾ cup diced banana
3 tablespoons grated, unsweetened
  coconut, toasted

*C*ombine tapioca, 2 tablespoons sugar, and skim milk in a medium saucepan. Cook over medium heat, stirring constantly, until mixture comes to a boil.

Beat egg yolk in a small bowl with a wire whisk. Gradually stir about one-fourth of hot mixture into egg; add to remaining hot mixture, stirring constantly. Cook over medium heat, stirring constantly, 1 minute. Stir in rum, and cook an additional minute, stirring constantly.

Beat egg white (at room temperature) in a small bowl at high speed of an electric mixer until soft peaks form. Gradually add remaining 3 tablespoons sugar, 1 tablespoon at a time, beating until stiff peaks form. Gently fold hot mixture into beaten egg white. Cool 20 minutes. Fold in banana. Spoon evenly into 6 individual dessert dishes. Sprinkle with toasted coconut. Yield: 6 servings (135 calories per serving).

PROTEIN 4.2 / FAT 2.7 / CARBOHYDRATE 24.3 / CHOLESTEROL 47 / IRON 0.4 / SODIUM 55 / CALCIUM 108

Caribbean Cream

⅓ cup water
1 medium mango, peeled and
  coarsely chopped
2 tablespoons brown sugar
2 tablespoons honey
2 tablespoons lemon juice
¼ teaspoon ground ginger
⅓ cup instant nonfat dry milk
  powder
2 tablespoons unsweetened flaked
  coconut, toasted
2 tablespoons sliced almonds,
  toasted

*P*lace water in a small, narrow glass or stainless steel bowl; freeze 25 minutes or until a ⅛-inch-thick layer of ice forms on surface.

Combine mango, brown sugar, honey, lemon juice, and ground ginger in container of an electric blender or food processor; top with cover, and process until smooth. Place mixture in a glass or stainless steel bowl; freeze for 10 to 15 minutes.

Add milk powder to partially frozen water; beat at high speed of an electric mixer 5 minutes or until stiff peaks form. Fold into mango mixture. Spoon into 4 stemmed dessert dishes. Top each serving with coconut and almonds. Yield: 4 servings (142 calories per ½-cup serving).

PROTEIN 4.4 / FAT 2.3 / CARBOHYDRATE 28.2 / CHOLESTEROL 2 / IRON 0.4 / SODIUM 57 / CALCIUM 141

Café au Lait Cream

2 tablespoons sugar
1½ teaspoons unflavored gelatin
¾ cup cold water
⅔ cup instant nonfat dry milk
  powder
2 eggs, separated
1 teaspoon instant espresso powder
2 teaspoons Kahlúa or other
  coffee-flavored liqueur
1 egg white
¼ cup sugar
Chocolate curls (optional)

Combine first 3 ingredients in a nonaluminum saucepan. Stir with a wire whisk until blended. Add milk powder, egg yolks, espresso powder, and liqueur; whisk until frothy. Cook over medium-low heat, stirring constantly, 4 minutes or until slightly thickened (mixture should reach 165°). Remove from heat. Chill for 15 minutes or until mixture is the consistency of unbeaten egg white, stirring occasionally.

Beat egg whites (at room temperature) in a large bowl at high speed of an electric mixer until soft peaks form. Add ¼ cup sugar, 1 tablespoon at a time, beating until stiff peaks form. Gently fold egg white mixture into chilled coffee mixture. Spoon into 4 individual dessert dishes. Chill 2 to 3 hours or until set. Garnish with chocolate curls, if desired. Yield: 4 servings (193 calories per ½-cup serving).

PROTEIN 12.1 / FAT 2.9 / CARBOHYDRATE 29.6 / CHOLESTEROL 141 / IRON 0.6 / SODIUM 156 / CALCIUM 267

Scandinavian Vanilla Cream

⅔ cup instant nonfat dry milk
  powder
1¼ cups water
⅓ cup sugar
1 envelope unflavored gelatin
½ cup low-fat sour cream
1 teaspoon vanilla extract
Vegetable cooking spray
¼ cup plus 2 tablespoons
Raspberry Chambord Sauce
  (page 226)

Combine first 4 ingredients in a small saucepan. Let stand 1 minute. Cook over medium heat until sugar and gelatin dissolve. Remove from heat; let cool 15 minutes.

Add gelatin mixture to sour cream in a medium bowl, stirring until smooth. Stir in vanilla. Pour into 6 individual dessert molds that have been coated with cooking spray. Chill at least 4 hours or until firm.

Unmold onto individual serving plates. Top each serving with 1 tablespoon Raspberry Chambord Sauce. Yield: 6 servings (140 calories per ⅓-cup serving).

PROTEIN 6.6 / FAT 3.1 / CARBOHYDRATE 21.2 / CHOLESTEROL 10 / IRON 0.1 / SODIUM 83 / CALCIUM 191

Coconut Blancmange With Dark Cocoa Sauce

1 teaspoon unflavored gelatin
2 cups skim milk
⅓ cup sifted powdered sugar
3 tablespoons cornstarch
½ teaspoon coconut extract
⅛ teaspoon almond extract
Vegetable cooking spray
Dark Cocoa Sauce
Edible flowers (optional)

Sprinkle gelatin over milk in a small saucepan; let stand 1 minute. Cook over low heat, stirring constantly, until gelatin dissolves.

Combine powdered sugar and cornstarch in a small bowl; stir well. Add to milk mixture, stirring until smooth. Cook over medium-low heat, stirring constantly, until mixture comes to a boil and thickens. Remove from heat; stir in coconut and almond flavorings. Pour into four 6-ounce custard cups that have been coated with cooking spray. Cover; chill 2 hours or until firm.

Unmold onto individual dessert plates. Spoon Dark Cocoa Sauce evenly over desserts. Garnish with edible flowers, if desired. Yield: 4 servings (187 calories per serving).

Dark Cocoa Sauce

¼ cup sugar
1 tablespoon light corn syrup
¼ cup plus 1 tablespoon water
3 tablespoons Dutch process cocoa
½ teaspoon vanilla extract
½ teaspoon chocolate extract

Combine sugar, corn syrup, and water in a small saucepan. Cook over medium heat until mixture comes to a boil, stirring constantly. Boil 1 minute; remove from heat, and add cocoa, stirring until smooth. Stir in vanilla and chocolate flavorings. Cover and chill 30 minutes. Yield: ⅓ cup.

PROTEIN 5.5 / FAT 1.4 / CARBOHYDRATE 39.3 / CHOLESTEROL 2 / IRON 0.5 / SODIUM 100 / CALCIUM 156

Lemon Blancmange

1 teaspoon unflavored gelatin
¼ cup lemon juice
⅓ cup sugar
3 tablespoons cornstarch
⅛ teaspoon salt
1¾ cups skim milk
1 teaspoon grated lemon rind

Sprinkle gelatin over lemon juice in a small bowl; let stand 1 minute. Combine sugar, cornstarch, and salt in a medium saucepan; stir in skim milk. Cook over medium heat, stirring constantly, until mixture comes to a boil; cook an additional minute, stirring constantly. Remove from heat. Add gelatin mixture and lemon rind, stirring until gelatin dissolves. Pour mixture into 4 individual dessert dishes. Cover and chill thoroughly. Yield: 4 servings (130 calories per serving).

PROTEIN 4.4 / FAT 0.2 / CARBOHYDRATE 28.4 / CHOLESTEROL 2 / IRON 0.1 / SODIUM 130 / CALCIUM 134

A rich-tasting chocolate sauce accompanies Coconut Blancmange for a simple but luscious finale to a meal.

Charlotte Russe

1 tablespoon unflavored gelatin
2 tablespoons sugar
1 cup skim milk
1 teaspoon almond extract
1/3 cup water
1/3 cup instant nonfat dry milk
  powder
2 egg whites
1/4 cup sugar
Vegetable cooking spray
8 vanilla wafers
Fresh raspberries (optional)

Combine gelatin, 2 tablespoons sugar, and skim milk in a small saucepan. Let stand 1 minute. Cook over medium heat, stirring constantly, until gelatin dissolves. Stir in almond extract. Chill until consistency of unbeaten egg white.

Place 1/3 cup water in a small, narrow glass or stainless steel bowl; freeze 25 minutes or until a 1/8-inch-thick layer of ice forms on surface.

Add milk powder to partially frozen water; beat at high speed of an electric mixer 5 minutes or until stiff peaks form.

Beat egg whites (at room temperature) at high speed of an electric mixer until foamy. Gradually add 1/4 cup sugar, 1 tablespoon at a time, beating until stiff peaks form. Gently fold whipped milk mixture and egg white mixture into chilled gelatin mixture.

Coat sides of an 8-inch springform pan with cooking spray. Place vanilla wafers evenly around side of pan with rounded side of wafers toward outside of pan. Spoon mixture into pan. Chill 3 to 4 hours or until firm. Remove sides of springform pan before serving. Garnish with fresh raspberries, if desired. Yield: 8 servings (94 calories per serving).

PROTEIN 4.8 / FAT 1.0 / CARBOHYDRATE 16.0 / CHOLESTEROL 2 / IRON 0.1 / SODIUM 73 / CALCIUM 103

Brandy Alexander Mousse

1/3 cup water
1 envelope unflavored gelatin
3/4 cup cold water
1/4 cup sugar
Dash of salt
2 egg yolks, beaten
2 tablespoons brandy
2 tablespoons crème de cacao
1/3 cup instant nonfat dry milk
  powder
3 egg whites
1/4 cup sugar

Place 1/3 cup water in a small, narrow glass or stainless steel bowl; freeze 25 minutes or until a 1/8-inch-thick layer of ice forms on surface.

Sprinkle gelatin over 3/4 cup cold water in a medium-size nonaluminum saucepan. Let stand 1 minute. Stir in 1/4 cup sugar and salt. Cook over medium-low heat, stirring constantly, until gelatin and sugar dissolve. Gradually stir about one-fourth of hot mixture into egg yolks. Add to remaining hot mixture, stirring constantly. Cook over medium-low heat 2 minutes, stirring constantly. Remove from heat; stir in brandy and crème de cacao. Place saucepan in refrigerator, and chill mixture 15 to 20 minutes or until slightly thickened, stirring with a whisk after 10 minutes.

Brandy Alexander Mousse
(CONTINUED)

Add milk powder to partially frozen water during last 5 minutes of chilling; beat at high speed of an electric mixer 5 minutes or until stiff peaks form. Gently fold chilled gelatin mixture into whipped milk mixture.

Beat egg whites (at room temperature) in a large bowl at high speed of an electric mixer until soft peaks form. Gradually add ¼ cup sugar, 1 tablespoon at a time, beating until stiff peaks form. Gently fold whipped milk mixture into beaten egg whites. Pour mixture into a 1½-quart soufflé dish or 12 individual dessert dishes, and chill until firm. Yield: 12 servings (75 calories per serving).

PROTEIN 3.0 / FAT 1.0 / CARBOHYDRATE 11.1 / CHOLESTEROL 46 / IRON 0.2 / SODIUM 45 / CALCIUM 47

Frosty Lemon Mousse Squares
(pictured on pages 210 and 211)

¾ cup quick-cooking pan-toasted oats, uncooked
2 tablespoons wheat germ
1 tablespoon brown sugar
3 tablespoons reduced-calorie margarine, melted
⅓ cup water
3 eggs, separated
½ cup sugar, divided
2 teaspoons grated lemon rind
3 tablespoons lemon juice
⅛ teaspoon salt
⅛ teaspoon cream of tartar
⅓ cup instant nonfat dry milk powder
Lemon rind bow (optional)

Combine oats, wheat germ, brown sugar, and margarine; place in a 15- x 10- x 2-inch jellyroll pan, and bake at 350° for 15 minutes, stirring occasionally. Reserve 2 tablespoons of mixture, and press remaining mixture into an 8-inch square baking pan. Freeze 15 minutes.

Place water in a small, narrow glass or stainless steel bowl; freeze 25 minutes or until a ⅛-inch-thick layer of ice forms on surface.

Beat egg yolks until thick and lemon colored. Gradually add ¼ cup sugar, lemon rind, and lemon juice, beating until well blended. Set aside.

Beat egg whites (at room temperature) at high speed of an electric mixer until foamy. Add salt and cream of tartar; beat until soft peaks form. Gradually add remaining ¼ cup sugar, 1 tablespoon at a time, beating until stiff peaks form. Fold into egg yolk mixture.

Add milk powder to partially frozen water; beat at high speed of an electric mixer 5 minutes or until stiff peaks form. Fold into egg yolk mixture. Pour mixture into prepared pan, and freeze until firm.

Sprinkle with reserved 2 tablespoons oat mixture; cut into squares and serve immediately. Garnish with lemon rind bow, if desired. Yield: 9 servings (174 calories per serving).

PROTEIN 6.3 / FAT 5.6 / CARBOHYDRATE 25.9 / CHOLESTEROL 92 / IRON 1.2 / SODIUM 120 / CALCIUM 76

Cranberry Mousse

3 cups fresh cranberries
1⅓ cups water, divided
2 envelopes unflavored gelatin
¼ cup cold water
4 egg whites
1 cup sugar
⅓ cup instant nonfat dry milk
  powder
Vegetable cooking spray
Fresh cranberries (optional)
Fresh mint sprigs (optional)

Combine cranberries and 1 cup water in a medium saucepan; bring to a boil, reduce heat, and simmer 6 to 8 minutes or until skins pop. Drain fruit, reserving juice; set fruit aside. Return juice to saucepan and boil until reduced to ½ cup.

Place ⅓ cup water in a small, narrow glass or stainless steel bowl; freeze 25 minutes or until a ⅛-inch-thick layer of ice forms on surface.

Place reserved berries in container of an electric blender. Top with cover, and blend until smooth. Strain and discard skins and seeds. Set puree aside.

Sprinkle gelatin over ¼ cup cold water. Let stand 1 minute. Add to hot juice in saucepan, stirring until gelatin dissolves. Add to puree.

Beat egg whites (at room temperature) in a large glass or stainless steel bowl at high speed of an electric mixer 1 minute. Gradually add 1 cup sugar, 1 tablespoon at a time, beating until stiff peaks form and sugar dissolves (2 to 4 minutes). Set aside.

Add milk powder to partially frozen water; beat at high speed of an electric mixer 5 minutes or until stiff peaks form. Fold milk mixture and egg white mixture into cooled cranberry mixture. Pour into an 8-cup mold that has been coated with cooking spray. Cover and chill 4 hours or until firm. If desired, garnish with cranberries and mint sprigs. Yield: 12 servings (97 calories per serving).

PROTEIN 3.4 / FAT 0.1 / CARBOHYDRATE 21.3 / CHOLESTEROL 1 / IRON 0.1 / SODIUM 36 / CALCIUM 45

Mousses and Bavarians are thickened fruit purees or custards to which gelatin has been added for stability. Whipped instant nonfat dry milk powder has replaced whipping cream to create a light and healthy low-fat dessert.

Garnish Cranberry Mousse with fresh berries and mint sprigs for a colorful, refreshing dessert.

Frozen Peach and Banana Mousse

1 large peach, peeled and sliced
½ cup unsweetened orange juice
1 medium banana, peeled and
  sliced
1 egg white
¼ teaspoon lemon juice
1 tablespoon crème de cassis

*P*osition knife blade in food processor bowl; add peach slices, orange juice, and banana. Top with cover, and process until smooth. Pour mixture into an 8-inch square baking pan; freeze until firm, at least 8 hours.

Let stand at room temperature 15 minutes to soften. Position knife blade in processor bowl; add softened frozen fruit mixture, egg white, lemon juice, and crème de cassis. Top with cover, and process 2 to 3 minutes until fluffy. Spoon mixture into baking pan; freeze until firm.

Remove from freezer; let stand at room temperature 5 minutes. Scoop into individual dessert dishes to serve. Yield: 6 servings (44 calories per ½-cup serving).

PROTEIN 1.1 / FAT 0.1 / CARBOHYDRATE 9.9 / CHOLESTEROL 0 / IRON 0.1 / SODIUM 9 / CALCIUM 5

Peach Mousse

¼ cup unsweetened orange juice
1 envelope unflavored gelatin
½ cup cold water
¼ cup sugar
1 cup sliced fresh peaches
1 (8-ounce) carton peach low-fat
  yogurt
2 egg whites
2 tablespoons sugar
¼ cup instant nonfat dry milk
  powder
Peach slices (optional)
Fresh mint sprigs (optional)

*P*lace orange juice in a small, narrow glass or stainless steel bowl; stir well. Freeze 25 minutes or until a ⅛-inch-thick layer of ice forms on surface.

Sprinkle gelatin over cold water in a small saucepan; let stand 1 minute. Add ¼ cup sugar; cook over medium heat, stirring constantly, until mixture comes to a boil and gelatin and sugar dissolve. Remove from heat; cool.

Place 1 cup sliced peaches in container of an electric blender; top with cover, and process until smooth. Gradually add gelatin mixture and yogurt; process until smooth. Chill 20 to 30 minutes or until mixture mounds from a spoon.

Beat egg whites (at room temperature) at high speed of an electric mixer until soft peaks form. Gradually add 2 tablespoons sugar, 1 tablespoon at a time, beating until stiff peaks form. Gently fold egg whites into peach mixture.

Add milk powder to partially frozen orange juice. Beat at high speed of an electric mixer 5 minutes or until stiff peaks form. Fold into peach mixture. Spoon mixture into a 6-cup mold; chill until firm. Unmold and, if desired, garnish with peach slices and fresh mint sprigs. Yield: 8 servings (102 calories per serving).

PROTEIN 4.5 / FAT 0.4 / CARBOHYDRATE 20.9 / CHOLESTEROL 2 / IRON 0.2 / SODIUM 51 / CALCIUM 93

Holiday Pumpkin Mousse Cups

3 eggs, separated
1/3 cup sugar
1/2 cup skim milk
1 envelope unflavored gelatin
1 tablespoon all-purpose flour
1 1/2 teaspoons grated orange rind
1/2 cup unsweetened orange juice
1 cup canned pumpkin
1/2 teaspoon ground allspice
1/3 cup water
1 tablespoon sugar
1/3 cup instant nonfat dry milk
powder

Combine egg yolks and next 5 ingredients in a large, heavy saucepan, stirring well. Cook over medium heat, stirring constantly, until mixture comes to a boil. Remove from heat; stir in orange juice, pumpkin, and allspice. Cover and chill 25 minutes or until syrupy.

Place 1/3 cup water in a small, narrow glass or stainless steel bowl; freeze 25 minutes or until a 1/8-inch-thick layer of ice forms on surface.

Beat egg whites (at room temperature) at high speed of an electric mixer until soft peaks form; add 1 tablespoon sugar, beating until stiff peaks form.

Add milk powder to partially frozen water; beat at high speed of an electric mixer 5 minutes or until stiff peaks form.

Fold egg whites and whipped milk mixture into pumpkin mixture. Spoon into 10 individual dessert dishes; chill until firm. Yield: 10 servings (93 calories per serving).

PROTEIN 4.8 / FAT 1.8 / CARBOHYDRATE 14.8 / CHOLESTEROL 83 / IRON 0.7 / SODIUM 51 / CALCIUM 83

Raspberry Mousse Parfaits

2 cups frozen raspberries, thawed
1 tablespoon cornstarch
1 tablespoon Chambord or other
raspberry-flavored liqueur
2 egg whites
1/4 teaspoon cream of tartar
1/4 cup sugar

Place raspberries in a saucepan. Bring to a boil over medium heat, stirring constantly. Cook 1 minute or until very soft. Remove from heat. Strain, reserving all pulp and juice to yield 1 cup; discard seeds. Return strained raspberry puree to saucepan. Combine cornstarch and liqueur, stirring well. Add to raspberry puree. Cook over medium heat until mixture comes to a boil and thickens, stirring constantly. Remove from heat. Let cool to room temperature.

Beat egg whites (at room temperature) and cream of tartar at high speed of an electric mixer until soft peaks form. Gradually add sugar, 1 tablespoon at a time, beating until stiff peaks form. Gently fold cooled raspberry mixture into egg white mixture. Spoon into 6 parfait glasses; chill thoroughly. Yield: 6 servings (70 calories per 1/2-cup serving).

PROTEIN 1 6 / FAT 0.7 / CARBOHYDRATE 15.6 / CHOLESTEROL 0 / IRON 0.3 / SODIUM 28 / CALCIUM 12

Raspberry-Yogurt Mousse

(pictured on pages 182 and 183)

2 cups frozen raspberries, thawed
2 (8-ounce) cartons
  raspberry-flavored low-fat
  yogurt
3 egg whites
¼ teaspoon cream of tartar
1 cup fresh raspberries

*P*lace 2 cups raspberries in container of an electric blender; top with cover, and process until smooth. Press puree through a sieve to remove seeds. Discard seeds. Add yogurt to puree in a large bowl, mixing well with a wire whisk.

Beat egg whites (at room temperature) in a large bowl at high speed of an electric mixer until soft peaks form. Add cream of tartar, beating until stiff peaks form. Fold into raspberry mixture. Spoon into 12 individual dessert dishes. Chill until firm. Arrange fresh raspberries evenly on desserts. Yield: 12 servings (58 calories per serving).

PROTEIN 2.6 / FAT 0.5 / CARBOHYDRATE 14.3 / CHOLESTEROL 2 / IRON 0.2 / SODIUM 37 / CALCIUM 59

Frosty Strawberry Mousse Squares

¾ cup quick-cooking oats,
  uncooked
2 tablespoons wheat germ
1 tablespoon brown sugar
3 tablespoons margarine, melted
⅓ cup water
1 pint fresh strawberries, hulled
¾ cup sugar
2 egg whites
2 tablespoons lemon juice
⅓ cup instant nonfat dry milk
  powder

*C*ombine first 4 ingredients; stir well. Spread mixture evenly on a baking sheet. Bake at 350° for 15 minutes or until toasted, stirring occasionally. Sprinkle two-thirds of crumb mixture evenly into a 13- x 9- x 2-inch baking pan; set pan and remaining crumbs aside.

Place ⅓ cup water in a small, narrow glass or stainless steel bowl; freeze 25 minutes or until a ⅛-inch-thick layer of ice forms on surface.

Place strawberries in container of an electric blender or food processor; top with cover, and process until smooth. Combine pureed strawberries, sugar, egg whites, and lemon juice in a large mixing bowl. Beat at high speed of an electric mixer 10 minutes or until glossy and stiff.

Add milk powder to partially frozen water; beat at high speed of an electric mixer 5 minutes or until stiff peaks form. Fold into strawberry mixture. Spoon mixture into prepared pan. Sprinkle with remaining crumbs. Cover and freeze at least 6 hours. Cut into 3-inch squares and serve immediately. Yield: 12 servings (146 calories per serving).

PROTEIN 3.9 / FAT 3.9 / CARBOHYDRATE 25.0 / CHOLESTEROL 1 / IRON 0.7 / SODIUM 61 / CALCIUM 54

Honey Bavarian

(*pictured on page 227*)

²/₃ cup instant nonfat dry milk powder
1½ cups cold water
1 tablespoon unflavored gelatin
2 eggs, separated
1 teaspoon vanilla extract
½ cup part-skim ricotta cheese
2 tablespoons low-fat sour cream
¼ cup honey
⅛ teaspoon salt
Vegetable cooking spray
Raspberry Chambord Sauce, page 226 (optional)

Combine milk powder, cold water, and gelatin in a nonaluminum saucepan; let stand 2 minutes. Bring to a boil over medium heat, stirring constantly, until gelatin dissolves.

Beat egg yolks in a small bowl. Gradually stir about one-fourth of hot mixture into yolks; add to remaining hot mixture, stirring constantly. Cook, stirring constantly, 2 minutes. Remove from heat; stir in vanilla. Chill until consistency of unbeaten egg white; fold in ricotta, sour cream, and honey.

Beat egg whites (at room temperature) and salt at high speed of an electric mixer until stiff peaks form. Fold egg whites into gelatin mixture. Pour into a 5-cup mold that has been coated with cooking spray; chill until firm. Unmold, and top with Raspberry Chambord Sauce, if desired. Yield: 8 servings (112 calories per serving).

PROTEIN 8.2 / FAT 2.3 / CARBOHYDRATE 14.9 / CHOLESTEROL 73 / IRON 0.4 / SODIUM 168 / CALCIUM 147

Vanilla Bavarian

(*pictured on pages 210 and 211*)

1 envelope unflavored gelatin
1½ cups cold water
²/₃ cup instant nonfat dry milk powder
⅓ cup sugar
2 eggs, separated
1 teaspoon vanilla extract
Dash of salt
½ cup part-skim ricotta cheese
2 tablespoons plain nonfat yogurt
Vegetable cooking spray
Red and green grapes (optional)

Sprinkle gelatin over cold water in a medium saucepan. Let stand 1 minute. Add milk powder and sugar, stirring gently. Cook over medium heat, stirring constantly, until sugar and gelatin dissolve.

Beat egg yolks until slightly thickened. Gradually stir about one-fourth of hot mixture into egg yolks; add to remaining hot mixture, stirring constantly. Cook 1 minute, stirring constantly. Remove from heat; stir in vanilla.

Beat egg whites (at room temperature) and salt at high speed of an electric mixer until stiff peaks form. Set aside.

Pour gelatin mixture into a medium-size metal bowl. Place metal bowl in a larger bowl of ice and water. Stir mixture until syrupy.

Combine ricotta and yogurt; stir into gelatin mixture. Fold beaten egg whites into mixture. Spoon mixture into a 3½-cup mold that has been coated with cooking spray. Cover and chill until firm. Unmold onto serving platter. Garnish with grapes, if desired. Yield: 8 servings (133 calories per serving).

PROTEIN 9.0 / FAT 3.1 / CARBOHYDRATE 17.0 / CHOLESTEROL 86 / IRON 0.4 / SODIUM 128 / CALCIUM 208

Mocha-Rum Bavarian

⅓ cup water
1 envelope unflavored gelatin
¼ cup cold water
½ cup unsweetened apple juice
¼ cup unsweetened cocoa
1 teaspoon espresso powder
2 eggs, separated
1 tablespoon plus 1½ teaspoons
   dark rum
⅓ cup instant nonfat dry milk
   powder
¼ cup sugar
Vegetable cooking spray

Place ⅓ cup water in a small, narrow glass or stainless steel bowl; freeze 25 minutes or until a ⅛-inch-thick layer of ice forms on surface.

Combine gelatin, ¼ cup cold water, and apple juice in a medium saucepan. Let stand 1 minute. Stir in cocoa and espresso powder. Cook over medium heat 5 minutes or until gelatin dissolves, stirring frequently. Beat egg yolks until thick; stir in rum. Gradually stir about one-fourth of hot mixture into yolk mixture; add to remaining hot mixture, stirring constantly. Cook over medium heat 1 to 2 minutes, stirring constantly. Remove from heat, and chill 20 to 30 minutes or just until slightly thickened, stirring occasionally.

Add milk powder to partially frozen water; beat at high speed of an electric mixer 5 minutes or until stiff peaks form.

Beat egg whites (at room temperature) in a medium bowl at high speed of an electric mixer until soft peaks form. Gradually add sugar, 1 tablespoon at a time, beating until stiff peaks form. Gently fold chilled mocha mixture into egg whites. Fold in whipped milk mixture. Spoon mixture into a 6-cup fancy mold that has been coated with cooking spray. Chill several hours or until firm. Yield: 10 servings (68 calories per serving).

PROTEIN 3.9 / FAT 1.5 / CARBOHYDRATE 9.7 / CHOLESTEROL 56 / IRON 0.6 / SODIUM 37 / CALCIUM 60

Blender Strawberry Bavarian

2 envelopes unflavored gelatin
¼ cup cold water
½ cup boiling water
2 cups halved fresh or frozen
   strawberries, thawed
½ cup instant nonfat dry milk
   powder
2 egg whites
⅓ cup sugar
1 cup crushed ice

Sprinkle gelatin over cold water in container of an electric blender or food processor; let stand 1 minute. Add boiling water; top with cover, and process 30 seconds. Add strawberries, milk powder, egg whites, and sugar; top with cover, and process until smooth. Gradually add crushed ice; cover and process until mixture is smooth and thickened. Pour into 8 individual molds. Chill 30 minutes or until gelatin is set. Yield: 8 servings (80 calories per serving).

PROTEIN 5.3 / FAT 0.2 / CARBOHYDRATE 14.8 / CHOLESTEROL 2 / IRON 0.2 / SODIUM 55 / CALCIUM 100

Creamy Spanish Bavarian

2 envelopes unflavored gelatin
1/2 cup sugar, divided
1/4 teaspoon salt
2 cups skim milk, divided
3 eggs, separated
1 1/2 teaspoons vanilla extract
1/4 teaspoon cream of tartar
Vegetable cooking spray

Combine gelatin, 1/4 cup sugar, and salt in a large saucepan; stir well. Add 1/2 cup skim milk, and let stand 1 minute. Stir in remaining 1 1/2 cups skim milk. Cook over medium heat, stirring constantly, until mixture comes to a boil and gelatin dissolves.

Beat egg yolks in a small bowl with a wire whisk. Gradually stir about one-fourth of hot mixture into yolks; add to remaining hot mixture, stirring constantly. Cook over medium heat, stirring constantly, 1 minute. Remove from heat; stir in vanilla. Chill, stirring occasionally, until mixture is consistency of unbeaten egg white.

Beat egg whites (at room temperature) and cream of tartar in a large bowl at high speed of an electric mixer until soft peaks form; gradually add remaining 1/4 cup sugar, 1 tablespoon at a time, beating until stiff peaks form. Gently fold into gelatin mixture. Spoon mixture into a 6-cup mold that has been coated with cooking spray. Chill at least 5 hours or until firm. Unmold onto a serving platter. Yield: 10 servings (87 calories per serving).

PROTEIN 4.7 / FAT 1.8 / CARBOHYDRATE 12.7 / CHOLESTEROL 83 / IRON 0.3 / SODIUM 112 / CALCIUM 69

Coconut Bavarian

2 egg yolks
3 tablespoons sugar
2 tablespoons all-purpose flour
1 cup skim milk
1 envelope unflavored gelatin
3 tablespoons cold water
1 teaspoon vanilla extract
1 teaspoon coconut extract
1/4 teaspoon almond extract
1/2 cup unsweetened grated
  coconut
3 egg whites
Vegetable cooking spray
1 (11-ounce) can unsweetened
  mandarin oranges, drained

Beat egg yolks at medium speed of an electric mixer in top of a double boiler until thick and lemon colored. Gradually add sugar; beat well. Add flour; beat until smooth. Add milk; beat well. Cook over boiling water, stirring constantly, until mixture coats a spoon.

Sprinkle gelatin over cold water; let stand 1 minute. Add to hot milk mixture, stirring until gelatin dissolves. Remove from heat, and transfer to a large mixing bowl; cool to room temperature. Stir in flavorings and grated coconut; chill to consistency of unbeaten egg white.

Beat egg whites (at room temperature) at high speed of an electric mixer until stiff but not dry. Fold into milk mixture; spoon into a 3 1/2-cup mold that has been coated with cooking spray. Chill until firm. Unmold onto a serving platter; top with orange sections. Yield: 6 servings (139 calories per serving).

PROTEIN 5.8 / FAT 6.3 / CARBOHYDRATES 14.6 / CHOLESTEROL 92 / IRON 0.7 / SODIUM 56 / CALCIUM 63

Cold Coffee Soufflés look delectable garnished with flowering quince.

Cold Coffee Soufflés

Vegetable cooking spray
1 envelope unflavored gelatin
1½ cups skim milk, divided
2 eggs, separated
⅓ cup sugar
2 tablespoons instant coffee
   granules
1 teaspoon vanilla extract
⅓ cup water
3 tablespoons sugar
⅓ cup instant nonfat dry milk
   powder
Edible flowers (optional)

*C*ut 6 pieces of aluminum foil or wax paper long enough to fit around 6 individual soufflé dishes, allowing a 1-inch overlap; fold foil lengthwise into thirds. Lightly coat one side of foil with cooking spray. Wrap foil around outside of each dish, coated side against dish, allowing it to extend 3 inches above rim to form a collar; secure with string.

Sprinkle gelatin over ¼ cup milk in a small dish; let stand 1 minute. Combine 1¼ cups milk, egg yolks, ⅓ cup sugar, and coffee granules in a medium saucepan; cook over low heat until slightly thickened, stirring constantly with a wooden spoon. Add gelatin mixture, stirring until gelatin dissolves. Remove from heat; stir in vanilla. Chill until consistency of unbeaten egg white.

Place ⅓ cup water in a small, narrow glass or stainless steel bowl; freeze 25 minutes or until a ⅛-inch-thick layer of ice forms on surface.

Beat egg whites (at room temperature) in a large bowl at high speed of an electric mixer until foamy. Gradually add 3 tablespoons sugar, 1 tablespoon at a time, beating mixture until stiff peaks form.

Add milk powder to partially frozen water; beat at high speed of an electric mixer 5 minutes or until stiff peaks form.

Gently fold beaten egg whites and whipped milk into gelatin mixture. Spoon into prepared dishes, and chill until firm. Remove collars before serving. Garnish with edible flowers, if desired. Yield: 6 servings (150 calories per serving).

PROTEIN 7.7 / FAT 2.2 / CARBOHYDRATE 24.2 / CHOLESTEROL 94 / IRON 0.5 / SODIUM 93 / CALCIUM 170

Cold Strawberry Soufflé

(pictured on pages 210 and 211)

Vegetable cooking spray
½ teaspoon sugar
2 envelopes unflavored gelatin
⅔ cup cold water
3 cups fresh strawberries, hulled
1 tablespoon lemon juice
2 tablespoons sugar
2 tablespoons crème de fraises or
   other strawberry-flavored
   liqueur
6 egg whites
Dash of salt
⅓ cup sugar
2 fresh strawberries, sliced
   (optional)
Fresh mint sprigs (optional)

Cut a piece of aluminum foil long enough to fit around a 1½-quart soufflé dish, allowing a 1-inch overlap; fold foil lengthwise into thirds. Lightly coat one side of foil with cooking spray, and sprinkle with ½ teaspoon sugar. Wrap foil around outside of dish, coated side against dish, allowing it to extend 3 inches above rim to form a collar; secure with string.

Sprinkle gelatin over cold water in a small saucepan; let stand 2 minutes. Cook over low heat, stirring constantly, until gelatin dissolves.

Place strawberries in container of an electric blender; top with cover, and process until smooth. Add gelatin mixture, lemon juice, 2 tablespoons sugar, and liqueur; top with cover, and process 1 minute.

Beat egg whites (at room temperature) and salt in a large bowl at high speed of an electric mixer until soft peaks form. Gradually add ⅓ cup sugar, 1 tablespoon at a time, beating until stiff peaks form. Fold egg white mixture into strawberry mixture. Spoon into prepared dish; chill 4 hours or until firm. Remove collar from dish. If desired, garnish with strawberry slices and mint sprigs. Yield: 8 servings (95 calories per serving).

PROTEIN 4.4 / FAT 0.3 / CARBOHYDRATE 17.5 / CHOLESTEROL 0 / IRON 0.2 / SODIUM 59 / CALCIUM 11

Overleaf: *A country garden surrounds (clockwise from left) Vanilla Bavarian (page 205), Frosty Lemon Mousse Squares (page 199), and Cold Strawberry Soufflé.*

Ginger Soufflés

⅓ cup water
1 envelope unflavored gelatin
¼ cup cold water
1 cup skim milk
¼ cup sugar
½ teaspoon ground cinnamon
½ teaspoon ground ginger
⅛ teaspoon ground cloves
⅛ teaspoon ground nutmeg
1 egg, separated
⅛ teaspoon cream of tartar
⅓ cup instant nonfat dry milk
  powder
2 gingersnaps, coarsely crumbled

*P*lace ⅓ cup water in a small, narrow glass or stainless steel bowl; freeze 25 minutes or until a ⅛-inch-thick layer of ice forms on surface.

Combine gelatin and ¼ cup cold water in a saucepan. Let stand 1 minute. Stir in skim milk and next 5 ingredients. Cook over low heat, stirring constantly, until gelatin dissolves.

Lightly beat egg yolk in a small bowl. Gradually stir about one-fourth of hot milk mixture into yolk; add to remaining hot milk mixture, stirring constantly. Cook 1 minute or until slightly thickened, stirring constantly. Remove from heat; chill 20 to 30 minutes or until consistency of unbeaten egg white, stirring occasionally.

Beat egg white (at room temperature) at high speed of an electric mixer until foamy. Add cream of tartar; beat until stiff peaks form.

Add milk powder to partially frozen water; beat at high speed of an electric mixer 5 minutes or until stiff peaks form.

Fold beaten egg white and whipped milk into gelatin mixture. Spoon into 8 individual dessert dishes; top with cookie crumbs. Chill until set. Yield: 8 servings (76 calories per serving).

PROTEIN 4.5 / FAT 1.1 / CARBOHYDRATE 12.0 / CHOLESTEROL 37 / IRON 0.3 / SODIUM 58 / CALCIUM 110

Cold Lemon Soufflé

(pictured on pages 182 and 183)

Vegetable cooking spray
⅓ cup water
2 envelopes unflavored gelatin
⅓ cup cold water
½ cup sugar
2 egg yolks
1 tablespoon grated lemon rind
¾ cup lemon juice
6 egg whites
¼ cup sugar
⅓ cup instant nonfat dry milk
  powder
2 tablespoons chopped pistachios
Lemon rind (optional)

*C*ut a piece of aluminum foil long enough to fit around a 1½-quart soufflé dish, allowing a 1-inch overlap; fold foil lengthwise into thirds. Lightly coat one side of foil with cooking spray. Wrap foil around outside of dish, coated side against dish, allowing it to extend 3 inches above rim to form a collar; secure with string.

Place ⅓ cup water in a small, narrow glass or stainless steel bowl; freeze 25 minutes or until a ⅛-inch-thick layer of ice forms on surface.

Sprinkle gelatin over ⅓ cup cold water in a small bowl; let stand 1 minute.

Combine ½ cup sugar, egg yolks, lemon rind, and lemon juice in top of a large double boiler. Beat at medium speed of an electric mixer until blended. Place over simmering water, and continue beating for 5 minutes or until thick and creamy. Beat in gelatin mixture. Remove from heat. Cover and chill 10 minutes or until thickened.

Beat egg whites (at room temperature) in a large glass or stainless steel bowl at medium speed of an electric mixer until soft peaks form. Gradually add ¼ cup sugar, 1 tablespoon at a time, beating until stiff peaks form. (Do not overbeat.)

Add milk powder to partially frozen water; beat at high speed of an electric mixer 5 minutes or until stiff peaks form.

Fold egg white mixture and whipped milk into chilled lemon mixture. Spoon into prepared dish. Cover and chill 2 hours or until set. Remove collar from dish. Gently press pistachios around sides of soufflé. Garnish with lemon rind, if desired. Yield: 10 servings (112 calories per serving).

PROTEIN 5.6 / FAT 1.8 / CARBOHYDRATE 19.3 / CHOLESTEROL 55 / IRON 0.3 / SODIUM 55 / CALCIUM 62

Warm Chocolate Soufflé

Vegetable cooking spray
1 tablespoon cornstarch
3 tablespoons sugar
2 tablespoons plus 1 teaspoon
   unsweetened cocoa
¾ cup skim milk
1 tablespoon crème de cacao
2 egg yolks
4 egg whites
½ teaspoon cream of tartar

Cut a piece of aluminum foil long enough to fit around a 1-quart soufflé dish, allowing a 1-inch overlap; fold foil lengthwise into thirds. Lightly coat one side of foil with cooking spray. Wrap around outside of dish, coated side against dish, allowing it to extend 3 inches above rim to form a collar; secure with string.

Combine cornstarch, sugar, cocoa, and milk in a large saucepan; stir well. Cook over medium heat, stirring constantly, until mixture comes to a boil and thickens.

Combine crème de cacao and egg yolks; stir well. Gradually stir about one-fourth of hot cocoa mixture into egg yolk mixture; add to remaining hot cocoa mixture, stirring constantly. Cook 1 minute; remove from heat. Set aside.

Beat egg whites (at room temperature) at high speed of an electric mixer until foamy. Add cream of tartar; beat until stiff peaks form.

Gently stir one-fourth of egg white mixture into cocoa mixture. Gently fold remaining egg white mixture into cocoa mixture. Spoon into prepared dish. Bake at 375° for 30 to 35 minutes or until puffed and lightly browned. Remove collar, and serve immediately. Yield: 6 servings (102 calories per serving).

PROTEIN 5.6 / FAT 2.7 / CARBOHYDRATE 12.5 / CHOLESTEROL 91 / IRON 1.2 / SODIUM 70 / CALCIUM 56

Hot Banana-Rum Soufflé

Vegetable cooking spray
1 tablespoon sugar
⅔ cup mashed ripe banana
1 teaspoon grated lemon rind
3 tablespoons lemon juice
⅓ cup all-purpose flour
1 cup skim milk
2 tablespoons dark rum
2 egg yolks
⅓ cup sugar
6 egg whites
⅛ teaspoon salt
½ teaspoon cream of tartar
Rum Sabayon Sauce

Cut a piece of aluminum foil or wax paper long enough to fit around a 2-quart soufflé dish, allowing a 1-inch overlap; fold foil lengthwise into thirds. Lightly coat one side of foil with cooking spray. Wrap foil around outside of dish, coated side against dish, allowing it to extend 3 inches above rim to form a collar; secure with string.

Coat soufflé dish and collar with cooking spray. Sprinkle with 1 tablespoon sugar, carefully shaking to coat bottom and sides of soufflé dish and collar. Set aside.

Combine banana, lemon rind, and lemon juice in a small bowl; stir well.

Combine flour and milk in a medium saucepan. Cook over medium heat, stirring constantly, until mixture comes to a boil. Add banana mixture, stirring well.

Combine rum, egg yolks, and ⅓ cup sugar in a small bowl, beating with a wire whisk. Gradually stir about one-fourth of hot milk mixture into egg yolk mixture; add to remaining hot milk mixture, stirring constantly. Cook 1 minute or until mixture thickens.

Beat egg whites (at room temperature) and salt in a large bowl at high speed of an electric mixer until frothy. Add cream of tartar; beat until stiff peaks form.

Fold rum mixture into egg white mixture; spoon into prepared dish. Bake at 375° for 35 to 45 minutes or until puffed and golden. Remove collar, and serve immediately with Rum Sabayon Sauce. Yield: 8 servings (152 calories per 1-cup soufflé and 3 tablespoons sauce).

Rum Sabayon Sauce

1 egg
¼ cup sugar
2 tablespoons dark rum
3 tablespoons plus 1 teaspoon
  water

Combine all ingredients in top of a large double boiler. Place over simmering water. Beat with a wire whisk until frothy. Continue beating for 10 minutes or until mixture has doubled in volume. Yield: 1½ cups (11 calories per tablespoon).

PROTEIN 5.8 / FAT 2.4 / CARBOHYDRATE 27.6 / CHOLESTEROL 103 / IRON 0.6 / SODIUM 114 / CALCIUM 53

Kahlúa Soufflé

¾ cup sugar

⅓ cup instant nonfat dry milk powder

¼ cup all-purpose flour

3 tablespoons unsweetened cocoa

⅛ teaspoon salt

¾ cup water

2 eggs, separated

2 tablespoons Kahlúa

1 teaspoon vanilla extract

Vegetable cooking spray

1 teaspoon powdered sugar

Combine first 5 ingredients in a large bowl; stir well. Combine water, egg yolks, Kahlúa, and vanilla; add to dry ingredients, stirring until smooth.

Beat egg whites (at room temperature) at high speed of an electric mixer until stiff peaks form. Gently fold egg whites into batter.

Spoon into a 1½-quart soufflé dish that has been coated with cooking spray. Set dish in a 13- x 9- x 2-inch baking pan; pour hot water into pan to a depth of 1 inch. Bake at 350° for 45 to 50 minutes or until top of soufflé looks like a cake and springs back when touched (bottom of soufflé will be a sauce).

Remove dish from water. Sprinkle with powdered sugar. Spoon cake-like top into serving dishes and spoon sauce from bottom of dish over each serving. Yield: 6 servings. (186 calories per serving).

PROTEIN 5.8 / FAT 2.4 / CARBOHYDRATE 35.2 / CHOLESTEROL 93 / IRON 1.0 / SODIUM 108 / CALCIUM 99

Lemon Soufflé

¼ cup all-purpose flour

¾ cup sugar

¼ teaspoon salt

2 eggs, separated

⅔ cup skim milk

1 teaspoon grated lemon rind

¼ cup lemon juice

1 teaspoon powdered sugar

Combine flour, sugar, and salt in a small bowl; stir well. Set mixture aside.

Combine egg yolks, milk, lemon rind, and lemon juice in a medium bowl; beat at low speed of an electric mixer until smooth. Gradually add flour mixture, beating well.

Beat egg whites (at room temperature) at high speed of an electric mixer until stiff peaks form. Gently fold egg whites into batter. Spoon into a 1-quart soufflé dish. Place dish in an 8-inch square baking pan; pour hot water into baking pan to a depth of 1 inch. Bake at 350° for 40 to 45 minutes or until slightly puffed and golden. Sprinkle with powdered sugar. Serve immediately. Yield: 6 servings (157 calories per serving).

PROTEIN 3.6 / FAT 2.0 / CARBOHYDRATE 32.1 / CHOLESTEROL 92 / IRON 0.5 / SODIUM 135 / CALCIUM 46

Serve Lemonade Skillet Soufflé straight from the oven for rave reviews.

Lemonade Skillet Soufflé

⅓ cup instant nonfat dry milk
    powder
¼ cup sugar
¼ cup all-purpose flour
⅛ teaspoon salt
1 cup lemonade
2 egg yolks
½ teaspoon grated lemon rind
6 egg whites
½ teaspoon cream of tartar
Vegetable cooking spray
1 teaspoon powdered sugar

Combine milk powder, sugar, flour, salt, and lemonade in a medium saucepan. Cook over medium heat, stirring constantly, until mixture comes to a boil. Remove from heat. Beat egg yolks until thick and lemon colored. Gradually stir about one-fourth of hot mixture into yolks; add to remaining hot mixture, stirring constantly. Stir in lemon rind; set aside.

Beat egg whites (at room temperature) and cream of tartar in a large bowl at high speed of an electric mixer until stiff peaks form. Fold into lemonade mixture. Spoon mixture into a 10-inch ovenproof skillet that has been coated with cooking spray. Bake at 375° for 25 to 30 minutes or until puffed and golden. Sprinkle with powdered sugar. Serve immediately. Yield: 12 servings (68 calories per serving).

PROTEIN 3.7 / FAT 1.2 / CARBOHYDRATE 10.9 / CHOLESTEROL 46 / IRON 0.3 / SODIUM 78 / CALCIUM 49

Omelet Soufflé

6 egg whites
1/4 cup plus 2 tablespoons sugar, divided
3 egg yolks
1 teaspoon grated lemon rind
1/2 teaspoon vanilla extract
1 tablespoon margarine
3 tablespoons lemon juice
2 teaspoons powdered sugar

*B*eat egg whites (at room temperature) in a large bowl at high speed of an electric mixer until foamy; gradually add 3 tablespoons sugar, 1 tablespoon at a time, beating mixture until stiff peaks form.

Beat egg yolks, 1 tablespoon sugar, lemon rind, and vanilla until thick and lemon colored. Gently fold yolk mixture into egg white mixture.

Melt margarine in a 10-inch ovenproof omelet pan or heavy skillet; add remaining 2 tablespoons sugar and lemon juice. Bring to a boil; cook 1 minute, stirring constantly.

Spoon egg mixture into skillet, and gently smooth surface. Cook over low heat 1 minute. Transfer to oven, and bake at 350° for 15 minutes or until a knife inserted in center comes out clean. Sprinkle with powdered sugar. Serve immediately. Yield: 6 servings (119 calories per serving).

PROTEIN 4.8 / FAT 4.7 / CARBOHYDRATE 14.5 / CHOLESTEROL 136 / IRON 0.5 / SODIUM 77 / CALCIUM 18

Orange Soufflé

1/4 cup all-purpose flour
3/4 cup sugar
1/4 teaspoon salt
2 eggs, separated
1/4 cup instant nonfat dry milk powder
1 teaspoon grated orange rind
1 cup unsweetened orange juice
Vegetable cooking spray
1 teaspoon powdered sugar

*C*ombine flour, sugar, and salt in a small bowl, stirring mixture well.

Combine egg yolks, milk powder, orange rind, and orange juice in a large bowl, stirring with a wire whisk. Add flour mixture to orange mixture, stirring well.

Beat egg whites (at room temperature) at high speed of an electric mixer until stiff but not dry. Fold beaten egg whites into yolk mixture. Spoon into a 1-quart soufflé dish that has been coated with cooking spray. Place soufflé dish in an 8-inch square baking pan; pour hot water into baking pan to a depth of 1 inch. Bake at 350° for 45 to 50 minutes until puffed and golden. Sprinkle with powdered sugar, and serve immediately. Yield: 6 servings (182 calories per serving).

PROTEIN 4.8 / FAT 2.1 / CARBOHYDRATE 37.2 / CHOLESTEROL 92 / IRON 0.6 / SODIUM 148 / CALCIUM 79

Flaming Grand Marnier Soufflé

Vegetable cooking spray
1/4 cup all-purpose flour
1/3 cup sugar
1 cup skim milk
1/4 cup Grand Marnier
2 egg yolks
1 tablespoon grated orange rind
1 teaspoon vanilla extract
1/8 teaspoon salt
6 egg whites
1/2 teaspoon cream of tartar
2 tablespoons Grand Marnier,
  warmed

Cut a piece of aluminum foil long enough to fit around a 1½-quart soufflé dish, allowing a 1-inch overlap; fold foil lengthwise into thirds. Lightly coat one side of foil with cooking spray. Wrap foil around outside of dish, coated side against dish, allowing it to extend 3 inches above rim to form a collar; secure with string.

Combine flour, sugar, and milk in a large saucepan; stir well. Cook over medium heat, stirring constantly, until mixture comes to a boil and thickens.

Combine 1/4 cup Grand Marnier, egg yolks, orange rind, vanilla, and salt; stir well. Gradually stir about one-fourth of hot mixture into egg yolk mixture; add to remaining hot mixture, stirring constantly. Cook 1 minute; remove from heat. Set aside.

Beat egg whites (at room temperature) at high speed of an electric mixer until foamy. Add cream of tartar; beat until stiff peaks form. Gently stir one-fourth of egg white mixture into cooked mixture. Gently fold remaining egg white mixture into cooked mixture. Spoon into prepared dish. Bake at 375° for 40 to 45 minutes or until puffed and lightly browned.

With a long match, ignite 2 tablespoons warmed Grand Marnier, and pour over top of soufflé. Remove collar, and serve immediately. Yield: 8 servings (99 calories per serving).

PROTEIN 4.7 / FAT 1.6 / CARBOHYDRATE 17.0 / CHOLESTEROL 69 / IRON 0.4 / SODIUM 105 / CALCIUM 49

Honey-Strawberry Soufflé

Vegetable cooking spray
2 cups fresh strawberries, hulled
2 tablespoons cornstarch
2 tablespoons water
1 tablespoon lemon juice, divided
3 tablespoons honey
1 egg yolk
4 egg whites

Cut a piece of aluminum foil long enough to fit around a 1-quart soufflé dish, allowing a 1-inch overlap; fold foil lengthwise into thirds. Lightly coat foil and bottom of soufflé dish with cooking spray. Wrap foil around outside of dish, coated side against dish, allowing it to extend 3 inches above rim to form a collar; secure with string.

Reserve 4 strawberries. Place remaining strawberries in container of an electric blender. Top with cover, and process until smooth. Dice reserved strawberries and stir into pureed mixture.

Dissolve cornstarch in water in a nonaluminum saucepan. Stir in strawberry mixture, 2 teaspoons lemon juice, and

Honey-Strawberry Soufflé
(CONTINUED)

honey. Bring mixture to a boil, stirring constantly. Reduce heat to low, and cook an additional 2 to 3 minutes, stirring constantly, until mixture is smooth and thickened.

Beat egg yolk in a small dish with a wire whisk. Gradually stir about one-fourth of hot mixture into egg yolk; add to remaining hot mixture, stirring constantly. Cook 1 minute; remove from heat. Transfer to a bowl. Cover and chill until mixture mounds from a spoon.

Beat egg whites (at room temperature) in a large bowl at high speed of an electric mixer until frothy. Add remaining 1 teaspoon lemon juice; beat until stiff peaks form. Stir about one-fourth of egg white mixture into chilled strawberry mixture. Gently fold in remaining egg white mixture. Spoon into prepared dish, and bake at 375° for 25 to 30 minutes or until set and puffy. Remove collar, and serve immediately. Yield: 8 servings (60 calories per serving).

PROTEIN 2.3 / FAT 0.9 / CARBOHYDRATE 11.3 / CHOLESTEROL 34 / IRON 0.3 / SODIUM 27 / CALCIUM 11

Salzberg Nockerl

6 *egg whites*
1 *tablespoon lemon juice*
¼ *cup sugar*
4 *egg yolks*
1 *teaspoon vanilla extract*
½ *teaspoon grated lemon rind*
1 *tablespoon all-purpose flour*
Vegetable cooking spray
1 *teaspoon powdered sugar*

*B*eat egg whites (at room temperature) and lemon juice in a large bowl at high speed of an electric mixer until foamy. Gradually add ¼ cup sugar, 1 tablespoon at a time, beating until stiff peaks form.

Combine egg yolks, vanilla, and lemon rind in a small bowl; beat at high speed of an electric mixer until thick and lemon colored. Stir flour into egg yolk mixture.

Partially fold egg white mixture into egg yolk mixture. (Mixture will have marbled effect.)

Spoon 6 mounds of egg mixture into a 13- x 9- x 2-inch baking dish that has been coated with cooking spray. Bake at 375° for 10 to 12 minutes or until golden brown. Sprinkle with powdered sugar. Serve immediately. Yield: 6 servings (101 calories per serving).

PROTEIN 5.3 / FAT 3.8 / CARBOHYDRATE 10.7 / CHOLESTEROL 182 / IRON 0.7 / SODIUM 56 / CALCIUM 21

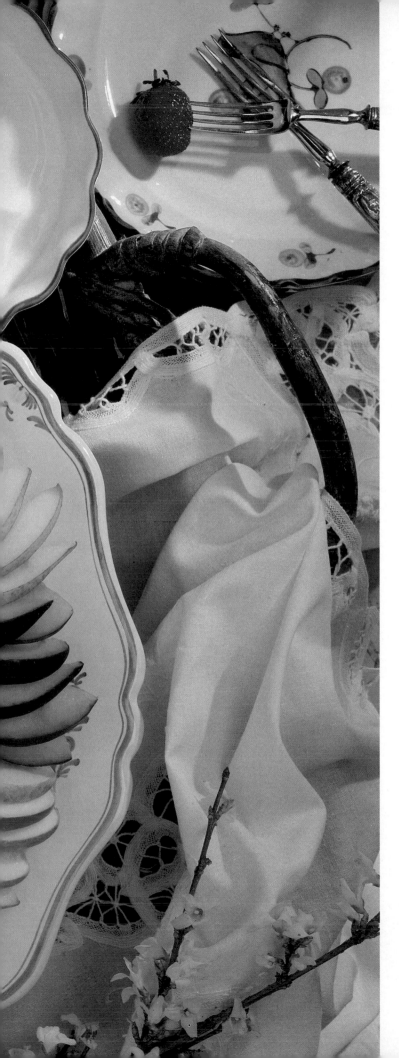

Sauces

Sauces can elevate a simple dessert to gourmet status. Besides blending with the texture, flavor, and character of a dessert, these light sauces are healthy alternatives to their richer counterparts.

Each recipe contains serving suggestions, although most of the sauces can be a tasty complement to ice milks, fruit, or simple cakes such as sponge or angel food. For entertaining, prepare a variety of sauces, selecting them for their color and contrasting flavor. Serve them with an arrangement of fresh strawberries, pineapple, and sliced pears for dipping.

Most of these sauces can be prepared a day or two ahead of serving time, and all of the pureed sauces can be frozen for later use.

Surrounded with colorful fresh fruit, Dessert Fruit Dip (page 226) is attractive enough to be a centerpiece.

Black Cherry Sauce

2 tablespoons cornstarch
1 cup water
¼ cup light corn syrup
2 teaspoons lemon juice
2 tablespoons kirsch or other
  cherry-flavored liqueur
¼ teaspoon almond extract
1 (16-ounce) package frozen sweet
  cherries, thawed

Combine first 4 ingredients in a medium saucepan. Bring mixture to a boil over medium heat. Stir in kirsch, and cook 1 minute. Remove from heat; stir in almond extract. Fold in cherries. Cover and refrigerate. Serve over ice milk or plain cake. Yield: 3 cups (15 calories per tablespoon).

PROTEIN 0.1 / FAT 0.1 / CARBOHYDRATE 3.3 / CHOLESTEROL 0 / IRON 0.0 / SODIUM 2 / CALCIUM 1

Blackberry Sauce

1 (16-ounce) package
  unsweetened frozen blackberries,
  thawed
¼ cup water
¼ cup corn syrup
2 tablespoons blackberry-flavored
  brandy

Combine blackberries and water in container of an electric blender; top with cover, and process until smooth. Press puree through a sieve to remove seeds. Discard seeds. Stir remaining ingredients into juice. Cover; chill thoroughly. Serve over ice milk or plain cake. Yield: 2 cups (16 calories per tablespoon).

PROTEIN 0.1 / FAT 0.0 / CARBOHYDRATE 3.6 / CHOLESTEROL 0 / IRON 0.1 / SODIUM 3 / CALCIUM 4

Kahlúa Cocoa Sauce

½ cup sugar
½ cup Dutch process cocoa
¼ cup light corn syrup
½ cup water
2 tablespoons Kahlúa
1 teaspoon vanilla extract

Combine first 4 ingredients in a medium saucepan, stirring well. Bring mixture to a boil over medium heat, stirring frequently. Stir in Kahlúa; cook 1 minute. Remove from heat and cool. Stir in vanilla. Cover and chill.

Serve over ice milk, raspberry ice, fresh raspberries, or angel food cake. Yield: 1⅓ cups (40 calories per tablespoon).

PROTEIN 0.3 / FAT 0.5 / CARBOHYDRATE 9.0 / CHOLESTEROL 0 / IRON 0.2 / SODIUM 20 / CALCIUM 3

Kahlúa Cocoa Sauce is guaranteed to be a winner when served over ice milk.

Chocolate Sauce

½ cup water
3 tablespoons sugar
2 tablespoons unsweetened cocoa
1 teaspoon cornstarch
1 teaspoon vanilla extract
2 tablespoons Chablis or other dry white wine

Combine first 5 ingredients in a medium saucepan, stirring until smooth. Cook over medium heat, stirring constantly, until smooth and thickened. Stir in wine, and cook 1 minute; let cool. Serve over ice milk or fresh fruit. Yield: ½ cup (28 calories per tablespoon).

PROTEIN 0.4 / FAT 0.2 / CARBOHYDRATE 6.0 / CHOLESTEROL 0 / IRON 0.3 / SODIUM 0 / CALCIUM 2

Cocoa-Sour Cream Topping

1 cup low-fat sour cream
3 tablespoons powdered sugar
2 teaspoons unsweetened cocoa
1 teaspoon vanilla extract
½ teaspoon chocolate extract

Combine all ingredients in a small bowl; stir well. Cover and chill thoroughly. Serve over angel food cake or fresh fruit. Yield: 1 cup (28 calories per tablespoon).

PROTEIN 0.5 / FAT 1.8 / CARBOHYDRATE 2.2 / CHOLESTEROL 6 / IRON 0.1 / SODIUM 6 / CALCIUM 16

Mango-Lime Sauce

2 tablespoons light corn syrup
1 tablespoon plus 2 teaspoons warm water
1 cup chopped ripe mango
2¼ teaspoons lime juice

Combine all ingredients in container of an electric blender; top with cover, and process until smooth.

Cover and chill thoroughly. Serve over ice milk or angel food cake. Yield: 1 cup (17 calories per tablespoon).

PROTEIN 0.1 / FAT 0.0 / CARBOHYDRATE 4.4 / CHOLESTEROL 0 / IRON 0.0 / SODIUM 3 / CALCIUM 1

Top angel food cake with the tropical flavor of Mango-Lime Sauce.

Dessert Fruit Dip

(pictured on pages 220 and 221)

1 (16-ounce) carton plain low-fat
yogurt
¼ cup sifted powdered sugar
1 tablespoon plus 1 teaspoon
raspberry or other fruit-flavored
schnapps

Line a colander or sieve with a double layer of cheese-cloth that has been rinsed out and squeezed dry; allow cheese-cloth to extend over outside edges of colander. Stir yogurt until smooth; pour into colander and fold edges of cheesecloth over to cover yogurt. Place colander over a large bowl; refrigerate 12 to 24 hours. Remove yogurt from colander and discard liquid.

Combine strained yogurt, powdered sugar, and schnapps in a medium bowl. Stir until well blended. Refrigerate until ready to serve. Serve with assorted fresh fruit. Yield: 1¼ cups (23 calories per tablespoon).

PROTEIN 1.2 / FAT 0.4 / CARBOHYDRATE 3.4 / CHOLESTEROL 1 / IRON 0.0 / SODIUM 16 / CALCIUM 42

Ginger-Yogurt Sauce

1 (8-ounce) carton plain nonfat
yogurt
1 tablespoon crystallized ginger,
finely minced
2 tablespoons honey
1 teaspoon lemon juice

Combine all ingredients in a small bowl. Stir until well blended. Cover and chill thoroughly. Serve over fresh berries or sliced fresh fruit. Yield: 1 cup (19 calories per tablespoon).

PROTEIN 0.8 / FAT 0.0 / CARBOHYDRATE 4.1 / CHOLESTEROL 0 / IRON 0.2 / SODIUM 11 / CALCIUM 30

Raspberry Chambord Sauce

2½ cups frozen unsweetened
raspberries, thawed
¼ cup water
2 tablespoons Chambord
2 teaspoons cornstarch

Place raspberries in container of an electric blender; top with cover, and process until smooth. Press puree through a sieve to yield ¾ cup juice; discard seeds. Combine juice and remaining ingredients in a small saucepan; stir well. Cook over medium heat, stirring constantly, until thickened and bubbly. Remove from heat, and cool completely. Serve over ice milk or fresh fruit. Yield: 1 cup (11 calories per tablespoon).

PROTEIN 0.2 / FAT 0.4 / CARBOHYDRATE 2.1 / CHOLESTEROL 0 / IRON 0.1 / SODIUM 2 / CALCIUM 3

Drizzle Raspberry Chambord Sauce over Honey Bavarian (page 205).

Rum-Cranberry Sauce

1 (16-ounce) can whole-berry
cranberry sauce
¼ cup light rum
2 tablespoons water

Combine all ingredients in a small saucepan. Bring to a boil; reduce heat, and simmer 1 minute, stirring gently. Serve over vanilla ice milk. Yield: 2 cups (21 calories per tablespoon).

PROTEIN 0.0 / FAT 0.0 / CARBOHYDRATE 5.5 / CHOLESTEROL 0 / IRON 0.0 / SODIUM 4 / CALCIUM 1

Rum Cream Sauce

⅓ cup water
⅓ cup instant nonfat dry milk
powder
1 cup vanilla ice milk, softened
1 tablespoon dark rum

Place water in a small, narrow glass or stainless steel bowl; freeze 25 minutes or until a ⅛-inch-thick layer of ice forms on surface. Add milk powder to partially frozen water; beat at high speed of an electric mixer 5 minutes or until stiff peaks form.

Combine ice milk and rum; stir well. Gently fold whipped milk into ice milk mixture. Serve immediately over baked or fresh fruit. Yield: 2½ cups (9 calories per tablespoon).

PROTEIN 0.5 / FAT 0.1 / CARBOHYDRATE 1.2 / CHOLESTEROL 1 / IRON 0.0 / SODIUM 8 / CALCIUM 17

Rum Sabayon Sauce

¼ cup sugar
1 egg
2 tablespoons dark rum
3 tablespoons plus 1 teaspoon
water

Combine all ingredients in top of a large double boiler. Place over simmering water. Beat with a wire whisk until frothy. Continue beating for 10 minutes or until mixture has doubled in volume. Serve over sliced fruit or baked soufflés. Yield: 1½ cups (11 calories per tablespoon).

PROTEIN 0.3 / FAT 0.2 / CARBOHYDRATE 2.1 / CHOLESTEROL 11 / IRON 0.0 / SODIUM 3 / CALCIUM 1

Sabayon Sauce

¼ cup sugar
1 egg
⅓ cup Sauterne

Combine all ingredients in top of a large double boiler. Place over simmering water. Beat with a wire whisk until frothy. Continue beating for 10 minutes or until doubled in volume. Remove from heat, and serve immediately over baked or fresh fruit or baked soufflés. Yield: ¾ cup (24 calories per tablespoon).

PROTEIN 0.5 / FAT 0.5 / CARBOHYDRATE 4.5 / CHOLESTEROL 23 / IRON 0.1 / SODIUM 6 / CALCIUM 3

Slim Crème Anglaise

2 cups skim milk
¼ cup sugar
2 tablespoons cornstarch
1 egg yolk, lightly beaten
1 teaspoon vanilla extract
½ cup vanilla ice milk, softened

Combine first 3 ingredients in a medium saucepan; stir well. Cook over medium heat, stirring constantly, until mixture comes to a boil; cook 1 minute, stirring constantly, until mixture thickens.

Reduce heat to low. Gradually stir about one-fourth of hot mixture into egg yolk; add to remaining hot mixture, stirring constantly. Cook an additional minute, stirring constantly. Remove from heat; stir in vanilla. Cover with plastic wrap, gently pressing directly on custard; chill thoroughly.

Before serving, stir in softened ice milk. Serve over fresh berries, baked apples, or baked puddings. Yield: 2 cups (18 calories per tablespoon).

PROTEIN 0.7 / FAT 0.3 / CARBOHYDRATE 3.2 / CHOLESTEROL 9 / IRON 0.0 / SODIUM 10 / CALCIUM 22

Strawberry Puree Sauce

¼ cup water
2 tablespoons sugar
1 pound fresh strawberries, hulled
1 tablespoon plus 1 teaspoon
  lemon juice

Combine water and sugar in a small saucepan. Cook over medium heat, stirring until sugar dissolves.

Place berries and sugar syrup in container of an electric blender. Top with cover, and process until smooth. Press puree through a sieve to remove seeds. Discard seeds. Add lemon juice to puree. Stir well. Serve over vanilla ice milk or angel food cake. Yield: 2 cups (7 calories per tablespoon).

PROTEIN 0.1 / FAT 0.1 / CARBOHYDRATE 1.8 / CHOLESTEROL 0 / IRON 0.1 / SODIUM 0 / CALCIUM 2

Party Desserts

Come one, come all and join the festivities! Whether the occasion is a backyard barbecue or a formal afternoon tea, *Light Desserts* can suggest a variety of foods appropriate for the occasion.

Each recipe in the chapter has been developed to serve at least twelve people. Serving suggestions and photographs of many of the dishes will offer hints on garnishing techniques that make the presentation of even the simplest dessert a memorable occasion.

Turn the page for beverages, cakes, pies, soufflés, and a variety of other desserts that are sure to be real party pleasers.

Combine the fresh flavor of blackberries in Blackberry Chiffon Pie (page 242) with coffee made from Instant Coffee Extract (page 233).

Festive Party Punch
(pictured on pages 244 and 245)

1 medium orange
10 whole cloves
6 (4-inch) sticks cinnamon
2 quarts unsweetened apple cider
2 (32-ounce) bottles
   reduced-calorie cranberry juice
   cocktail
2 cups Burgundy or other dry red
   wine
½ cup cinnamon schnapps

Stud orange with cloves; place in a 10-ounce custard cup. Bake at 275° for 2 hours. Transfer to a nonaluminum Dutch oven.

Add remaining ingredients; cook over low heat 30 minutes. Serve warm or chilled. Yield: 4½ quarts (45 calories per ½-cup serving).

PROTEIN 0.1 / FAT 0.1 / CARBOHYDRATE 10.8 / CHOLESTEROL 0 / IRON 1.4 / SODIUM 4 / CALCIUM 9

Percolator Glogg

3 (32-ounce) bottles
   reduced-calorie cranberry juice
   cocktail
1 (25.4-ounce) bottle Burgundy
   or other dry red wine
1 tablespoon whole cloves
4 (3-inch) sticks cinnamon
12 whole cardamom pods, cracked
¼ cup sugar
1 cup port wine

Combine cranberry juice cocktail and Burgundy wine in a 30-cup electric percolator; place cloves, cinnamon sticks, and cardamom pods in percolator basket. Perk through complete cycle of electric percolator. Add sugar and port wine to cranberry mixture, stirring well. Yield: 4 quarts (38 calories per ½-cup serving).

PROTEIN 0.0 / FAT 0.0 / CARBOHYDRATE 7.6 / CHOLESTEROL 0 / IRON 2.1 / SODIUM 4 / CALCIUM 7

Slimmer Eggnog

2 cups sugar
2 tablespoons all-purpose flour
3 quarts skim milk, divided
10 eggs
¼ cup vanilla extract
Light rum or rum extact
   (optional)
Freshly grated nutmeg

Combine sugar and flour in a large Dutch oven; stir well with a wire whisk. Slowly add 6 cups milk to sugar mixture, stirring well with a wooden spoon. Cook over low heat 30 to 40 minutes, stirring constantly, until mixture is slightly thickened.

Beat eggs in a large bowl with a wire whisk until frothy. Gradually stir about 1 cup hot milk mixture into eggs; add to remaining hot milk mixture, stirring constantly. Cook over medium heat 5 minutes or until thickened, stirring constantly. Add remaining 6 cups milk and vanilla; stir well. Cover; chill 8 hours.

Add rum or rum extract to taste, if desired. Sprinkle with nutmeg. Yield: 4 quarts (113 calories per ½-cup serving).

PROTEIN 5.1 / FAT 1.9 / CARBOHYDRATE 18.0 / CHOLESTEROL 87 / IRON 0.4 / SODIUM 69 / CALCIUM 122

Instant Coffee Extract

(pictured on pages 230 and 231)

1 pound ground coffee
2 quarts plus 1 cup cold water

*P*lace coffee in a large container. Pour water over coffee, stirring just until coffee is moistened. Cover and let stand at room temperature 12 hours.

Place colander or sieve in a large container. Line colander with a double layer of cheesecloth that has been rinsed out and squeezed dry, allowing cheesecloth to extend over outside edges of colander. Carefully pour coffee into colander; discard grounds. Pour strained coffee into a container; refrigerate until ready to use. Yield: 7 cups extract (1 calorie per tablespoon).

Coffee: Use 1 or more tablespoons coffee extract per cup of coffee. Add hot water to fill cup.

Café au Lait: Use 1 or more tablespoons coffee extract per cup. Add hot skim milk to fill cup.

Note: Extract will keep in refrigerator for 1 week, or pour into ice cube trays; freeze until firm. Use 1 cube per cup of coffee. Add hot water to fill cup.

PROTEIN 0.0 / FAT 0.0 / CARBOHYDRATE 0.0 / CHOLESTEROL 0 / IRON 0.0 / SODIUM 0 / CALCIUM 0

Spicy Gingerbread Cutouts

(pictured on pages 6 and 7)

$2/3$ cup margarine, softened
$2/3$ cup firmly packed brown sugar
$2^{1/2}$ cups all-purpose flour
$1^{1/2}$ teaspoons baking soda
1 tablespoon ground cinnamon
2 teaspoons ground ginger
1 teaspoon ground cloves
2 to 3 tablespoons water
Vegetable cooking spray

*C*ream margarine and sugar, beating at medium speed of an electric mixer until light and fluffy.

Combine flour, soda, cinnamon, ginger, and cloves; add to creamed mixture, stirring well. Add water, 1 tablespoon at a time; stir with a fork until dry ingredients are moistened. Cover and chill at least 1 hour.

Divide dough in half. Roll half of dough to $1/8$-inch thickness between 2 sheets of heavy-duty plastic wrap. Remove plastic wrap. Cut dough with a 2-inch round or shaped cookie cutter, and place on cookie sheets that have been coated with cooking spray.

Bake at 375° for 7 to 9 minutes or until lightly browned. Cool on wire racks. Repeat procedure with remaining half of dough. Yield: 7 dozen cookies (35 calories each).

PROTEIN 0.5 / FAT 1.5 / CARBOHYDRATE 4.9 / CHOLESTEROL 0 / IRON 0.2 / SODIUM 32 / CALCIUM 7

Blueberry Brunch Cake

2 cups all-purpose flour
½ cup sugar
⅓ cup instant nonfat dry milk
  powder
2 teaspoons baking powder
½ teaspoon baking soda
½ teaspoon salt
1 egg
⅔ cup water
⅓ cup margarine, melted
2 tablespoons lemon juice
Vegetable cooking spray
2 cups fresh blueberries
⅓ cup sugar
⅓ cup all-purpose flour
½ teaspoon ground cinnamon
3 tablespoons cold margarine

Combine first 6 ingredients in a large bowl. Make a well in center of mixture; add egg, water, ⅓ cup margarine, and lemon juice, stirring just until moistened. Spoon batter into a 13- x 9- x 2-inch baking pan that has been coated with cooking spray. Sprinkle with blueberries.

Blend ⅓ cup sugar, ⅓ cup flour, and cinnamon in a small bowl. Cut in 3 tablespoons margarine with a pastry blender until mixture resembles coarse meal. Sprinkle crumb mixture evenly over blueberries. Bake at 375° for 35 to 40 minutes or until a wooden pick inserted in center comes out clean. Yield: 16 servings (194 calories per serving).

PROTEIN 3.6 / FAT 6.6 / CARBOHYDRATE 30.5 / CHOLESTEROL 18 / IRON 0.7 / SODIUM 226 / CALCIUM 71

Fruit-Topped Celebration Cake

Vegetable cooking spray
1¾ cups sifted cake flour
¾ cup sugar
2 teaspoons baking powder
½ cup water
¼ cup vegetable oil
2 teaspoons vanilla extract
6 egg whites
1 teaspoon cream of tartar
1 quart fresh strawberries, sliced
1 pint fresh blueberries
½ cup imitation apple jelly,
  melted
2 tablespoons Cointreau or other
  orange-flavored liqueur
Fresh mint sprigs (optional)

Coat a 15- x 10- x 1-inch jellyroll pan with cooking spray; set pan aside.

Sift together flour, sugar, and baking powder in a mixing bowl. Make a well in center of mixture; add water, oil, and vanilla. Beat at medium speed of an electric mixer until smooth.

Beat egg whites (at room temperature) at high speed of an electric mixer until foamy. Add cream of tartar; beat until stiff peaks form. Gently fold egg whites into batter. Spread batter evenly in prepared pan. Bake at 350° for 20 to 25 minutes or until cake springs back when lightly touched. Let cool.

Arrange strawberries and blueberries over top of cake. Combine jelly and liqueur; stir well. Brush jelly glaze over fruit. Garnish with mint sprigs, if desired. Yield: 20 servings (127 calories per serving).

PROTEIN 2.0 / FAT 3.1 / CARBOHYDRATE 20.2 / CHOLESTEROL 0 / IRON 0.2 / SODIUM 57 / CALCIUM 28

For summertime freshness at its fullest, try Fruit-Topped Celebration Cake.

Kiwifruit Savarin

1½ cups all-purpose flour
¼ cup sugar
¼ teaspoon salt
1 package dry yeast
½ cup water
¼ cup margarine
3 eggs
Vegetable cooking spray
Rum Syrup
2 kiwifruit, peeled and thinly
  sliced
Topping (recipe follows)

Combine flour, sugar, salt, and yeast in a large mixing bowl; stir well. Combine water and margarine in a small saucepan; heat until margarine melts, stirring occasionally. Cool to between 120° and 130°.

Gradually add cooled mixture to flour mixture, beating well at medium speed of an electric mixer until batter is smooth. Beat an additional 2 minutes. Add eggs, one at a time, beating well after each addition.

Spoon batter into an 8-cup ring mold that has been coated with cooking spray. Cover and let rise in a warm place (85°), free from drafts, 30 minutes or until doubled in bulk. Bake at 350° for 30 minutes or until a wooden pick inserted in center comes out clean.

Invert onto a serving plate. Spoon Rum Syrup over hot cake. Top with kiwifruit slices. Spoon 1 tablespoon topping over each serving. Yield: 16 servings (147 calories per serving).

Rum Syrup

½ cup sugar
¼ cup water
2 tablespoons dark rum

Combine sugar and water in a small saucepan; bring to a boil, and cook until sugar dissolves. Cool mixture; stir in rum. Yield: ⅔ cup.

Topping

¼ cup water
⅓ cup instant nonfat dry milk
  powder
2 teaspoons powdered sugar
1 teaspoon vanilla extract

Place water in a small, narrow glass or stainless steel bowl; freeze 25 minutes or until a ⅛-inch-thick layer of ice forms on surface. Add milk powder, sugar, and vanilla to partially frozen water; beat at high speed of an electric mixer 5 minutes or until stiff peaks form. Yield: 1 cup.

PROTEIN 4.0 / FAT 4.1 / CARBOHYDRATE 22.5 / CHOLESTEROL 52 / IRON 0.8 / SODIUM 97 / CALCIUM 43

Chocolate Layered Loaf Cake

Vegetable cooking spray
1 cup sugar
2 eggs
1 teaspoon vanilla extract
½ cup water
2 tablespoons margarine
1 cup all-purpose flour
¼ cup unsweetened cocoa
1 teaspoon baking powder
¼ teaspoon salt
1 tablespoon unsweetened cocoa,
   sifted
Chocolate Filling
2 teaspoons powdered sugar

Line a 15- x 10- x 1-inch jellyroll pan with wax paper. Coat with cooking spray.

Combine sugar, eggs, and vanilla in a large bowl. Beat at high speed of an electric mixer 2 minutes. Combine water and margarine in a saucepan. Bring to a boil over medium heat.

Combine flour, ¼ cup cocoa, baking powder, and salt. Add to sugar mixture alternately with boiling water mixture, beginning and ending with flour mixture. Pour batter into prepared pan. (Batter will be thin in pan.)

Bake at 350° for 20 to 25 minutes or until a wooden pick inserted in center comes out clean. Invert cake onto a pastry cloth that has been dusted with 1 tablespoon sifted cocoa. Peel off wax paper. Let cake cool.

Cut cake crosswise into 4 equal strips. Place one cake layer on a serving plate. Top with one-third of Chocolate Filling. Repeat layers and filling twice, ending with cake layer. Cover and chill thoroughly. Before serving, sift powdered sugar over cake. Yield: 16 servings (172 calories per serving).

Chocolate Filling

1 teaspoon unflavored gelatin
½ cup cold water
3 tablespoons sugar
3 tablespoons margarine
2 tablespoons unsweetened cocoa
1 cup instant nonfat dry milk
   powder, divided
⅓ cup water
1 teaspoon vanilla extract

Soften gelatin in ½ cup cold water in a medium saucepan. Add sugar, margarine, and cocoa. Cook over medium heat until sugar dissolves and margarine melts, stirring constantly. Remove from heat.

Place ⅔ cup milk powder in a large bowl. Add gelatin mixture, beating at low speed of an electric mixer until blended. Let chill 15 to 20 minutes or until slightly thickened, stirring occasionally.

Place ⅓ cup water and vanilla in a small, narrow glass or stainless steel bowl; freeze 25 minutes or until a ⅛-inch-thick layer of ice forms on surface. Add remaining ⅓ cup milk powder. Beat at high speed of an electric mixer 5 minutes or until stiff peaks form. Gently fold into chilled chocolate mixture. Cover and chill until set. Before spreading filling on cake, stir with a wire whisk until mixture is smooth. Yield: 1½ cups.

PROTEIN 5.3 / FAT 4.8 / CARBOHYDRATE 27.0 / CHOLESTEROL 36 / IRON 0.8 / SODIUM 147 / CALCIUM 116

Chocolate Pots de Crème

(pictured on cover)

2/3 cup sugar
1/2 cup unsweetened cocoa
1/4 cup cornstarch
1 envelope unflavored gelatin
2 cups instant nonfat dry milk
   powder
1 quart water
2 eggs, lightly beaten
2 teaspoons vanilla extract
1 teaspoon chocolate extract
1 tablespoon plus 1 teaspoon
   chopped pistachios
Edible flowers (optional)

Combine first 4 ingredients in a medium saucepan. Combine milk powder and water; stir well. Gradually add milk mixture to dry ingredients, stirring well. Cook over medium heat, stirring constantly, until mixture thickens.

Gradually stir about one-fourth of hot mixture into beaten eggs; add to remaining hot mixture, stirring constantly. Cook over low heat, stirring constantly, 3 to 4 minutes (do not boil). Remove from heat; stir in flavorings.

Spoon mixture into small cordial glasses or demitasse cups. Cover and chill thoroughly. Top each serving with pistachios. Garnish with edible flowers, if desired. Yield: 12 servings (165 calories per 1/3-cup serving).

PROTEIN 10.0 / FAT 2.1 / CARBOHYDRATE 26.2 / CHOLESTEROL 50 / IRON 0.9 / SODIUM 120 / CALCIUM 263

Orange-Poached Pears

12 medium-size ripe pears (about
   5 pounds)
1 1/2 cups water
1/2 cup sugar
1/4 cup lemon juice
3/4 cup Chablis or other dry white
   wine
1/4 cup plus 2 tablespoons Grand
   Marnier or other
   orange-flavored liqueur
3 whole cloves
2 (3-inch) strips orange rind
1/4 cup cognac
Orange rind twists (optional)

Peel pears and core from the bottom, cutting to, but not through, stem end. Combine water, sugar, and lemon juice in a Dutch oven; bring to a boil over medium heat, stirring until sugar dissolves. Add pears; cover, reduce heat, and simmer 10 minutes. Combine wine, liqueur, cloves, and orange rind strips; pour over pears. Simmer an additional 5 minutes or until pears are tender. Remove from heat. Transfer pears and liquid to a large bowl; cover and chill thoroughly.

To serve, strain poaching liquid, reserving 1 cup. Place each pear in an individual dessert dish; spoon 2 tablespoons reserved poaching liquid over each pear. Drizzle 1 teaspoon cognac over each pear. Garnish each pear with a twist of orange rind, if desired. Yield: 12 servings. (94 calories per serving).

PROTEIN 0.4 / FAT 0.4 / CARBOHYDRATE 21.2 / CHOLESTEROL 0 / IRON 0.3 / SODIUM 1 / CALCIUM 12

Peaches in Minted Orange Sauce

¾ cup water
3 tablespoons sugar
1 tablespoon plus 1½ teaspoons
  fresh mint leaves, minced
9 medium-size ripe peaches,
  peeled and sliced (about 2¼
  pounds)
1½ cups unsweetened orange juice
3 tablespoons slivered almonds
¼ cup Grand Marnier or other
  orange-flavored liqueur
Fresh mint sprigs (optional)

Combine water and sugar in a small saucepan; bring to a boil. Cook, uncovered, over medium heat until liquid is reduced to ¼ cup. Add mint; cover and remove from heat. Let stand 30 minutes. Strain liquid; discard mint leaves.

Divide peaches evenly among 12 individual dessert dishes. Spoon 2 tablespoons orange juice over each serving. Top each serving evenly with mint sauce, slivered almonds, and liqueur. Garnish with fresh mint sprigs, if desired. Yield: 12 servings (95 calories per serving).

PROTEIN 1.4 / FAT 2.0 / CARBOHYDRATE 16.9 / CHOLESTEROL 0 / IRON 0.2 / SODIUM 1 / CALCIUM 16

Fresh Fruit Compote for a Party
(pictured on pages 244 and 245)

2 medium bananas, peeled and
  sliced
3 tablespoons lemon juice, divided
½ cup sifted powdered sugar,
  divided
2 small apples, cored and cut into
  thin wedges (about ¾ pound)
2 medium-size oranges, peeled,
  sliced crosswise, and seeded
  (about 1¼ pounds)
3 medium pears, cored and cut
  into thin wedges (about 1¼
  pounds)
1 cup seedless red grapes, halved
4 medium peaches, peeled and
  sliced (about 1 pound)
1 cup seedless green grapes,
  halved
1 pint fresh strawberries, hulled
  and halved
½ cup unsweetened orange juice
½ cup Triple Sec or other
  orange-flavored liqueur

Arrange banana slices in bottom of a 10-cup trifle bowl or individual dessert compotes. Sprinkle with 1 tablespoon lemon juice and 1 tablespoon powdered sugar. Layer apples and next 5 ingredients, sprinkling each layer with 1 teaspoon lemon juice and 1 tablespoon powdered sugar. Top with strawberries. Combine orange juice and liqueur. Pour over fruit. Cover and chill 3 hours. Before serving, sprinkle with remaining 1 tablespoon powdered sugar. Yield: 20 servings (105 calories per ½-cup serving).

PROTEIN 0.8 / FAT 0.4 / CARBOHYDRATE 23.5 / CHOLESTEROL 0 / IRON 0.3 / SODIUM 1 / CALCIUM 18

Fruit Flambé

1½ cups vanilla ice milk
¼ cup plus 2 tablespoons
   Chambord or other
   raspberry-flavored liqueur,
   divided
1 tablespoon margarine
1 medium apple, peeled, cored,
   and sliced
1 large pear, peeled, cored, and
   sliced
1 large banana, peeled and
   diagonally sliced
2 tablespoons brown sugar
⅛ teaspoon ground cinnamon
⅛ teaspoon ground nutmeg
2 cups fresh strawberries, hulled
   and quartered
2 kiwifruit, peeled and sliced

Combine ice milk and 3 tablespoons liqueur; stir until creamy. Place in freezer 30 minutes before serving.

Melt margarine in a large, heavy skillet over medium heat. Add sliced apple, pear, and banana; cook 2 minutes or just until fruit is thoroughly heated. Remove from heat. Combine brown sugar, cinnamon, and nutmeg; sprinkle over fruit. Add strawberries and kiwifruit, tossing gently.

Place remaining 3 tablespoons liqueur in a small, long-handled pan; heat just until warm. Ignite with a long match; pour over fruit, and stir gently. Remove ice milk mixture from freezer, and stir to soften. Spoon fruit into individual serving dishes; top each with 2 tablespoons ice milk mixture. Serve immediately. Yield: 12 servings (94 calories per ½-cup serving).

PROTEIN 1.2 / FAT 2.0 / CARBOHYDRATE 17.0 / CHOLESTEROL 2 / IRON 0.4 / SODIUM 25 / CALCIUM 35

Orange Angel Pie

2 (9-inch) Crumb Pie Crusts
   (page 130)
1 tablespoon unflavored gelatin
⅓ cup cold water
¾ cup skim milk
3 egg yolks, lightly beaten
1 (6-ounce) can frozen orange
   juice concentrate, thawed
6 egg whites
⅛ teaspoon salt
⅓ cup sugar
Orange curls (optional)
Edible flowers (optional)

Prepare Crumb Pie Crusts; set aside.

Sprinkle gelatin over cold water in a small saucepan; let stand 1 minute. Stir in milk and egg yolks. Cook over medium-low heat, whisking constantly, until mixture comes to a boil. Remove from heat, and whisk in orange juice concentrate. Chill 20 minutes.

Beat egg whites (at room temperature) and salt in a large bowl at high speed of an electric mixer until soft peaks form. Gradually add sugar, 1 tablespoon at a time, beating until stiff peaks form; fold into chilled orange juice mixture.

Spoon evenly into prepared crusts, and chill until firm. If desired, garnish with orange curls and edible flowers. Yield: 16 servings (161 calories per serving).

PROTEIN 3.7 / FAT 8.1 / CARBOHYDRATE 18.5 / CHOLESTEROL 51 / IRON 0.7 / SODIUM 193 / CALCIUM 31

For a grand finale, serve Orange Angel Pie to guests.

Blackberry Chiffon Pie

(pictured on pages 230 and 231)

2 (9-inch) Crumb Pie Crusts
(page 130)

6 cups fresh or frozen
blackberries, thawed

1 tablespoon unflavored gelatin

1¼ cups cold water, divided

¼ cup lemon juice

½ cup instant nonfat dry milk
powder

1 tablespoon lemon juice

5 egg whites

Dash of salt

¾ cup sugar

Fresh mint sprigs (optional)

*P*repare Crumb Pie Crusts; set aside.

Reserve a few firm blackberries. Place remaining blackberries in container of an electric blender or food processor; top with cover, and process until pureed. Press puree through a sieve; discard seeds.

Sprinkle gelatin over ¾ cup cold water in a medium saucepan; let stand 1 minute. Add blackberry puree and ¼ cup lemon juice; cook over medium heat, stirring constantly, 5 minutes or until gelatin dissolves. Remove from heat. Refrigerate for 1 hour and 15 minutes or until mixture is syrupy.

Place remaining ½ cup cold water in a small, narrow glass or stainless steel bowl; freeze 25 minutes or until a ⅛-inch-thick layer of ice forms on surface. Add milk powder to partially frozen water; beat at high speed of an electric mixer 5 minutes or until stiff peaks form. Beat in 1 tablespoon lemon juice.

Beat egg whites (at room temperature) and salt in a large bowl at high speed of an electric mixer until soft peaks form. Gradually add sugar, 1 tablespoon at a time, beating until stiff peaks form.

Place blackberry mixture in an extra-large bowl. Fold whipped milk and egg whites into blackberry mixture. Spoon mixture evenly into prepared crusts, mounding high in center. Top with reserved blackberries, and garnish with fresh mint sprigs, if desired. Freeze 4 hours or until firm. Remove from freezer 10 minutes before serving. Yield: 16 servings (179 calories per serving).

PROTEIN 3.9 / FAT 7.1 / CARBOHYDRATE 25.5 / CHOLESTEROL 1 / IRON 0.7 / SODIUM 193 / CALCIUM 66

Chiffons are gelatin-based puddings made light and airy by folding beaten egg whites into the mixture. A make-ahead dessert that requires no last-minute preparation, a chiffon pie is a popular dish to serve company.

Lemon-Raspberry Mousse

(pictured on pages 244 and 245)

2 envelopes unflavored gelatin
1 cup cold water
2 teaspoons cornstarch
2 egg yolks, beaten
1 teaspoon grated lemon rind
1 tablespoon lemon juice
⅓ cup prepared lemonade
2 cups frozen unsweetened
  raspberries, thawed
1 tablespoon sugar
1½ teaspoons cornstarch
1 tablespoon cold water
⅓ cup instant nonfat dry milk
  powder
6 egg whites
¼ cup sugar
Vegetable cooking spray
2 cups fresh raspberries
Fresh mint leaves (optional)

Combine gelatin, 1 cup cold water, and cornstarch in a medium saucepan, stirring well. Cook over medium heat, stirring constantly, until mixture is thickened and gelatin dissolves. Gradually stir about one-fourth of hot mixture into egg yolks; add to remaining hot mixture, stirring constantly. Cook over medium-low heat 1 to 2 minutes, stirring constantly. Remove from heat. Stir in lemon rind and lemon juice. Pour mixture into a medium bowl, and chill 30 minutes or just until slightly thickened, whisking occasionally.

Place lemonade in a small, narrow glass or stainless steel bowl; freeze 25 minutes or until a ⅛-inch-thick layer of ice forms on surface.

Place raspberries in a small saucepan. Cook over medium heat until very soft and juicy, stirring frequently. Remove from heat. Press raspberries through a sieve; discard seeds. Return strained raspberries to saucepan. Add 1 tablespoon sugar. Combine cornstarch and 1 tablespoon cold water, stirring well. Add to saucepan. Cook over medium heat until thickened and bubbly, stirring frequently. Transfer to a small bowl, and let cool.

Add milk powder to partially frozen lemonade. Beat mixture at high speed of an electric mixer 5 minutes or until stiff peaks form.

Beat egg whites (at room temperature) in a large bowl at high speed of an electric mixer until soft peaks form. Gradually add ¼ cup sugar, 1 tablespoon at a time, beating until stiff peaks form. Gently fold chilled gelatin mixture into egg whites. Fold in whipped mixture. Spoon ⅓ of mixture into a 9-cup fancy mold that has been coated with cooking spray. Drizzle with half of raspberry mixture. Cut through mixture with a knife to create a marble effect. Repeat procedure. Top with remaining ⅓ of whipped mixture. Cover and chill several hours or until firm. Unmold and top with fresh raspberries and, if desired, fresh mint leaves. Yield: 18 servings (56 calories per ½-cup serving).

PROTEIN 3.2 / FAT 0.8 / CARBOHYDRATE 9.4 / CHOLESTEROL 31 / IRON 0.3 / SODIUM 31 / CALCIUM 39

Overleaf: (clockwise from left) Lemon-Raspberry Mousse, Fruit Compote for a Party (page 239), and Festive Party Punch (page 232) make a luscious combination for entertaining.

Grasshopper Soufflé

Vegetable cooking spray
1 teaspoon sugar
2 packages unflavored gelatin
½ cup sugar, divided
1⅓ cups cold water
⅓ cup light process cream cheese
    product
¼ cup green crème de menthe
¼ cup crème de cacao
2 egg yolks, beaten
8 egg whites
¼ teaspoon cream of tartar
2 chocolate wafer cookies, halved
Edible flowers (optional)

Coat bottom of a 1½-quart soufflé dish with cooking spray. Sprinkle with 1 teaspoon sugar. Cut a piece of aluminum foil long enough to fit around soufflé dish, allowing a 1-inch overlap; fold foil lengthwise into thirds. Coat one side of foil with cooking spray. Wrap foil around outside of dish, coated side against dish, allowing it to extend 3 inches above rim to form a collar; secure with string.

Combine gelatin, ¼ cup sugar, and cold water in a medium saucepan. Let stand 1 minute. Cook over low heat, stirring constantly, until gelatin dissolves.

Beat cream cheese until smooth. Add 1 tablespoon crème de menthe, beating well. Stir in remaining crème de menthe and crème de cacao. Add to gelatin mixture. Cook over low heat 3 minutes or until thoroughly heated.

Gradually stir about one-fourth of hot mixture into egg yolks; add to remaining hot mixture, stirring constantly. Remove from heat; transfer to a large bowl, and chill 45 minutes or until mixture mounds slightly when dropped from a spoon, stirring occasionally.

Beat egg whites (at room temperature) and cream of tartar in a large bowl at high speed of an electric mixer until soft peaks form. Gradually add remaining ¼ cup sugar, 1 tablespoon at a time, beating until stiff peaks form. Gently fold beaten egg whites into chilled mixture. Spoon mixture into prepared dish. Cover and chill until firm. Remove collar; top with cookies. Garnish with edible flowers, if desired. Yield: 16 servings (72 calories per ½-cup serving).

PROTEIN 3.3 / FAT 1.7 / CARBOHYDRATE 7.3 / CHOLESTEROL 35 / IRON 0.1 / SODIUM 60 / CALCIUM 12

Garnished with chocolate and edible flowers, Grasshopper Soufflé makes a memorable dessert.

Appendices

CAKE BAKING PROBLEM CHART

Any one or a combination of the following may cause a cake failure

PROBLEM	CAUSE	PROBLEM	CAUSE

Low volume	Batter underbeaten
	Batter overbeaten
	Too much liquid
	Pan too large
	Not enough leavening
	Oven too cool
		Cake is heavy, compact	Mixed too slowly after
			  adding milk
			Use of flour with too much
			  gluten
			Too much shortening
			Too little baking powder
			Baked too slowly
			Baked too fast

Wet or soggy layer	Batter underbeaten Batter overbeaten Too much liquid Oven too cool	Extreme shrinkage	Too much water in batter Batter overbeaten
Dry, crumbly cake	Not enough liquid Not enough shortening Oven too hot Overbaked Too much flour Too much baking powder	Cake peaked on top	Pan too small Oven temperature too hot Too much liquid in batter Batter overmixed
Coarse texture	Batter underbeaten Batter overbeaten Ingredients not thoroughly mixed Too much sugar Too much leavening	Sticky top	High humidity Underbaked Too much liquid Too much sugar
Cake fell	Underbaked Pan too small Oven too hot Oven too cool Too much leavening Too much liquid Too much sugar Too much shortening Loss of oven temperature during baking	Cake not level on top	Too much flour Oven rack not level Oven heat uneven Pans too close to oven sides
		Cake sticks in pan	Pan not properly greased Cake cooled in pan too long
		Cake cracked on top	Pan too deep Oven too hot Batter overmixed Flour has too much gluten

PASTRY PROBLEM CHART

Technique and good judgment are most important when preparing pastries. Pastries for Light Desserts *have been developed with less than the classic 1 to 3 ratio of fat to flour. For success, be careful to follow the directions in each recipe. Follow the directions on page 11 to roll out the pastry.*

PROBLEM	CAUSE	PROBLEM	CAUSE
Tough, dry, hard crust	Too much flour Too little water Too much water Overmanipulation of pastry Too much gluten in flour	Pastry will not roll out evenly between plastic	Too little water
Crust crumbly	Too little water Too much shortening	Pastry shrinks too much	Overmanipulation of pastry Not chilled before rolling Pastry was stretched to fit the pan
Sticky, hard to handle	Too much water Ingredients too warm	Pastry cracks while baking	Too little water Pastry not chilled before baking

BAKING PANS AND SUBSTITUTION CHART

Shape	Dimensions	Capacity	Substitutions
Rectangular	10- x 6- x 2-inch	5 cups	8- x 1½-inch round
	11- x 7- x 1½-inch	8 cups	8- x 8- x 2-inch
	12- x 8- x 2-inch	10 cups	9- x 9- x 2-inch
	15- x 10- x 1-inch	10 cups	9- x 9- x 2-inch
	13- x 9- x 2-inch	15 cups	two 9-inch round
			or
			three 8-inch round
Square	8- x 8- x 2-inch	8 cups	11- x 7- x 1½-inch (rectangular)
	9- x 9- x 2-inch	10 cups	9- x 5- x 3-inch (loaf) or
			two 8-inch round
			12- x 8- x 2-inch
Round	8- x 1½-inch	5 cups	10- x 6- x 2-inch (rectangular)
	8- x 2-inch	6 cups	8½- x 4½- x 3-inch (loaf)
	9- x 1½-inch	6 cups	9- x 2¼-inch pie pan
			8 x 2-inch round
Tube	10- x 4-inch	12 cups	10-inch ring mold or cake mold
Loaf	9- x 5- x 3-inch	8 cups	9-inch ring mold or three 3- x 5-inch loaf pans
	8½- x 4½- x 2½-inch	6 cups	8-inch ring mold or two 3- x 5-inch loaf pans
Pie Pan	8- x 1½-inch	3 cups	No substitution unless tart pans are used
	9- x 1½-inch	4 cups	
	10- x 1½-inch	6 cups	
Cookie Sheet	15½- x 12-inch		Baking sheet or jellyroll pan
Jellyroll Pan	13- x 9-inch		Do not substitute baking sheet for jellyroll pan
	15½- x 10½-inch		

ALCOHOL SUBSTITUTION CHART

Liqueurs, spirits, and wines add special flavor to desserts that is difficult to replace. Alcohol itself evaporates at 172° F, leaving only its flavor behind. However, this chart gives ideas for substitution of alcoholic ingredients should you choose to change the recipe. Remember, also, that most extracts, including vanilla, are about 40% alcohol (which translates to 80 proof). Extracts, however, are used in small amounts, usually not more than 1 tablespoon. So, we've based this chart on substitutions starting at 2 tablespoons (1 ounce).

IF THE RECIPE CALLS FOR:	SUBSTITUTE:
2 tablespoons Grand Marnier or other orange-flavored liqueur	2 tablespoons unsweetened orange juice concentrate or 2 tablespoons orange juice and ½ teaspoon orange extract
2 tablespoons rum or brandy	½ to 1 teaspoon rum or brandy extract for recipes in which liquid amount is not crucial. Add water if it is necessary to have specified amount of liquid.
2 tablespoons amaretto	¼ to ½ teaspoon almond-flavored extract
2 tablespoons sherry or bourbon	1 to 2 teaspoons vanilla extract
2 tablespoons Kahlúa, coffee or chocolate-flavored liqueur	½ to 1 teaspoon chocolate extract plus ½ to 1 teaspoon instant coffee in 2 tablespoons water
¼ cup or more port, sherry, rum, brandy, or fruit-flavored liqueur	Equal measure of unsweetened orange juice or apple juice plus 1 teaspoon of corresponding flavored extract or vanilla extract
¼ cup or more white wine	Equal measure of white grape juice or apple juice
¼ cup or more red wine	Equal measure of red grape juice or cranberry juice

Index